AID TO THE READER

Some persons have expressed to the author that they find the text difficult to read, with words of which they are not familiar. The concepts expressed here are important to us to determine what makes us human.

I suggest the reader "skip over" those words temporarily and proceed on to grasp the thoughts intended. I also suggest the reader devote most attention, and even consider to commence reading the book at Part IV, dealing with the soul. That is really the "heart" of the book.

The book is a unique, comprehensive and complex explanation of our cosmos, world, extra dimensions and accompanying spirituality. The person who devotes effort to reading and understanding the concepts will be rewarded with a rich understanding of life and what makes us human.

The author

T0354532

Do We Live In Two Worlds?

Reconciling Science and Soul

Second Edition

by

Robert Greenough

Order this book online at www.trafford.com
or email orders@trafford.com

Most Trafford titles are also available at major online book retailers.

Printed in the United States of America.

ISBN: 978-1-4669-6584-3 (sc)
ISBN: 978-1-4669-6585-0 (hc)
ISBN: 978-1-4669-6583-6 (e)

Library of Congress Control Number: 2012920450

Trafford rev. 10/24/2013

 www.trafford.com

North America & international
toll-free: 1 888 232 4444 (USA & Canada)
fax: 812 355 4082

Dedication . . . . and Thanks

. . . . to my wife
   . . . . to my family
      . . . . to my acquaintances
         . . . . and to the other authors whose
                  input formulated understanding
                  of a more complete existence.

—Robert Greenough

And . . . . Thanks to Hazel, Don, and Kathy, with their editorial staff at Proctor Publications, LLC. They performed what I must consider a "production miracle" in transforming word processed pages, with numerous errors, to become this finished book. I know they must have been exasperated by the many "hold the presses" additions written to clarify different topics.

Table Of Contents

THOUGHTS

I am convinced that theoretical physics is actually philosophy.

Max Born

As often in science, the incredible theory of one age becomes the everyday image for its successors.

J. Bronowski, *The Ascent of Man*

Every sentence that I utter should be regarded by you not as an assertion but as a question.

Neils Bohr, in addressing his students

I reserve the right to be inconsistent as long as I become more enlightened.

President Jimmy Carter

An essence of science is that if you ask an impertinent question, you are on the way to the pertinent answer.

J. Bronowski, *The Ascent Of Man*

I think that in discussion of physical problems we ought to begin not from the authority of scriptural passages, but from sense-experiences and necessary demonstrations . . . . Nor is God any less excellently revealed in nature's actions than in the sacred statements of the Bible.

Galileo Galilei, 16th Century

Your Galileo has ventured to meddle with things that he ought not to and with the most important and dangerous subjects which can be stirred up in these days.

and

His Holiness charges the Inquisitor at Florence to inform Galileo, in the name of the Holy Office, that he is to appear as soon as possible in the course of the month of October at Rome before the Commissary-General of the Holy Office.

Pope Urban VIII, Year 1632 (from *The Ascent Of Man*)

The imagination is a telescope in time. What we call cultural evolution is essentially a constant growing and widening of the human imagination. In every age there is a turning point, a new way of seeing and asserting the coherence of the world.

J. Bronowski, *The Ascent Of Man,* 1973

He drew a circle that shut me out,
Heretic, rebel, a thing to flout,
But love and I had the wit to win,
We drew a circle that took him in.

Edwin Markham

Fort Worth, Texas—Bill Moyers to Southern Baptists, "Lighten up!" The broadcaster says conservatives are clinging to an "alien ideology" by leaning towards a literal interpretation of the Bible and a close-minded philosophy. Speaking at the Baptist General Convention of Texas, Moyers—a Baptist minister—blasted the conservative faction for pushing a belief system that is "less a set of ideas than it is a pathological distemper, a militant anger over the fact that the universe is not closed and life is not static." He told 1,700 people at Tuesday's meeting that Baptists must accept other religions and reject conservative legislation that is not inclusive.

From the <u>Associated Press,</u> in <u>The Ann Arbor News</u>. November 14,1996

It's easy to be visionary, or to be creditable. It's hard to be both.

Geoffrey Landis,
Researcher in Space-Time at NASA

I'm not sure I totally buy this idea—it's outrageous, but it's the only idea that explains the action that is observed.

Anonymous

"The most beautiful and most profound emotion we can experience is the sensation of the mystical. It is the sower of all true science. He to whom this emotion is a stranger, who can no longer wonder and stand rapt in awe, is as good as dead. To know that what is impenetrable to us really exists, manifesting itself as the highest wisdom and the most radiant beauty which our dull faculties can comprehend only in their most primitive forms—this knowledge, this feeling is at the center of true religiousness."

"My religion consists of a humble admiration of the illimitable superior spirit who reveals himself in the slight details we are able to perceive with our frail and feeble minds. That deeply emotional conviction of the presence of a superior reasoning power, which is revealed in the incomprehensible universe, forms my idea of God."

—Albeit Einstein
From *The Universe and Dr. Einstein*
by Lincoln Barnett, William Morrow & Co., 1949

"THE UNEXAMINED LIFE IS NOT WORTH LIVING."
Socrates, *fifth century B.C.*

PART I

INTRODUCTION

- Introduction
- Scope
- Prelude
- The Case For God's Existence
- A Scenario In Unity
- Interdisciplinary Fertilization
- Anatomy Differences In Origins Of Families
- Is This Possible?

"Whom do people say that I am?" Jesus once asked his disciples according to the Gospel of Matthew. The disciple's answered, "Some say John the Baptist, others say Elijah . . . or one of the prophets." This reveals how, even then, there was little consensus over the identity of the enigmatic preacher from Galilee. And the controversy endures today. Some modern scholars say that historical evidence reveals a much different portrait of Jesus than the one in the Christian creeds.

The historical quest has been denounced by some as a frontal assault on Christian faith and an attempt to undermine the Bible's authority. Yet proponents find in it hope for a more rational basis for belief and a clearer essence of Jesus's teachings. Many scholars think the gospels are unreliable records since they were written as proclamations, not objective history, decades after Jesus's death. (Excerpted from *In Search of Jesus,* U.S. News and World Report, April 8,1996.)

Reporting of religious events in Paleo-time could only be told by the word of God, as related in the Book of Genesis. But Biblical and historic man has misinterpreted the time frame into something within their conceivable history. We may have a variance between the actualities of an event and the Biblical interpretation.

In comparison with the technological knowledge available as we enter the 21st Century, two and three

Do We Live In Two Worlds?

thousand years ago there was incredible ignorance and lack of knowledge regarding nearly all phases of science, physical, social, and theological in comparison with the state of knowledge as we know it today.

In light of these developments, some theologians are actually a part of the problem in their rigid, dogmatic mind sets. It was only in year 1996 that Pope John Paul II acknowledged that evolution may be a possibility. The Roman Catholic Church now recognizes, as St. Augustine did in about year 600 and St. Thomas Aquinas did in about year 1250, that soul and body exists within the same human. This concept has been termed for hundreds of years as "dualism". It has been said, "There are laws in the background and contingency in the details."

The reader will see conflict between the rationalist and the mystic—between the person who believes in the conventional thought, and the mystic who is searching for something beyond conventional thought in an attempt to explain and to understand.

In writing these pages, I do not portray myself in any way as a scientist, and I think this is the strength of this book.

A scientist would feel compelled to protect his professional reputation, to give lengthy support for the hypothesis presented, and to provide unquestioned documentation for any statements made.

As the author, I do not feel constricted to these limits. I am a layman—a businessman by training, who has wide interests in many fields. This diversity in background has fomented and developed a universal, or wide-scope view in approaching possible solutions to the questions presented in this book.

My thought mechanisms seem to want a desire to link advancements in science to a cause that is spiritual and which has a spiritual motivation. In many ways this study is a reconciliation of science and theology. The two are not as widely opposed as some people in the past have thought.

It seems that all fields of knowledge present a system of how each concept in their respective discipline develops. The fields of knowledge are like brothers and sisters in a family, all of the same parents, with differences in their nature, yet held together by their like genes. So, many knowledge, cultural, and religious systems are different, yet alike.

These concepts many times seem to be related to one another. Social science rules have their parallel in proven rules of physical science: rules of accounting state that for every debit there is a credit, and these have parallels in nuclear theory that for every electron there is a proton, the business transaction that triggers accounting entries is parallel to the neutron from which electrons and protons emanate.

I see at least three ways to study science: 1) The academic, laboratory, experimental way, to prove or disprove some question or hypothesis—necessary, but mundane. 2) The theoretical method, employed by physicist and mathematicians—the real fun of the chase. 3) The way of reason, multi-disciplinary association, and gut feeling, a way used in brainstorming, where conventional limitations are dismissed from mind in order to create new solutions, or at least new questions to be studied later.

In industry, these three styles might be illustrated by: 1) the worker, who is operational and actually makes the product, 2) the manager or foreman who coordinates the efforts in a sensible way, and 3) the executive or planner, who is paid to be creative and come up with better ways to run the enterprise, considering the multiple challenges that exist in the universe of marketing, finance, future, and practicalities of actual existence. An executive will sometimes, faced with many subjects vying for his time, employ separate specialized entities, perhaps a researcher or planner, to concentrate on a particular aspect of his responsibilities.

So, in science, experts will explore in depth certain specialized topics. I see future research, experimentation, and exploration as confirmation (and some rejection) of theories and analysis presented here.

I visualize intuitive insight into how something might be, to infer, theorize, or simply speculate on its exact nature. I have tried to be a futurist, using cognitive subjects for wellspring ideas.

I hope to present a meeting ground for fundamentalist advocates who hold that words stated in the Bible stand without question, and the evidence before us that disputes some aspects given in the Bible, if taken literally.

I hope to present an integrated and plausible theory of how and when souls were created by God, how they functioned over the many eons to be God's messengers, acting to shape evolution.

Jesus, an intellectual and moral spiritual leader of His time, was tried and crucified because He was facing an establishment in which religion was simply an arm of government. One can compare the joint functioning of laws in present-day Moslem countries and present-day Christian oriented governments that separate church and state in this regard.

One can also contrast a world in which science and government are separate, versus that existing in a country where science and government are interrelated, heavily subsidized, and acting almost as one. In the latter, will science evolve to be a tool of government, controlled by government, and without freedom and independence of thought?

It has been said that a mind once stretched by a new idea, never regains its original dimensions. It also can be taken that in the wondrous creation of earth and life over the many eons, all things which can occur, have, and do occur.

I suspect that even God has experienced some failures in his development of life and biological trials. We can cite evolutionary regression, or loss of developed mutations in the evolved biological anthropology of man as an example. The record lies in the genes of mankind.

From failures improvements evolved. I don't think God is through with mankind yet. There is bound to be further refinements, and perhaps some failures, as there has been for over 4 1/2 billion years, when, I believe God first manifested Himself with life forms in this cosmos.

Do We Live In Two Worlds?

Part I - Introduction

I imagine that most men and women feel that they would like to retain and remember all of the knowledge to which they have been exposed—the information or experiences which they have read, or heard, or seen, or analyzed, or have been the subject of their associated thoughts. This, however, is impossible. If I read the whole 20 volumes of the Encyclopedia Britannica on the shelf of my living room, I could retain and absorb only a fraction of the information contained therein.

But the association of bits of information and essence of knowledge regarding various fields that relate to one another is, I believe, the essence of learning. The bits of information then cease to be only bits, but become an integral part of the more complete understanding of the various subjects associated.

It is like the supply of individual bricks, sitting at a construction site (the bits of information), finally serving a more complete service when the mason has assembled them to become a whole building (the essence of knowledge and understanding of a field). Each bit of information supports and relates to each other bit of information in the whole to become a significant, recognizable, rational and logical structure. In this way, a city is built, although it will probably never be completed. From such structuring and analysis, wisdom is built.

A basic tenet of science is that there is a reason for everything. With this tenet, we need only to find what that reason is. Without action or change, we have inertia only to remain at rest.

I suggest that if the reader disagrees with some aspect presented here, that he (or she) separately pick out exactly what is disagreed with, and not throw out the entire concept. Perhaps an improvement in the reasoning process will result. The modern-day automobile was inconceivable in the initial years of its conception. Continual honing of the ideas were required to attain our present state of usefulness. To cite a cliche, *"Rome wasn't built in a day."*

We will all die. It is just a matter of when, where, and the circumstances. Death levels all things.

In the story of "We live In Two Worlds", the author reflects and recognizes the teachings of past philosophers that soul exists within, but separate and distinct from the body, and that soul continues on in existence after the body has died.

These ideas are not new. It may be that it is only one's personal realization that is new, of the idea that we are living in two worlds. The concept of a soul existing within man goes back at least to Plato and Aristotle, to Pope Gregory, St. Augustine, Thomas Aquinas, to the Stoics of Ancient Greece, and to leading church men in history, as well as to many religious followers. Some persons, even today, have not come to the realization that man is more than an animal body, that he, or she, has a soul, a spirit of God, that exists within his material body.

The idea of the origin of the soul may be new and unique with this writing. Less unique may be the idea of the existence and appearance of the soul during our own lifetime, as well as at times in the past, and the eventual victory of the soul, which may in fact replace Cro-Magnon man on earth, as Homo sapiens had replaced Neanderthal man in the past.

The author proposes how the soul came into existence during the particle physics evolution prior to, during, and after the "Big Bang". He proposes the preexistence of God as an intelligence in a prior cosmos, and that souls are a microcosm, or micro-division of God.

Souls, therefore, have existed as long as has the earth's creation. This book suggests that all living organisms since creation have the potential of having soul, and that souls perhaps have undergone an evolutionary process, much as the primate body has evolved to Homo sapiens.

I first composed my theory espoused here in about 1990 after spending a lone weekend at my family cabin and then driving the four hour trip back to my home. Readings in scientific journals since that time have elaborated and supported various aspects of my theory and given encouragement that other aspects may not be as ridiculous as I first believed. My thoughts were not publicly expressed for fear of ridicule.

Readings on evolution of *"Black Holes"* parallel my theory.

The Big Bang development, cosmic and earth formation, physical and chemical creation of life, evolution of species, events in parapsychology, and historic and Biblical readings, all played a part in trying to resolve questions through reason and analysis.

The studies in depth to prepare for this book were much more grand than my simplified, conceptual overview and scheme. The scope of the book is somewhat all-encompassing and I found it necessary in many cases to summarize the findings, rather than add to the complexity of this "panorama of thought".

Now I find even today yet another study (Scientific American, November, 1994, *The Self-Reproducing Inflationary Universe)* that parallels and supports an element in my theory that perhaps many "Big Bangs" did exist and created various portions of the cosmos.

There are distinct and separate qualities of souls that are characterized in the qualities of the mind, as opposed to those of the brain alone. The brain functioning permits life for animals to live, eat, digest, be mobile, and otherwise serve as living creatures on earth, somewhat as a biological-electrical machine with computer-like programming.

However, the soul exists and is manifested in the mind of Homo sapiens, demonstrating qualities of affection, planning, emotion, insight, intuition, and like qualities beyond what a mere machine or computer could perform in the parallel functioning.

The existence of mind and souls within man is presented. Souls, sometimes called spirits or even ghosts, have been reported, documented as best possible, for hundreds and thousands of years.

Souls play a part in guiding and directing the minds and bodily functioning of each of us, as they have directed the functioning of living bodies since the first algae and amoeba life on earth.

The tool for biological change has been manipulation of RNA and DNA. It is the author's belief that God, operating through souls that manipulated the RNA and DNA of all living organisms, did, in this way, create and evolve the life forms on the earth, including man.

The author proposes that a change in religious dogma should take place that accommodates the practical existence of soul, and proposes interpretation of the reporting in the

Bible that would be consistent with these presentations. After all, much of our religious dogma was developed after the time of Christ.

The continuum of humanoid evolution is projected forward many millenniums to a state when, as the Bible states, *"The meek shall inherit the earth."* Just as pre-humans evolved in many phases to Neanderthal, then replaced by Homo sapiens and Cro-Magnon man, our present form of humanoid existence may, *"in another 50,000 years or so, evolve into an existence only of souls, human bodies having then become extinct."*

With rational, philosophical thought, society has moved away from the supernatural and the unexplainable. Faith is needed only for the unexplainable. We have come to realize that there is more than one way to look at things. We realize that exploration into new thoughts requires an open mind, a willingness to investigate unconventional ideas, theories, and new areas in which to gain knowledge.

This book is presented as an effort to reconcile principles of theology with facts known to science. It has been said that God is the greatest scientist. The magnitude of this concept is being revealed even further in the current era by revelations in particle physics, a field of science not even suspected at the early part of our current century. (See *Part II—Creation*).

Other facts presently known have been revealed over the past 2,000 years since the days of Christ on this earth.

Do We Live In Two Worlds?

Part I - Introduction

It is safe to state that further revelations in science, and I believe applicable to theology, will come to be known in the future.

Presented here is a complex theory: A theory of what differentiates modern man from animals. A theory of how and why man, with conscience and ethics, evolved to be different from other animals, including Simians, a theory springing from accepted biologic, geographic, and otherwise scientific development of the tangible earth and its contents of metallic, as well as organic life, that we call matter.

A theory is presented of when and how our very souls were created into an exotic world of antimatter, coexistent with the world of matter. A theory is presented of how the souls, under the direction of a preexisting God, directed the evolution of plant and animal life from protozoa and algae, through formation of worm-like organisms, then to functional combinations, developing into complex organs of animal and plant life, all acting by manipulation of RNA and DNA, by these messengers from God. In this sense God was the Creator. (See *Part IV—The Soul*).

There is presented an outline of those qualities possessed by all animals having ability to motor (move by themselves), whether worms, reptiles, fish or animal. Presented also is an additional outline of qualities possessed by Cro-Magnon man. These latter qualities are not exhibited by animals other than man, and these qualities are those that make man unique in this world. *(See Part IV—The Soul)*.

Evidence of coexistence of man and souls are suggested by recognized events in parapsychology. Some in the field of what we call religion.

Projection into eons of the future, too, are suggested, that a new world, without animate forms of man, may transpire, as radical, or more so, than the pre-history replacement on earth of Neanderthal man by Homo sapiens. (See *Part V—To The Future).*

This theory ties together and could explain the wonderment of man's existence that science, theology, and philosophy have debated for thousands of years. A reasonable continuum would explain where and why life exists, and perhaps the future of mankind on this earth.

Beliefs, practices in theology, formulated by minds with the limits of knowledge existing 2,000 to 2,600 years ago (when the individual books of the Old Testament were written) are challenged in light of information obtained since those times.

Many holdings in religious dogma should be updated to reflect not mystical events, but rational events. This reinterpretation would serve, not to destroy faith and confidence in religious beliefs, but in fact, bring this to a state of realism and understandable comprehension with today's state of information.

The concept of God changed during the reign of Solomon, from the militant, fearsome, omnipotent "Yahweh" of old, to the omnipotent Father who loved His children. So too, our concept was made more clear of how the organization of Heaven's ways could now be better understood.

Do We Live In Two Worlds?

Part I - Introduction

This book is intended to present a message as an overview. The author feels that the scope of the story, ranging in "time before time", to a period of evolution when humans have become extinct, and an attempt to relate tangibility to the intangible as it relates to antimatter, is "deep" enough as it is. I prefer not to make this book more complex.

Considerable research and reporting has been performed and is available in all of the component aspects of this story. One can read extensively in fields of the Bible, particle physics, geology, anthropology, archeology, philosophy, psychology, medicine, anatomy, brain and mind, natural science, zoology, social relationships, cosmology, astronomy, theology, Newtonian, Einsteinian and general science, mathematics, history of art, and really all other fields of knowledge. Individuals have made careers in each of these academic fields, and elaboration here in depth would require volumes, with thousands of pages to adequately explain each field.

In 1989 COBE (Cosmic Background Explorer Satellite) was launched into space. COBE looked for, and found, the faint afterglow of cosmic radiation left by the Big Bang, proving once and for all that a massive explosion and expansion brought the universe into being.

I recall a dream when I was about age 8 that either influenced or predicted my future interest. In this dream I experienced a loss, and later control, of gravity. Loss of gravity meant eternal falling through space. However, in my dream, I was able to control gravity by turning two valves, much like temperature of water can be controlled at a sink by adjusting the hot and the cold valves. I have experienced an interest in science ever since, with a special respect for gravity.

I also experienced the childish question of "whether the world goes away when I shut my eyes?" Recent thoughts in philosophy and multiple universes gives, strangely, some credence to this thought, that life is not real but merely an event in a "single time existence". An unseemly rule of particle physics holds that when an existence is not observed it does not exist, and does exist only when it is being observed. This is a strange concept but is indicative of the strangeness of particle physics, that we are on the threshold of trying to understand.

Science is leading us into completely new ventures in theology and spiritualism. We are "on the verge" of travel to the universe of antimatter. To compare our progress towards this enlightenment with cultural evolution, we stand somewhere between the years of the Dark Ages and those of the Renaissance. We presently are like coming out of the dark ages of history, approaching that state of year 1492 (or 1,000 AD when Vikings first touched North America, or even 1,000 BC or so when Orientals, Egyptians, or Asians first entered the North and South America continents, or perhaps 10,000 to 30,000 BC when early Africans may have crossed a land bridge to Antarctica and to South America presenting evidence of human life existence at Tierra del Fuego). This first physical presence was followed by a social intercourse that would dramatically change the world and ways of life.

Do We Live In Two Worlds?

Part I - Introduction

As science continues to identify aspects and qualities of antimatter, it will only need to devise a means of actual travel to the universe of antimatter and return, and I believe to the actual universe inhabited by souls and God. *(See Part V, A Research Project In Fiction)*

Science, almost monthly, reports new findings in publications such as <u>Science</u>, <u>Scientific American</u> or <u>Discovery</u> magazine on advancements in knowledge regarding antimatter. In June of the year 2000 we read of new findings concerning the quark-gluon *(DISCOVERY magazine, July 2000)*. We, not long ago, learned of the quark and how three quarks are present on the proton, neutron, and electron particles, components of what we once thought were the smallest forms of matter, the atom.

In terms of travel, we are seeking a "symbolic seaworthy ocean-traveling ship to replace the canoe and small boats formerly used to travel our rivers and small seas". We are approaching the state when we know where to go and have an idea what we will find, but do not have the vehicle to travel there. It is like space travel to the outermost planets, or to another galaxy. We presently have a concept of what environment exists on planets and other celestial bodies. Sooner or later, we will be able to make that travel. A whole new way of existence will occur.

The idea of dualism in body and soul has existed for at least 2,500 years. The ancient Greek philosophers, Socrates and Plato, spoke of a twofold existence within the body, of all intangible soul that proceeds on to an afterlife when the physical body is deceased.

Others echoed and reasoned that a spirit or soul exists within the human body. In the 13th Century, Thomas Aquinas wrote of the dualistic existence as an official view of the Holy Roman Church, and this doctrine continued on through the Protestant Reformation.

The author here recognizes the existence of body and soul, and goes further to propose the origin of the soul, acts of souls causing protein changes in DNA that result in biological change in living things, manifestations of the soul in the daily existence of human beings, that the soul continues on in existence after human death, and the existence in the God-substance of souls, to be reincarnated for future life on earth, working towards rejoining the soul world for an eventual oneness with God. God, Jesus Christ, and the soul of each of us are all part of the same substance.

The author proposes that souls were initially created during the Big Bang creation of this and other galaxies, and even that God may well have existed prior to a "Big Bang". He further proposes that there may have been a series of Big Bangs, each creating a separate galaxy, and each originating from a "pre-current cosmos" Black Hole.

Do We Live In Two Worlds?

Part I - Introduction

Elemental, or particle physicists have reasoned and researched in our current century that antimatter, the virtual opposite of all forms of matter, does exist.

Leading particle physicists have somewhat agreed that an extraordinary substance of Grand Unification existed at the very beginning that contained all of the elementary components of the cosmos, except space. Created from the Grand Unification were galaxies, stars, our sun, planets, moons, other physical matter of the cosmos, as well as the four elemental forces, called the 1) Weak Force, 2) Strong Force, 3) Electro Magnetic Force, and 4) Gravity.

Time did not exist during the Grand Unification, but upon activation of expansion, with creation of matter into space, time came into existence.

Quarks, electrons, protons, neutrons, Baryons, W Forces, Z Bosons, and other sources of energy were released and formed in the moments following the initial expansion, creating matter. For every electron, there was a proton, but a process of annihilation of most protons by electrons took place, to be the creation of matter.

The annihilated protons became antimatter, an existence little understood until our current century.

The author proposes that this world of antimatter is the world of God, and the world of souls. There is evidence of the subtle, marginal coexistence and interrelationship between matter and antimatter in studies of parapsychology and in reason, which man attempts to present in rational, understandable, and elementary terms.

Human-like creatures have existed for millions of years, evolving anatomically and biologically through many stages of evolution. At a point in earth-time, souls were incarnated to the humanoid form, to become Homo sapiens (thinking man). Perhaps in the far future, Homo sapien man will, too, become extinct, and souls will inherit the earth. The Bible states, *"The meek shall inherit the earth.'"*

The author proposes that this reasoning is all compatible with the Bible, but that historic church leaders have, in many circumstances, misinterpreted the essence of the Bible.

That man was created in God's image refers to creation of soul, and not to creation of the animal body. The death of Jesus Christ has been interpreted incorrectly now for 2,000 years, and the Genesis account of Adam and Eve is symbolic rather than literal, as are many other stories and parables.

An alternate interpretation of the Bible will go far in gathering and encouraging all variations of believers into religion and give rational basis for present disbelievers in the existence of God, to embrace the tenets of religion as a guide to directing their own way of life.

The author proposes that an alternate interpretation of the Bible provides a compatibility with the present state of knowledge of our current late 20th Century, and with known principles and evidence in physics, geology, anatomy, biology, and even parapsychology.

He proposes a tangible approach to religion and oneness with God, based on physical evidence that we can rationally observe today. He proposes a lesser need for faith, where knowledge provides evidence that clarifies

Do We Live In Two Worlds?

Part I - Introduction

the truth. Pure faith is needed today for a lesser number of events because of the increase in scientific knowledge in the past 20 to 26 centuries.

This is not necessarily a religious book, in the normal meaning of that term, but it is meant to be a practical view of how the existence of physical man and spiritual man can and does meld together. It is an attempt to explain how events that we experience in our lifetime, that we have previously acclaimed to faith alone, are understandable in our present state of knowledge, advanced from that preexisting state of 2,000 years knowledge, through knowledge gained, and an ability of reason that God has given to us and to mankind.

By attaining this understanding, each of us can achieve awareness and a state of bliss. We can reclaim the field of pure knowledge and conceive a new world into reality. An ability exists in all of us that is untapped, and can lead to immortality.

As Deepak Chopra has stated in, and about, his spiritualistic books and lectures, *"I'm not saying anything that hasn't been said before. This is advice on feeling good, feeling good about ourselves, achieving spiritual fulfillment, for expanding personal boundaries, and discovering our potential. This is a self-help approach to a mind-body-spirit concept in feeling a spiritual void and to provide real meaning to our lives."*

This book isn't intended as a textbook on the various sciences of geology, botany, biology, chemistry, medicine, anatomy, particle physics, physical or social sciences. Each of these topics, of course, is a specialty of knowledge in itself, and a wealth of information is available in the annals of each field.

This book is an attempt to show, in somewhat summary form, how the known facets of the various fields of knowledge can fit together to reveal a continuous and coordinated whole. This presentation is complex enough without bringing in the specific technicalities and nomenclature of the many sciences and fields of knowledge involved.

This book attempts to tell the evolution and development from a prehistory cosmology of Black Holes, evolving to the Big Bang, the resulting formation and existence of matter and antimatter, to formation of the cosmos, presence of hydrogen, helium, and oxygen elements, formation in the cosmos of amino acids, other known elements, and the start of basic life, the evolution of specialty biological and botanical cells, the formation of early primordial plants and animals, development of those into complex cells, plants and animals, and development of fish, reptiles, mammals, and humanoid animals.

I attempt to theorize the existence of God, and a subdivision into souls, that would be incarnated into the existing humanoid forms, and the possibility, purpose, and goals that souls have in their own existence. Projection is presented of what the end result of advanced existence on earth might be, in some far advanced eon, of Heaven, consisting of souls in a "world" or universe of antimatter, the ultimate World of God on earth in His own being. A physical existence of earth, changed perhaps by some

Do We Live In Two Worlds?

cosmic catastrophe, would have no bearing on the theorized "Heaven on Earth" home of souls living in antimatter.

These are not new thoughts. Each aspect has been discussed by philosophers and scientists, dating from near the beginning of civilization. The philosopher, Plato (428-348 BC) advocated a spirit world and life beyond death of the biological body, and Thomas Aquinas (1225-1274) further advocated this dual existence. Tremendous advancements in knowledge have evolved in all fields of science, especially since the 16th Century.

Our own 20th Century has been a stage for only the beginning in the field of particle physics for recognition and understanding of the components and qualities of elementary particles that make up what was once thought to be the smallest particle in existence, the atom, but which is now revealed as having components within itself.

I have merely brought these findings in science and evolution into a form of linear program, a continuum, that I believe is rational, conceivable, and understandable.

This book is not heretical. The author is by no means an Atheist. I believe in God, and hope to present here an understanding of God that is somewhat tangible, or at least understandable. Ideally, it would bring persons, who cannot quite fathom some of the irrational events presented by modern day religions, into their own world of realism.

If a bridge can be made from what has previously been known as mystical, to a state of realism, I believe more persons on our earth can and will come to recognize and accept God, and consequently compose a better life for themselves in our existence.

Not everyone is particularly interested in the extreme before and the extreme hereafter. But they are very interested in their own lifetime, their own physical existence, the nurturing of their own soul, and the immediate hereafter of the soul.

This book presents a theory of where one's soul came from, its existence within the humanoid body, the recognition of our soul by its qualities, and what will become of the soul, once our biological body has deceased.

In this book the author attempts to reconcile the traditional conflict of theology versus science in the creation and development of life and our existence on earth.

Geology and nature presents undisputed evidence of the evolution of the firmament, fauna and flora. Yet, in the conflict, the origin, existence and evolution of creature life is debated, along with the existence of soul and spirit. Intelligence exists, to varying extent, in all creatures.

The existence of souls is recognized in the teaching of past philosophers that soul exists within, but separate and distinct from, the body and that the soul continues on in existence after the body has died.

As stated earlier, these ideas are not new. It may be that it is only one's personal realization that is new, of the idea that we are living in two worlds.

The concept of a soul existing within man dates back through centuries, well before the time of Jesus, with noted, historic philosophies and religious personalities expressing the concept of dualism. However, some persons, even today, have not come to the realization that man is more than an animal body, that he, or she, has a soul, a spirit of God, that exists within his natural body.

The idea of the origin of the soul may be unique with this writing. The author proposes how the soul came into existence during the particle physics evolution prior to, during, and shortly after the "Big Bang". He proposes the perpetual existence of God as an intelligence in a prior cosmos, and that souls are a microcosm or micro-division, of God. Souls have existed therefore, at least as long as has the earth's creation.

The "Big Bang" theory is generally accepted by science as an original occurrence. The author tells of the creation of both our present electron-oriented universe, but also of a proton-oriented universe resulting from annihilation of protons during the early moments of the Big Bang.

The Annihilation created a universe of antimatter (primarily protons) and the universe of antimatter houses the existence of soul, spirit, and God. The universe of antimatter exists in our presence, but invisible and intangible to human beings.

To some persons it will seem illogical that certain powers emanating from Heaven can and will physically effect the biology and well-being of a living organism. Others will have no trouble accepting this concept.

However, if we can accept the existence of soul, that miracles do in fact happen everyday, it seems somewhere on earth, that the sick and lame have actually been cured (the wonder of Lourdes Cathedral), that persons are in fact saved from death when medical physicians have performed all treatment that they feel is possible, that sincere prayers are answered, that events are preordained, and that all persons possess a soul, then we should be able to accept that DNA of individuals can be manipulated in a mystical way by the soul within us, and this relationship of spiritual and physical will be understood. Evidence and case histories exist, with verified reports, of both medical and religious events, that "miracles", or unexplained good happenings, do, in fact, happen.

God, acting through the created souls and having the spirit of God, directed and shaped evolution from the moment of the first elemental cell to the later complex sea plant life, fish and sea animals, reptiles and amphibians, mammals, and eventually primates, leading to Homo habilis, Homo erectus, Neanderthal Man, and eventually to us, Homo sapiens and Modern Man.

Only in our current half century has the existence and knowledge of RNA and DNA become known. This RNA and DNA was the means that souls could direct biological changes to take place within the body of mammals and plants.

Souls can effect biologic change to take place in DNA that result in "miracles" of bodily change attested to in medical science and in theology.

Present Homo sapien man was the result of an evolutionary, directed development "engineered" by God, and performed by His kingdom of souls.

In analogy, every deviation in biology and botany was an evolutionary step that industry today calls an "engineering change", a series of inventions that improves the product.

Do We Live In Two Worlds?

Part I - Introduction

The souls of the antimatter, in a Godly world, manipulated cells and bodily processes to affect the desired changes. Charles Darwin was right in his stated theory of evolution, and the mechanics of direct change is shown. However, Darwin did not show specifically how, or the biologic detail, the "mechanics", of exactly what happened to bring the evolutionary changes about. The science of DNA and RNA was not even thought of in Darwin's time.

God is the Creator, but in a sense different from the "ZAP theory" fomented by folklore in multitudinous cultures of the world, presently and in the past.

Homo sapien man, or Modern Man, embodies the spirit of God. God is defined here as an energy, intelligence and consciousness. The body and brain of man is a biologic development, but the intangible mind of man bridges into the antimatter universe.

We can derive analogies of this dimension by citing the wonder of today's computer, that can be programmed to perform any logical sequence. The mind of man exceeds the programmed limits of the computer to allow judgment, love and emotions, sense of a higher spirit, aesthetics, and numerous dimensions greater than logic. Therein lies the difference between man and machine, and between spirit and body.

We need to rethink the dogma of religion and theology that has been offered, in excess, for over 2,000 years. The facts may be there, but the interpretations of church leaders must be reexamined to show, not mystical happenings, but happenings based on scientific principles, understood now, but that were not known centuries ago. Biology, botany, geology, and yes, social science, biological science, and physical science, including Quantum Theory and particle science, were basically the same 2,000 years ago as they are today, but are now better understood and explainable as we enter the 21st century after Christ.

Some people express that they don't know if there is a God or not. They are called Agnostics. I personally have no question regarding this matter and firmly believe that there is a living God, but not in our secular form.

The point for the thinking of an Agnostic is perhaps well taken. After all, there is little hard, tangible evidence of the existence of God.

Fundamentalists point to the existence of day and night, the mountains and beautiful skies, the trees and flowers, the sunshine and weather, events in history, result of any prayer, food on the table, and many other examples they maintain are provisions of God.

I personally believe each of those items are explained by the physics, the mechanics, weather system, geology and geologic development, botanical evolution, anatomy and biology, culture, and economic systems that have come to be more understood today than they were 2,000 years ago. There is no need for faith in these matters that are now explained by rational happenings, and not by miracles.

---

1) In my mind, there has to be more than simply being born, living, and dying. Are we nothing more now than an extension of microbes, algae, bacteria, or virus that first inhabited the earth? Are we nothing more now than a complex conglomerate of cellular material grown over five million years in a mishmash of evolution? Reason tells me that this cannot be so.

2) The function of the human body and human mind is magical, mystical, and more than what could have serendipitously developed over eons, without some direction, without some master plan. Present day life could not possibly have evolved by simply a series of "accidents" or random mutations in chromosomes.

3) The process of birth itself and the technicalities of functioning of the body proper, the eye and visual system, the heart and pulmonary system, the nervous and blood systems, and other complexities of the human body, is so miraculous that a guiding hand must have been present, in my opinion, in the formulation of the process. Otherwise, today's plant and animal configurations would appear ridiculously grotesque and dysfunctional.

4) The human mind has so many intangibles, imponderables, and impreciseness in chosen alternatives that no machine-like, automatic process could operate such a system. How can a process, that so far has not even been duplicated in science by a computer, have been purposely designed and made operational?

5) There is apparent direction and guidance in one's life that supports a dogma that a guiding force is in existence. Some force motivates us, movement by movement, to manifest certain actions. Some actions are reactionary as in all mammals, but other actions follow thoughtful consideration, unique only to man.

6) Greater minds than mine, and many academic, philosophical and theological thinkers in history have pondered this same question for at least 3,000 years,

Do We Live In Two Worlds?

Part I - Introduction

The Case For God's Existence

and have come to the conclusion that a supreme power does exist.

7) Reinterpretation of the Bible, as an authentic source of historic and spiritual information, can be made in light of present day knowledge of how Biblical events could logically have happened, and to weed out illogical, and I believe erroneous in their detail, reports of events that only serve to disenfranchise millions of persons from belief in God.

8) I believe there is an explanation to life and death, that involves God and His processes, that is explainable, and which I have attempted to set forth here.

9) I submit that the world of insects, bacteria, parasites, and deep sea life are examples of evolution that was created, grows, and reproduces without a plan to its genetic evolution. Chaos has produced a wide variation in grotesque body types and existence patterns in these exotic worlds.

True, parents in these insect, bacteria, parasite and sea life families produce identical offspring, and mutations do occur as needs arise (cite changes almost yearly in the influenza viruses that cause continual need to research and develop new vaccines to combat new strains of influenza virus). Yet there seems to be no overriding pattern that leads to a complex "superbug" evolving in a planned or systematic way, as has a basic structure in the mammal family and the human body, as a new strain of outgrowth from a predecessor strain of life. There seems to be no ultra, complex mind-functioning evolution such as exists in humans or even mammals.

Complexities do exist in lifestyle and procedures in living characteristics of these organisms. Study of parasites reveal systems whereby parasitic animals and plants live and thrive in a systematic conveyance through its host, and even more than one host, during the life cycle of the parasites in this world of matter.

I have, I hope, by God-given observation, study and reasoning, provided here a scenario of perhaps when God first existed; when and how souls first existed, continue to exist and their duties; how the physical body of mammals and primates developed from elementary plants and animals; the incarnation of soul to man, and perhaps when soul joined perhaps Homo sapien man, or later, Modern Man; what differentiates man, that has the qualities of soul, from pure animal existence; the being and mission of the soul in afterlife; the possibility of reincarnation; and perhaps even what the longtime future of "mankind" will be.

Hopefully, both the believer in God, and a person who may be Agnostic, will, after reading this book, have gained a more realistic understanding of his God and the hereafter.

We live in two worlds—the world of human beings, which includes other mammals, fish, organic and inorganic beings, and the world of the spirit. The human world and the spirit world have been superimposed upon each other to make a human body with a spirit, as integral parts of each other. There is soul incarnated with the host body.

The human body has evolved over 4 1/2 billion years since the earth became somewhat firm following the Big Bang and solidification of the cosmic gasses emanating and coalescing from that event of 12 to 20 billion years ago.

The story of evolution of algae, amoeba, plants, fish, reptiles, mammals and intelligent man is well documented. The evolution and creation of the spirit is not as well known, but open to speculation.

At the moment of the Big Bang, elementary particles are theorized by physicists to have divided and become uniquely defined after the Grand Unification of the four basic forces in nature. Electrons and protons became basic parts of atoms that make up all physical things, which we call matter.

The opposite part of the split elementary particles, the positively charged electrons, called positrons, and the protons of opposite charge, called anti-protons, went into a somewhat mystical element called antimatter. This is a world invisible to us. The world of antimatter may be somewhat parallel to our own physical world.

I can't help but believe that another world does exist, evidenced by unexplained happenings, sometimes called parapsychology. Events occur in thought transmission, ghosts, sixth sense, deja vu, sensing a feeling, perhaps divine guidance, and who knows what other potential of our intelligence.

I believe this intelligence is the world of the antimatter. I believe the world of antimatter is the world of the spirits, souls and the Holy Ghost.

I believe the soul is in a state of evolution, or refinement, leading to an eventual stage of oneness with God.

I feel that I must respect the tenets of all major religions or thought cultures that have existed over the centuries. Each represents the directed thought of its philosophers, or leading thinkers of that time, after considerable analysis, and was able to continue for a substantial period of time. These should not be summarily dismissed by "moderns" simply because they do not nicely merge with our own accepted doctrines.

Consequently, I give credence to basic thoughts, not only of Christianity, but also to Judaism, Hinduism, Buddhism, philosophies of India, those of American Indians, ancient Egypt, and other mythologies, because, in their respective ages, they have all withstood the tests and trials of their times. Many of the mythologies have fallen from grace simply because a new dogma seemed stronger in the age-long "battle of conventional thought".

I believe we can look beyond accepted modern day theology into a world of possibility. This could be a world that reconciles all known thought—that of the physical world, as well as the metaphysical world.

Do We Live In Two Worlds?

Part I - Introduction

In many ways this reconciled thought theology "shoots down" some of the accepted dogma expressed by many churches today. It is radical. It might hold that Jesus Christ's body was merely mortal—the same as yours and mine, born, raised, died, and decomposed, like yours, mine, and others have and will. The difference is in the spirit or soul of Jesus Christ, His being closer to the oneness with God than that of others.

Jesus Christ taught that the soul can be directed. Civilizations and cultures over the past 2,000 years have paraphrased and interpreted this to mean (in our human, egotistical way) that the actions of the body can be directed. In some ways they are parallel, but I believe the physical status and activity of the body, in contrast to the development of the soul, are distinct and separate. The human body is the vehicle for the actions that manifest the refinement of the soul, and the means of proof that the soul has, in fact, undergone the living experience.

The human body has evolved over the past 4 1/2 billion years. Charles Darwin has largely spelled out the mechanics of how biological changes in living organisms have been manifested, and scientists are only now unwrapping the secrets of genes that control our development. But logic would dictate that there must have been a guiding force. Billion and billions of mutations have affected changes in living organisms since the start of life. But without a "master" guiding force, a master plan, a direction of the system, the miracle of life of birds, fish, reptiles, mammals, and man could not have come about. I believe that force to be God.

One needs to look only at the organs and systems of the living body, including the brain mechanism, versus the mind, that exceeds any other biological-electrical system, that will reflect the soul of God, to be amazed at the intelligence required to "engineer" such a marvel.

Postscript

In November 1996, Pope John Paul II announced a possible existence of both body and soul in man. This was reported in the November 4, 1996 issue of U.S. News and World Report, page 12.

Historically, fundamentalist churches, and especially the Roman Catholic Church, tenaciously upheld dogma that God created mankind in His image, in contrast to an opposing theory that humans evolved from animals, as Darwin theorized nearly 150 years ago.

In November 1996, the Pope announced that "evolution may be the better explanation". The Pope declared that evolution is "more than just a theory and is fully compatible with the Christian faith".

In a letter to the Pontifical Academy of Sciences, he also reaffirmed church teachings that, while the human body may have evolved gradually, the soul "is immediately created by God" in each person.

In 1950, Pope Pius XII called evolution a "serious hypothesis" worthy of study. As early as the 5th Century, St. Augustine warned against a literal reading of the Genesis creation account.

But John Paul II went further than previous Popes in declaring that a "convergence" of scientific evidence gathered in the past 50 years makes "a significant arguments in favor of this theory".

This isn't the Pope's first attempt to reconcile religion and science. In 1988 he called for ongoing dialogue between theologians and scientists. In 1992, he declared that the church had erred in condemning Galileo Galilei in 1633 for asserting that the earth revolves around the sun."

Especially in this present day, with its intense state of knowledge gained over millenniums, persons of recognized specialties in knowledge must, of necessity, limit their scope of research to those aspects that border on their own field of expertise. It seems that we no longer find the alchemist, or the sage, or the oracle, that portend to be all knowing in all fields (perhaps because knowledge in these many fields was limited at the time of their heyday in history).

Like medicine, surgery, engineering, and most other fields of knowledge, these specialties have evolved into subspecialties. Nearly all fields have developed their own specialized areas of knowledge and expertise, many times forgoing the generalist approach to their profession.

Because of the steadily increasing wealth of technical information arising in all fields of knowledge, even the broad scope "Renaissance Man" was limited to those persons who must be concerned with economic and intellectual advancement only in their chosen profession, rather than those persons who wished to follow studies in multiple-discipline knowledge areas.

As for myself, I feel that my academic degrees and experience in business (MBA, The University of Michigan, 1967), with a wide interest and diverse reading in many fields of interest, has worked to my advantage in presenting this academic exploration.

Perhaps because of my lack of an academic degree and credentials in science that might provide me as a recognized authority in some academic fields outside of those that I possess, and without a professional, academic reputation to piously protect against challenges from academic peers, I actually can demonstrate an advantage in radical exploration of independent thoughts.

I can afford to go off, some might say "half cocked", much as a participant might do in a "think tank", without practical constraints that restrict the thinking process before it is allowed to really get started. If my intuition is wrong on some particular attitude, so be it. Maybe some offshoot variation might lead to a more realistic truth. My scientific career and means of livelihood will not be ruined. I was only an interested amateur looking for a truth anyway!

Conceivably, and I'm sure this sounds egotistical, some of my hypotheses are wrong, and will be proved in error over time. But if some are new and found to be possible, perhaps a new truth will be found and later proven.

I do not claim to have scientific evidence for these findings, nor do I see scientific evidence that these concepts could not occur.

My hypotheses are based solely on a wide experience in reading and upon reason, formulated from observed phenomena in living experiences and knowledge of happenings.

For example, there is no tangible evidence to prove the existence of ghosts, or spirits, or soul, sensory perception, deja vu, reincarnation, alien intelligent beings and travel, time warps, time variance phenomena, power of prayer, existence of God, accuracy of biblical events, folklore in various cultures, creation of the world and universe, Heaven or Hell and many other unexplained phenomena.

Interdisciplinary Fertilization

There is considerable fact available in history, at least as recorded with the various biases of historians, to provide some basis for judgment in probable events in fields of geology, chemistry, physics and cultural history. More and more truths are becoming known in other fields of medical science and biology, astronomy and cosmology, evolution, social sciences, mentality, animal behavior, ecology, economics, geography, and, yes, theology.

Intense specific research by academicians, including scientists in all fields, is the wellspring of advancement in knowledge. Bless the efforts of these specialized, intensive, "wet chemistry" type academic researchers and their concentrated, specialized research, with quests for hard evidence to support their hypotheses.

The generals in an army can postulate and theorize a battle attack plan, but it is the foot soldiers who must do the actual shooting and slog in the mud. Likewise, these academic researchers will, given enough time, effort and funds, arrive at the truths.

My contribution (and the reader may choose to parallel this contribution with his or her own research towards this study) is the observed continuity, broadness, and interrelationship of various disciplines of chemistry, geology, physics, biological science, anthropology, and theology. Study resulted in an evolution of knowledge in fields of human, animal and plant anatomy, culture, history, and even to observing a generality in occupations that different individuals follow occupations with similar traits, (i.e., persons who choose to be accountants usually prefer a precise nature in the work they perform, whereas artists often prefer a more loose structure in their occupational mental functioning).

Nothing happens without a reason, consciously or unconsciously, understood or not understood. There is a purpose in life. There are possibilities of new knowledge through speculation into unexplained events.

Science needs a "think tank approach" to creativity where there are no constraints to what minds might create. The mechanics of how research, testing and implementation will be accomplished can be confronted afterwards. A think tank approach will begin with free thought, not constraints.

It is the author's considered opinion that, from the eon of first life on earth, there existed Intelligent Evolution. This evolution, guided by a body of intelligence, was orchestrated by angels, acting under the direction of God, purposely effecting the RNA and DNA in living cells, and subsequently the organs of basic plants and primitive animals (virus and amoeba).

Intelligent Evolution progressed in the evolutionary paths to ever-increasing complexity in anatomical and biological existence.

Animal evolution was paralleled by botanical evolution in flora of the earth.

In the mid-1800s, Abraham Lincoln stated that all men are created equal. This is ideally true in the United States in a political sense, but it is far from true biologically on a worldwide scale.

We observe differences in average height of persons from western South America, with Peruvian Indian heritage as an example. Also, many persons of ancient Japanese heritage, some whose families migrated to Japan perhaps 2,000 and 4,000 years ago from the China mainland and from what is now the Korean Peninsula, are also shorter than persons on a worldwide average in height.

Many of those persons also have a racial distinction in face, eyebrow, and skin pigmentation, with tendency for eyesight limitation, and with other biological strengths and weaknesses.

Other skin color variation occurs in what might be described as Mongolian, Indian, African, Native North American, and European. Scientists have found certain biological differences in blood, chromosome, RNA and DNA characteristics, with subsequent tendencies for, and protections against, certain disease types, biological strengths and weaknesses, and body variation.

We can observe another geographical, anatomical variation in the idealistic shaped breasts of women. The ancient statues of Romanesque cultures carved in stone, of which there are many, are amazing in their lifelike realism for detail of persons in the art of ancient Rome, Greece, India, the Orient, and even possibly Spain and southern France. There seems to be a belt of civilization through the area described by those historic origins that all display this common feature in anatomy.

There was a pretty legend in ancient Greece that the first cup was molded upon Helen's (of Troy) breast. (Source: *The Life Of Greece,* Will Durant, Simon and Shuster, 1939)

The formation of female breasts, in what we might call northern European origins, are somewhat triangular in shape, with the upper portion of the breast starting the formation fairly high on the chest, near the collar bone. However, in statues of women in Roman and Greek art, as well as art of ancient India and China, the breasts are noticeably more conical, round, nearly saucer shape. The shape of breasts on these statues seem not to be unique only to youth, because some characteristics of the female models are those of women well beyond the age of puberty. (In reality, perhaps many females were utilized as models in a composite for the sculptor to form an idealistic feminine form.)

Geographic origin of one's historic family (ancestry) can be observed today in some females by the shape of their breasts, albeit cross marriages occurring during the past 2,000 years have many times diluted this distinction of whether breasts were conical or triangular in shape.

Two characteristics can be observed in breasts of African females. The conical shape is noticed in some teenage persons, while in older persons, who have experienced child birth and breast feeding, the breasts seem to become elongated, functional to contain an adequate supply of mother's milk for child nurturing in successive births.

Romanesque origins can sometimes also be associated with a ruddy skin complexion and strong facial features frequently seen today in Italian and Greek people.

This variation in human anatomy, physiology and biology in humans at different regions of earth gives credence to the school of thought that creation of humans did not occur in only one location on earth as argued among anthropologists.

Instead, various forms of Homo sapiens had developed in multiple areas, each area encouraging specific characteristics through evolution and development of distinctive characteristics in anatomy, physiology and biology.

The soul and mind were later incorporated into each Homo sapien body on earth to form Cro-Magnon man in a total system of God, implemented by angels working through the intricacies of DNA and RNA, and acting at the direction of God.

This explanation of the cause and effect relationship of soul and genes will be considered by many as outrageous—in their minds it just does not seem to stand up to reason. I defend my theory only on the basis, at this time, that it happens!

That souls exist, most thinking humans including theologians, psychologists and many physical and medical scientists will agree.

That genes in the DNA sequence change and subsequent changes in one's biology occur in a predictable manner, is now a fact proven by geneticists and medical researchers.

My thesis that souls manipulate genes in an intelligent and purposeful manner is the premise of my theory, outrageous in their reasoning or not!

The world of science, and the greater world of knowledge in general, are abundant with events that at first appear outrageous. Nearly all developments were once considered outrageous by conservative-thinking contemporaries. With proven development, the breakthrough of new thought has been shown to be reality. This is shown in all fields of study from construction of skyscrapers to heart surgery.

In this book the author has proposed some ideas and concepts that he realizes are quite radical from generally accepted beliefs. He has raised questions:

1.) Is there a universe that exists separate, and unknown to us on earth that incorporates the existence of souls and of God?

2.) The universe that we now live in was the result of the "Big Bang", some 14.7 billion years ago. What action resulted in the creation of this other universe that is different from the one that we know?

3.) Where did the protons go, that equaled in number the electrons, that are the base of our known universe?

4.) Was God in existence as a predecessor of the "Big Bang"?

5.) Are souls existent in the world of antimatter?

6.) Can souls manipulate the genes of a living organism?

7.) Will there be an end to life as we know it?

8.) Remaining questions can be answered by rational thinking that is not bound to confusing theological dogma which has been assembled in a hegemony of beliefs over a period of 2,000 to 6,000 years.

To question #1—Is there another universe?

Our known universe resulted from, and continues to be determined from, a series of "decision tree" events. Philosophers reason as follows: A child is born, and lives. The alternative is that the born child does not live. The child matures and marries a certain person, parenting certain children. As an alternative, the child may have married someone else and parented entirely different children. The matured person accomplishes certain goals in his or her lifetime. If these situations have not been accomplished, would they have been accomplished at all, or who would have accomplished the goal: If Christ had not been born, would someone else have represented God on earth.

Each of the events that happen were either a (+) or a (-) in the sequence of events. The (+) alternatives are those events that we have realized during our lifetime. The (-) alternatives are those that might have been. Philosophers in recent years have theorized that each event decision constitutes a different alternative universe, a different existence from that of which we remember. Thus there are innumerable multiple universes, of which our five senses tell us of only one.

To question #2—What action created a universe other than our known universe?

Our known universe was created at the Big Bang. This was an "event decision". The Big Bang either happened, or it didn't happen. We can realistically state that from this event that physically happened, our universe was created. From the events that did not happen to our senses, but happened in the world of antimatter, another universe may well have come into existence.

To question #3—Where did the excess protons go following the "Big Bang"?

In the Grand Unification prior to the Big Bang, an equal number of electrons and protons existed. At the moment of the Big Bang, annihilation of protons by electrons took place, leaving a universe of electron-based matter, that we know in physics, chemistry, metallurgy, and geology are evidenced in the records within rocks and metals preserved on earth.

The annihilated protons continued on in existence, but now in a different universe. This is the universe of antimatter, and consists virtually of the opposite being of the various events and qualities that comprise our electron-based universe.

To question #4—Was God a predecessor of the "Big Bang"?
(Set: How Old Is God?)

God is an existence of energy, intelligence, and consciousness. God is omnipotent. However, there is no physical existence of God.

The existence of God could very well have transcended the Big Bang, having an existence prior to this event, and reigning in a universe prior to the Big Bang.

To question #5—Are souls existent in the world of antimatter?

Through evolution, living matter evolved from inorganic, or metallic matter, by a combination of electrons, protons, neutrons, and sub-components evolving from the Big Bang, such as quarks, leptons, muons, pions, and various forces that modern-day particle physicists have discovered. These are called weak force, strong force, electromagnetic force, and gravitation.

Do We Live In Two Worlds?

Part I - Introduction

Flat, two dimensional cells evolved and formed into tubular three dimensional worms, having a food intake at one end, energy conversion in the middle, and waste expulsion at the other end. From this basic intestine other organs evolved having specialty functions of nerves and brain, heart and circulatory, renal functions, reproduction, skeletal, protective skin, and the many other organs of living organisms. Perhaps, as is proposed in this book, this was accomplished by the "genetic engineering" manipulation of souls acting at the direction of God.

In each of the qualities and energies found in matter, science has discovered comparable, but opposite, qualities in antimatter.

As life eventually formed in the universe of matter, comparable but opposite existent qualities evolved into the form of souls, within the universe of God.

The soul is that intangible part of a person's mortality that exceeds his physical being. It is the person's liaison and connection to a world or universe beyond our own that exhibits worthiness and perpetual being.

Angels exist as messengers within this perpetual universe. They are souls and are designated by the Almighty God to serve as His representative in Heaven and on Earth. They carry the spirit, or concept of the existence of God, with powers to affect change.

This book will elaborate in more detail on the existence, definition, and description of souls, angels, and spirit. *(See Part IV-The Soul)*

Cultures of the world have recognized the soul of man ever since deceased persons have been buried, going back to at least the era of 10,000 BC. By this recognition, that cultures separated the human existence from that of an animal, which is left where it died, its body to be consumed by other wildlife as an animal of the forest.

Egyptian culture, dating back to at least 4,000 BC presents evidence of recognition and attempt to preserve one's mortality. Great thinkers and philosophers of this world, including Socrates, Plato, and Aristotle of 600 to 200 BC did espouse the existence of duality and soul existing within man.

Biblical records are rich in discussing and defining the soul, mentioning the existence in the Book of Genesis describing Adam and Eve and subsequent personalities of both the Old and New Testaments. Angels are cited, as well as the Spirit of God.

Specters have been reported as existing throughout our civilization, a manifestation of ethereal existence from a dimension different from what we understand in our own universe, and outside of our defined tangible matter.

Christianity, Hebrew, Moslem, Buddhism, American Indian, Hindu, and "dark religions" of so-called uncivilized societies all recognize the existence of soul, or a dimension of one's existence beyond his physical being.

Soul, angels, and spirit are all manifestations of existence within a mystical being incorporating the world of God.

To question #6—Can souls manipulate the genes of a living organism?

Do We Live In Two Worlds?
Part I - Introduction

Is This Possible?

The existence of God and of souls is mystical. It is impossible to state precisely what events are within the power of God and souls. It is generally accepted in most religions of the world that there is no limit to the powers of the Almighty. Souls, acting from God, and in an antimatter universe, can exert genetic engineering within life organisms, just as modern-day science is now on the verge of making physical changes and/or direction by cloning in the microbiology of living organisms.

We see this in the grafting of trees to form new qualities in the new variety. We see this in the study of genetics and offspring formed when a man and a women unite to form an offspring containing qualities derived from each, the man and woman. We see this in biological accomplishments of only recent years in which a perfect clone is formulated in producing an exact copy of a mother sheep.

Can we not say that souls, acting as representatives of God, and working in a mystical way, cannot accomplish the same results that are known to modern day science?

To question #7—Will there be an end to life as we know it?

Catastrophe is bound to happen again, sooner or later. Nearly all life forms existent at the time have been wiped clear from the surface of the earth several times since earth has evolved from a gaseous state to firmness, and from basic life forms to multicell animals, and from sea life with plants and fish to land mammals and reptiles. Mass extinctions have taken place, as shown in the geologic record of rocks and fossils at periods of 438 million years ago, 367 mya, 248 mya, 208 mya, and the extinguishing of dinosaurs at about 65 million years ago.

Environmental changes following physical catastrophe and changes seemed to account for the K-T collapse and explosion (at about 100,000,000 years ago between the Cretaceous and Tertiary periods of geologic time) of new life forms, as well as at the extinction of dinosaurs, believed to have been prompted by an asteroid from outer space colliding with earth.

An earlier extinction resulted from an imbalance of oxygen proportion in the atmosphere which actually poisoned life forms on earth. The author has presented a number of events (see Appendix) that could happen, some of which already have, and which could extinguish life on the earth as we know it.

What would be the form of existence on earth following another mass extinction? The author proposes that all life on land and water could become extinct, with continuation of existence being in a nonphysical form, that of a universe of antimatter and souls. God and souls, consisting of nonphysical energy and intelligence, would survive secular catastrophe to form a new world far different from life as we know it.

No one can predict when such a catastrophe might happen. The inter-periods of 71 million, 119, 40, and 143 million years seem to reveal little towards a frequency study. It could be argued that frequency is, on average, about every 100 million years, and with 65 million years transpired since the last mass extinction, we are due for another mass extinction at about 35 million years from now. On the other hand, catastrophe could happen as early as next year.

In anthropology, tracing backwards, Modern Man, or Homo sapiens with features of Modern Man, succeeded Neanderthal man at about 35,000 years ago. Neanderthal had come upon the world scene with a taller and larger brain, succeeding Homo erectus, at about 125,000 years ago.

Before, was the transitional and innovative, alert, intelligent, tool-using Homo habilis, whose fossil remains date to 1.8 million years, and the then contemporary Austropithicus boesei dates to 1.5 to 2.5 million years ago.

The last two inter-periods between the present, 35,000 years ago, and 125,000 years ago, averages 62,500 years.

By this reasoning, earth is due for a momentous anthropological change at about 45,000 years from now. We need lose no sleep that anthropological change will occur in our lifetimes, although cultural changes occur step by step with changes observed each century, and even more often.

It is not a case of *Will* this happen again, but *When* catastrophe changes the course of mankind. The Cambrian period was a time of incredible evolutionary experimentation. In the space of a few tens of millions of years, there evolved not only the ancestors of everything alive today, but also dozens of lineages that were simply wiped out in mass extinction. Ninety six percent of all species living during the middle Cambrian period, 530 million years ago, became extinct.

First primates bearing human features, Australopithecus afarensis, appeared between 3.9 and 3 million years ago, and is considered the common root of the human family tree. This specie lived for almost a million years in a region that ranged from Ethiopia in the north to the end of Africa in the south.

Many geologists believe life could not have had a permanent toehold on the earth until the meteor bombardment subsided about 3.9 billion years ago. The dating of the earliest known life forms allowed about 500 million years for the presumable development of living cells.

To question #8—Remaining questions

Questions remaining can be answered, at least in concept, by rational thinking that is not bound to confusing, theological dogmas that have been assembled over a time period of 2,000 to 6,000 years—or more, and that was limited by the lack of scientific knowledge contrasted with that we possess today.

Dogmas were shaped by a variety of cultures that sought and created their own answers to questions peculiar to their time and needs. Dogmas were presented, some of a mystical nature, some as a compromise of various favorite beliefs of different subcultures and religious centers, and some assembled as political, self-serving dogma of church leaders taking place over thousands of years in order to satisfy prominent religious or secular power centers of the time. History has exposed numerous situations where church policy was bent, and perhaps even contrary to certain Biblical "facts", to seek agreement with powerful personalities. How far are we today from that truth that existed 2,000 years ago, 6,000 years ago, and perhaps 12 billion years ago?

Over the years various cultures sought and created answers to questions peculiar to their time and needs, some of a mystical nature, some as a compromise of various favorite beliefs from different religious centers, and some assembled as political, self-serving dogma that would satisfy prominent religious power centers at the time.

Regardless of how one accepts the answers outlined here, the reasoning is certainly no more preposterous than some of the events and miracles reported in the Bible, and other native folklore that have been handed down for ages in tribal legends of various cultures throughout the world.

Some readers may feel that a concept of mystical manipulation of DNA genes in chromosomes is absurd. In opposition, the author proposes that it is not absurd, but that it is only a new concept.

In looking back through the decades and centuries of history in medicine, biological science, and research providing new information, each idea at its outset, seemed preposterous. It seemed preposterous that any cure or prevention routine could be had for leprosy. This condition existed probably for centuries and was reported in the Bible. It was thought to be part of the system of God and human existence.

Bubonic Plague was probably rationalized by some in the Middle Ages as a message from God and a part of God's plan. It was deemed a means to reduce the number of people on earth, and Middle Ages economists reasoned that it brought the number of people in the world into balance with the world's ability to produce food.

It was preposterous to think that milk and foods could and should be pasteurized—that change in methods of food processing was against "God's way".

Smallpox vaccination, resulting from biological research into cause and prevention of that disease, was a "miracle of the day". Inoculating children against smallpox seemed to be the only logical, humane action to take. Very few, if any, felt that protecting children from smallpox was "against God's way", or that it was attributed to a miracle rather than advancement in medical and biological science.

Tuberculosis and Infantile Paralysis (known as Polio), debilitating diseases throughout the world, have been largely conquered through 1) medical research to identify the disease and microscopic germs that attack the body, 2) discovery of an action (inoculation and drops) that would prevent persons from acquiring the condition, and 3) doing something about it, in the form of an extensive program of inoculation and drops that has all but eliminated the disease in North America, and is rapidly being eliminated world-wide.

Do We Live In Two Worlds?

Part I - Introduction

These marvelous discoveries of how to prevent or alleviate human suffering have been and are heralded by societies since the time of Christ and before as refinement, and in their time, as "miracles promoting God's way" in human, animal, plant, fish, and insect ecology and development.

Discovery of the operation of RNA and DNA during the mid-1900s, and the result from gene engineering following the discovery has resulted in biological change that will affect mankind on a worldwide scale.

The main "preposterous" event that remains in this topic is "how" the act of soul in angels can manipulate genes of the chromosomes. (The motivation of "why" such acts are undertaken as a macro-plan lies deeper into philosophical thought.) Studies by Charles Darwin and others in the late 1700s and 1800s introduced evidence that biological and physical changes in birds and life in general are prompted by an environmental need. What were the "biological mechanics" surrounding need for change, say, in a more or less, massive bill or longer bill on birds, and the actual biological change that came about? There was an action (call it mystical if you wish; the author sees it as a rational and logical operation of a physiological system) that affected genes of the specie, that in turn produced physical change.

Likewise, the author here tries to illuminate that manipulation of genes occurred and was accomplished by "force" applied by soul and angels of God, in an inter-universe action paralleling our universe of matter and a universe of particle science, both becoming more understood by our world of science as each year passes.

This similar force is recognized and deemed as power of God, similar to acts resulting from and recognition of, and faith in, a Supreme Being. It is action of particle science, acting in a parallel universe of antimatter.

The "preposterous" supposition has turned to one of possibility, when our limits of existence are stretched to reveal new knowledge. The author asks that the reader prospect and consider that there are possibilities that arise from new knowledge, and that those possibilities extend to "mystical" manipulation of genes in living organisms.

HOW OLD IS GOD?

The question of "How Old Is God?" is imponderable. Was God in existence prior to the Big Bang? Or was God created at time of the Big Bang, when it is theorized in this book that the world of antimatter was created upon annihilation of positive-based elementary particles, separated from negative-charge particles that formed matter?

Logic would dictate that everything has a beginning. If so, it would be logical that God came into existence from antimatter at moment identical to time that did the essence of first souls. From that celestial moment forward God existed, guiding physical and antimatter progress to Earth, to Heaven, and possibly to some greater scope, such as to other galaxies.

Do We Live In Two Worlds?

Part I - Introduction

In advocating God's first existence at time of our Big Bang, and advocating that numerous Big Bangs occurred to create other galaxies, either before or after our Milky Way Galaxy was created, the question arises of whether those created galaxies also had a created world of matter, antimatter, souls, and a god.

The author suggests that the reader be at least as open-minded in considering these possibilities as he, or she, has demonstrated in accepting theological dogma and ritual in the past. There is today rational explanation for the phenomena which in times before we were forced to attribute to faith.

If some academic person promotes some alternative, I say "more power to him or her. These surely may be alternative thoughts to the concepts presented here. I accept that.

PART II

CREATION

We have heard the term "created" almost since the start of our exposure to religious training. One version of the answer to the child's question of, "Where did we come from", is the common parental reply that "God created the Heavens and the Earth".

This event was supposedly the bringing into existence—something out of nothingness. Later, our religious exposure states, God created man from earth and breathed life into him. In like manner, woman was created out of the rib of Adam.

In the story *"Pinochio"*, the wood craftsman, Gepetto, carved a marionette from wood, which miraculously acquired life, to be the son that Gepetto had always wanted.

In the story of *"My Fair Lady"*, modeled after the Greek drama, and a later play, *"Pygmalion"*, by George Bernard Shaw, a refined lady, Liza Doolittle, is created by Professor Higgins from an ordinary "street urchin" who had origins in the environment of London's impoverished area, and lower social strata.

My Webster's dictionary states that creation is *"an act of creating, or fact of being created; specifically, the act of causing to exist, or fact of being brought into existence, by divine power, especially, the act of bringing the world into existence out of nothing"*.

To bring the event into real, understandable, and tangible terms, I believe we can relate "creation" as akin to the similar concept of "invention". An engineer, mechanic, or even an untrained man (or woman) creates an automobile, for example, by bringing together factors that already exist, of iron, rubber, oil, electricity, and even fabricated parts made of steel sheets, iron castings and forgings, rubber tires, gaskets, gears, lubricating oils, explosive gasoline vapors, spark plugs, and other elements to make the scheme work.

By adding the steam engine to the preexisting boat hull, Jacques C. Perier, in France, 1775, created a steamship. By adding steam power to a wheeled vehicle, Richard Trevithick, in England, 1804, created a railroad locomotive, useful to move passengers and freight along metal rails.

By adding an electrical vacuum tube to make simple "yes" or "no" reactions, electronic computers were created.

There is the Biblical "creation" of the earth, seas, and the air. These masses are really elements that had evolved in a physical, geological, and chemical sense as evolution over billions of years from cosmic clouds after the Big Bang. Animal and living organisms had evolved botanically and biologically from first organisms of algae and amoeba into complex plants, animals, and insects.

Therefore, creation can be merely adding life to an already existing complex, and not necessarily creating the elements of the complex itself.

I believe this is what God did in creating man. He added life, in the form of soul, to an already existing complex of an anatomical, or animalistic body.

Judeo-Christian doctrine has, I believe, jumped to the conclusion that creation means making presence where nothing existed before. I believe that this is not necessarily so. Adding a concept to an already existing being is also creation.

In the terminology that *"God created man in His own image"*, the concept more likely refers to bringing the added presence of soul to man, and not to bringing existence of man's animalistic body.

Rather than the wisdom stated in the Book of Genesis that God created man in His own image, it might more properly be said that God created souls in His own image. Souls are the essence of God, and upon total refinement of their morality, will join God in a oneness.

Souls evolved from particles of antimatter to incarnate with the complex organism of Homo sapiens to form a completed entity known as Cro-Magnon, aka Modern Man.

Let us keep our concepts of "creation" clear, and not be open to "fuzzy thinking" in this regard, especially when it comes to theology. Science holds that matter can be neither created nor destroyed.

Knowledge existing at the present day proposes a realistic theory of how matter came into existence from the moment of the Big Bang, and before. I have further proposed in this presentation how possibly the world, or a universe, of souls, from an existence in a world of antimatter, came into individual existence, souls emanating out of the "God-substance" itself.

I also propose here that God could well have existed in a cosmos prior to the Big Bang. Such prior existence of a cosmos would have previously been condensed by a Black Hole into a Grand Unification. The Grand Unification Theory (GUT) comprised the very essence and origin of the Big Bang, or possibly several GUTs, causing several Big Bangs.

It is the author's contention that the elements of physical creation were present at the moment that matter was placed into existence, and that the elements of mystical creation were present at the moment that soul was incarnated into the animal body, that became Cro-Magnon man. The origin of physical matter, and the origin of antimatter with the accompanying creation of souls, is explained in later chapters.

Cro-Magnon man developed from Homo sapiens at sometime between 25,000 and 12,000 BC. This coincides with the general period that civilization is said to have started on earth, with early beginnings in cultivation agriculture, hunting and social groups organized with common goals, and writing or pictures as a form of tangible communication. This creation was like "the Garden of Eden" in the evolution of Modern Man.

Note: *The contents of this chapter are important to understanding this book and form basic premises to the theses developed here. The author has attempted to present the material in a nontechnical manner to facilitate the reader understanding the concepts. Further reading in each of the technical fields alluded to here are available for research in the literature.*

I maintain that the world of souls, Heaven if you wish, the world of God-substance, was created in the moments of the "Big Bang". I will try to present here, as simply as I can, some complex physics that theoretical physicists have uncovered in the past half to three-quarters of this century.

Particle Physicists, or Elemental Physicists (those scientists that delve into the minute components of atoms, including electrons, protons, neutrons, and within these, quarks, in turn having various forces and "colors", and a wide variety of other forces and phenomena) work in a field of knowledge relatively new, developing only within the latter part of our current century. The specialized field of study in the components and qualities of atoms is sometimes called the area of Quantum Mechanics, Particle Physics, Elemental Physics or Quantum Field Theory, all names for this relatively new field of physics.

It may be difficult to fathom, but scientists in these fields theorize that all the particles of the universe could be condensed into a "unification", having the absence of space between.

Do We Live In Two Worlds?

This is understandable when we visualize the vast distances in our own solar system, for example, the 93 million miles (one Astronomical Unit, or A.U.) distance between our Sun and Earth, or greater by about 40 astronomical units, between our Sun and the furthest known planet, Pluto.

One astronomical unit represent 8.3 minutes of travel at the speed of light. It takes about 5.5 hours for light to travel from our Sun to the planet Pluto at this same speed of light.

To better comprehend this space, if a dime were to be laid on the ground to represent our Sun, Earth would be two yards away. Pluto would be 75 yards away, and 15 miles away would be the Oort Cloud at the very edge of our Solar System. The Oort Cloud is the origin of many comets.

The extent of space void between Earth and our closest cosmic neighbor, the galaxy Andromeda, is 900,000 light years. This is nearly an inconceivable number of astronomical units, as may be even the 40 astronomical units of distance to Pluto.

An atom might be visualized as like a solar system, with electrons circling a nucleus, further containing protons and neutrons, much like our sun contains particles of hydrogen and solids. Visualize the relative (I stress relative) minimal space taken up by the mass or solids in our solar system once the intra-molecular space, in between, is taken out. Once this space within an atom is removed, there is a tremendous reduction in relative size.

We can think further of our own earth, made up of uncountable atoms in everything having physical presence (rocks, water, soil, metals, the telephone on the wall, and all items that comprise matter on the earth, planets, comets, and dark matter in our solar system).

In addition to the solar system (our Sun and planets) being compressed, the atoms of the solid portion of the universe (other stars and celestial bodies such as comets, asteroids, dark matter, moons, satellites, etc.) would also be compressed, void of all space, and leaving only elementary particles.

Thirdly, imagine our Sun, a constantly exploding mass of hydrogen, helium, and solids, undergoing a similar compression, with distance between each atom reduced to zero space.

Fourth, electrons and protons are made up of elementary particles, called quarks, with space, infinitesimal as it would seem, separating each of the three quarks in each electron and proton. These too would be reduced to elementary particles with a void of space between.

Science may determine other particles, within quarks, which also exist, with certain distance between each of these particles. Additional findings in this field will be revealed by science research in the future.

With this multiple compression, we can visualize a substance, or mass, containing only what physicists refer to as Elementary Particles. These are particles that were present at, or momentarily after, the initial moments of the "Big Bang". It has been theorized that, with all space removed, the elementary particles remaining in the entire cosmos would occupy a size no larger than a modern-day basketball. However, the mass of this substance would be astronomically great, as would be the temperature of the substance before and upon its expansion.

In addition, the inherent qualities and nature of these elementary particles changed during the milliseconds of the "Big Bang" event. Other "opposites" came into existence to form anti-quarks and similar abnormalities. (Anti-electrons, anti-protons, anti-neutrons, anti-photons, etc.)

The "Big Bang" supplied a disc of dust and debris, called the planetary nebula, out of which the planets and stars originally formed. The inward migration of dust and debris resulted from the basic physics governing the motions of orbiting material and gravitation.

Solidification, through gravitation, amalgamated, condensed and changed the elements comprising the solid bodies of stars, planets and satellites to be what they are today, even though transition was and is still in progress.

Into the gases that had gravitated to the cosmic solid, later to be called earth, fell also solid debris from space, including asteroids, remains of broken planets, moons, comets, and whatever else that came within the horizon of earth's gravitation.

The elementary particles present at the initial moment of the "Big Bang" may be the end result of a compression that took place in a "Black Hole", acting as a swirling cosmic funnel collecting matter from perhaps some previous universe or cosmos, as if it were some type of enormous centrifuge.

Temperatures in the "Big Bang" were likely in the magnitude of millions of degrees Celsius or more as particles of atoms, and atoms themselves, would strive for position and thus cause such tremendous heat.

I theorize that the unification of the four forces of nature, (Strong force, Weak force, Electromagnetic, and Gravitation) and the consequent "Big Bang", was the end result of a "Black Hole". (For further discussion, see the chapter, "A *Black Hole Theory*" later in this book.)

There may even have been, in the wildest stretch of our imagination, an earlier generation of universes, like various generations of stars that cosmos scientists now know form, explode and then reform with new, more complex elements and heavier metals.

At the very beginning, the initial moment of the "Big Bang", electrons and protons did not exist. The "father" of these two particles was known as a Neutron. As the neutron "aged", in milliseconds, equal charges of negative and positive electric forces were created. Negative electrical forces formed electrons, and positive electrical forces formed protons.

For every negative force, there was a positive force. Negatively charged elementary particles canceled out nearly all positively charged elementary particles of like nature. The negatively charged electrons became matter. The remaining positively charged electrons (positrons), became antimatter. This elimination, with nearly equal numbers of negative and positive forces, is called "annihilation", that is, negative forces annihilated positive forces.

Annihilation of electrons in excess of protons is called the "CP Violation". This has been observed in the laboratory. Annihilation occurred about a millionth of a second after the incident of the "Big Bang". (Further discussion of these topics can be found in two excellent books, *The Left Hand Of Creation* by John D. Barrow and Joseph Silk, published by William Heinmann, Ltd., London, England, and *Virtual Dust* by Christian de Duve, Published by Basic Books, NY, NY. The reader is also referred to *Cosmic Antimatter* in Scientific American magazine, April, 1998.)

The result was a net balance in number of electrons over protons. The electrons in atoms, circling the nucleus made up of protons and neutrons, are the base of matter in the universe—the items that we can see and touch (or at least visualize and study when they are deep within the earth, the seas, or in the atmosphere).

With a net balance of electrons that formed matter, and understanding that for every electron there was a proton, we can theorize that anti-protons, which were eliminated from matter during the annihilation process, and anti-electrons, known in physics as positrons, made their own world of antimatter.

The antimatter is opposite in all ways of physics to matter. It is not physical, has no dimension or weight, and cannot be seen as a physical entity. As electrons exist in matter, positrons, which are anti-electrons, exist in antimatter. The makeup of "atoms" in antimatter are basically the same, but opposite in terms of physics and qualities, as it is in matter.

My thesis is that a world of antimatter was created at the moment of the Big Bang, as was matter, and the world of antimatter is the world of Heaven, if you will. Further, the population of that world of antimatter are souls. The souls evolved from a God-substance.

Souls were combined, or incarnated, into the parallel developing humanoid forms at some time in the history of the world. Perhaps this time was with the development of species leading to the present day Cro-Magnon, or Modern Man. Predecessors of Cro-Magnon and Homo sapiens on earth, anthropologists tell us, were Neanderthal Man, who lacked certain advanced qualities of Homo sapiens. Fossils of Homo sapiens date back nearly 35,000 years BCE (Before Current Era).

Neanderthal Man populated the earth during the years from nearly 250,000 BC to about 35,000 years ago. There was a common period from about 100,000 to 35,000 BC when both Neanderthal and Homo sapiens inhabited the earth, with Neanderthal eventually becoming extinct as a species and Homo sapiens arising to prominence.

Fossil remains have been discovered over the past 100 to 150 years by anthropologists to form a story of continuous humanoid evolution, with progressive complexity in successive types of predecessor man leading to Modern Man.

Anthropologists generally date the start of civilization, as defined by development of language, special purpose tools, organized wild animal hunts for community food supplies, forms of agriculture, and animal husbandry, at about 10,000 BCE, although arrowheads and stone points for cutting and striking have been unearthed dating to 30,000 BCE, and before. Writing is said to have begun in Sumer (in now southeast Iraq), with the pre-semitic population of the lower Euphrates valley.

Since this event, soul and man, I contend, have existed on earth as one, with eventual separation at time of the human death. I further contend that there is reentry of a soul (reincarnation) at the time of various events including childbirth, possibly at formation of the fetus, or during life through salvation of some pathetic, wayward human, or animal, or even plant existence. *{See Appendix for discussion of reincarnation.)*

These concepts were inconceivable two and three thousand years ago. At that time there was a wide boundary between ignorance and knowledge that was only gradually bridged over the entire period of our civilization, and most rapidly in the past 500 years.

Popular thought, though controversial, is that Homo sapiens appeared on this earth about 35,000 years ago, evolving in Africa, migrated into the Levant (Mideast), and later into Europe, about 90,000 years ago. For a time they coexisted with Neanderthal Man. Cro-Magnon, or Modern Man as we are sometimes called, came into existence at perhaps 100,000 to 20,000 years ago.

A projection from before time, indicated at the start of this chapter, to a time past Armageddon, might include that body form would change in the future, although no drastic change has essentially occurred in perhaps 20,000 years, aside from pure growth, simple enlargement, and refinement.

At that future time, conceivably, a new entity of earth occupation might exist. Body form would have become extinct, and souls only shall have inherited the earth. (For further and recent discussions on this subject, please see *Antiatoms: Here Today.* Discovery Magazine. January, 1997, Pages 74-75.

After the initial brilliance of the "Big Bang", the cosmos was generally black. There was not, at that era, a conglomeration of gases and solids of matter to form stars and other substances that would serve as sources of light as we see today. Instead there was only a glow from cosmic radiation.

This condition lasted for about 200 millions, continuing billions of years until eventually increasing self-generated gravity (attraction of elements) brought together the selection of basic elements into stars, quasars, and other cosmic phenomena that generated light sources, and non-star substances of planets, asteroids, comets, and the like.

Our concept of "day" evolved only when earth, and other planets, revolved, to expose one surface of the sphere at a time to the source of light. With earth, of course, this was mostly the sun. Light in the cosmos and on earth evolved gradually over millions and billions of years.

Periodic Table Of The Elements

Group	O	I	II	III	IV	V	VI	VII	VIII
Series									
1		H 1 1.008							
2	He 2 4.003	Li 3 6.94	Be 4 9.02	B 5 10.82	C 6 12.01	N 7 14.008	O 8 16	F 9 19	
3	Ne 10 20.183	Na 11 22.997	Mg 12 24.32	Al 13 26.97	Si 14 28.06	P 15 30.98	S 16 32.06	Cl 17 35.457	
4 A	Ar 18 39.944	K 19 39.096	Ca 20 40.08	Sc 21 45.10	Ti 22 47.90	V 23 50.95	Cr 24 52.01	Mn 25 54.93	Fe 26 55.85 Co 27 58.94 Ni 28 58.69
B		Cu 29 63.57	Zn 30 65.38	Ga 31 69.72	Ge 32 72.6	As 33 74.91	Se 34 78.96	Br 35 79.916	
5 A	Kr 36 83.7	Rb 37 85.48	Sr 38 87.63	Y 39 88.92	Zr 40 91.22	Nb 41 92.91	Mo 42 95.95	Tc 43 (97.9)	Ru 44 101.7 Rh 45 102.91 Pd 46 106.7
B		Ag 47 107.88	Cd 48 112.41	In 49 114.76	Sn 50 118.7	Sb 51 121.76	Te 52 127.61	I 53 126.92	
6 A	Xe 54 131.3	Cs 55 132.91	Ba 56 137.36	Rare Earths 57-71	Hf 72 178.6	Ta 73 180.88	W 74 183.92	Re 75 186.31	Os 76 190.2 Ir 77 193.1 Pt 78 195.23
B		Au 79 197.2	Hg 80 200.61	Tl 81 204.39	Pb 82 207.21	Bi 83 209	Po 84 (209)	At 85 (210)	
7 A	Rn 86 (222)	Fr 87 (223)	Ra 88 226.05	Ac 89 228	Th 90 232.12	Pa 91 231	U 92 238.07		

Rare Earths 57-71

La 57 138.92	Ce 58 140.13	Pr 59 140.92	Nd 60 144.27	Pm 61 (145)	Sm 62 150.43	Eu 63 152	Gd 64 159.9
Tb 65 158.9	Dy 66 162.46	Ho 67 164.94	Er 68 167.2	Tm 69 169.4	Yb 70 173.04	Lu 71 174.99	

The natural elements too are products of evolution. From the gaseous unions of first hydrogen and helium, extremes of temperature caused by pressures within the roily gases, and later within earth, plus volcanic action and star reformation forced joining of atoms that would form new and more chemically complex atoms having greater atomic weight, more electrons, and different properties as a new element.

Successively, the created atoms with incomplete orbiting of electrons joined other atoms having incomplete shells to make new, even more complex atoms. The newly created atoms had an increased number of electrons in their shells, or electron rings, a greater atomic weight and entirely new properties of a new element.

All elements of earth and our cosmos have a certain and unique atomic weight. In analysis, when each atom is charted in a table following the order of complexity in number of electrons, atomic weight, and by the number of shells or electron rings, it was discovered that each element had certain families, or relationships of elements. These are seen in their properties, in their order on the periodic table, and in the electron composition of their various shells.

Properties of atoms have distinct relationships with other atoms. These are made evident in a periodic chart. Values of melting point, density, hardness, excess or voids in a full complement of electrons in their respective shells (valence), complexity of respective atoms, stability or instability of the atom, or its willingness to share electrons of a particular atom.

Existence of certain elements and their properties can be predicted from voids in the Periodic Chart. Indeed, many elements were discovered only after being theorized from the periodic table.

In the beginning of star generations was the Neutron Star, a dead star that has previously exploded and now has pulled back in within itself, to be very small (relative to its former size), and extremely dense in its death throes, the star had exploded, sending energy waves and matter outwards, and then its own gravitation had pulled the star substance back and reconstituted the smaller and more dense neutron star into its new subatomic particle qualities.

The collapsed neutron star will then form into a pulsar, that is a spinning neutron star that emits pulses of radiation, perhaps at a frequency of 1,100 times per second, or else as an X-ray Binary, where the neutron star draws energy and matter from an adjacent star, or alternatively will form into the theoretical, but still not observed, Black Hole, where all forms of matter and energy, including light, are attracted in by gravitation, to be reduced to an end-form of Grand Unification. Black Holes have as much as a billion times the mass of our sun—a beast capable of swallowing entire stars.

Neutron stars receive additional spin each time matter or energy crashes back onto its surface, much like a beach ball in water can be caused to spin, faster and faster, by quickly striking a side of the ball with one's hand on a tangent edge. Thus do pulsars acquire their tremendous velocity of spin.

Do We Live In Two Worlds?

PART II - Creation

A Black Hole Theory

A "Black Hole" is thought by physicists to be the result of a collapsed neutron star, or a star that once existed, has since exploded, growing to a size many volumes greater than its original dimensions, and subsequently fallen within itself in its "old age".

Other matter from space, including whole stars and their possible planetary systems, would have also been attracted to the Black Hole, due to its tremendous gravitational force, and would have contributed to the growth and potential energy of the Black Hole.

The outward-going force created by the fusion energy (explosion) of a diminishing supply of hydrogen in its core would have been followed by its own force of gravity, amplified tremendously as its particles fell back to its own core.

A Black Hole can be visualized as a tremendously large "funnel" of energy in the cosmos. Matter is drawn into the "larger end" of the funnel (the event horizon) by gravitational forces, so strong that not even light can escape.

Note: Recent theory holds that matter was not drawn into the Black Hole, because there was no matter in original space. Instead the Black Hole attracted cosmic energy, from which matter later evolved. (Albert Einstein proposed that, in the beginning energy and matter were interchangeable.)

All things of matter within the "event horizon" (the area above and within a horizontal plane or "bowl-shaped" force sitting on the funnel opening) are drawn into the Black Hole, to be elongated, squeezed, otherwise physically and chemically changed, and reduced to a near inconceivably small volume, with a comparable increase in ratio of mass to volume.

As matter, and cosmic energy that is scattered throughout inner-galactic space, is drawn into a Black Hole by gravitation, all aspects of space between particles are reduced, leaving only solids of elements.

Further gravitational effect causes space within molecules to be reduced to that of atoms only, and further reduction to the components of matter, elementary particles, and quantum forces.

Then space within atoms is reduced to a single unified mass of electrons, protons, and neutrons.

These too, in turn, are reduced in minuscule space and matter, to leave only quarks, and thence further elementary particles, with absolutely zero space between those elementary particles.

There is then only a small physical existence with tremendous mass remaining, known as a "Grand Unification" of energy, or sometimes called unification, of all the fundamental forces of nature, which are gravitation, strong force, weak force, and electromagnetic force. This mass is theorized to be, at the apex, or "small end" of the "gravitational funnel", containing all matter formerly existing in a complete galaxy, then no larger than a modern-day basketball.

This tremendous reduction in size, combined with a near inconceivable increase in mass (think weight) and temperature is described at the chapter, *"The Beginning . . .".*

At the state of Grand Unification, in the absence of space, time would be zero. (Albert Einstein posited that space and time are equal. Zero space equals zero time lapse between one atomic particle and other particles.)

This, then, is the Grand Unification that would, in time, be "triggered" and the source of a "Big Bang". The "Big Bang" is the result of the effects of a "Black Hole".

It is conceivable that, instead of one "Big Bang" in our cosmos, perhaps there were a number of "Big Bangs", each recreating a new galaxy, and also creating the heavier metals, with resulting stars, gases, and eventually even planets, moons, comets, and all other celestial aspects that are experienced or may be found in galaxies.

Perhaps each galaxy that astronomers view are results of separate Big Bangs, and to be crude for matter of illustration, are located "like cow plops in a pasture field". In this theory, there would be no relationship between the location of one galaxy to the location of other galaxies, each being created independently by output of individual Black Holes. Location of galaxies within the cosmos would be determined strictly by rules of chaos and chance.

Since Earth possesses a large number of different elements, and each element was formed from a previous generation of elements, it would follow that Earth (and possibly other planets of our Solar System, as well as the sun) would have experienced star formations, neutron star explosions, possibly through quasar formation, and reformation into a star, and multiple cycles of this nature. (An alternative would be cycling through tremendous pressure and heat totally within the planet itself.)

Rebirth of a star might also have occurred through a variation of the Black Hole and Unification cycle, or through creation of a new primordial soup, preliminary to forming a new, solid celestial body.

This theory further implies a cosmos that existed prior to the start of our present cosmos, currently estimated at 14.7 billion years ago. It is only conjecture of whether God existed prior to moments of a Big Bang, with God defined here as an intelligence and energy. With absence of material existence, there certainly would be no physical reason to prevent this transition by God.

This is a tremendously simplified portrayal of a momentous cosmic scenario. It is shown to visualize, to the reader, in simplicity, how an event, or series of events, might have happened.

Albert Einstein worked extensively in general relativity and developed the formula, $E=MC^2$. From this, one can imagine that tremendous potential energy buildup in a Black Hole will result when tremendous mass is held at tremendous gravitational pressure.

The resulting energy, when released from a Black Hole, is expressed as $E=MC^2$, where E is energy released, M is units of mass, and C is the speed of light, squared.

One can only partially imagine the tremendous forces of energy released when masses of stars, radiation, planets, comets, and other like matter in the cosmos are collected into a Black Hole by gravity, and then amplified into potential energy by multiplying the product of this mass by the speed of light (186,000 miles per second) and squaring that number (multiplying by its own number).

Stephen Hawking has developed momentous work in Quantum Mechanics regarding the theoretical existence and workings of Black Holes. To date, no other Black

PART II - Creation

Holes have been positively identified, although they theoretically exist.

Since Earth possesses a large number of chemical elements, and that each element was formulated from a previous generation of elements in nuclear activity, it would follow that Earth (and possibly other planets of our solar system, as well as our sun) would logically have experienced a countless number of star formations, neutron star expansions, reformation into a star or subsequent planets, with multiple cycles of this nature.

Rebirth of a star might also have occurred through a variation of a Black Hole and Unification, or through creation of a new primordial soup and celestial matter preliminary to forming a new solid celestial body of star or planet.

An alternative theory would involve cycling through tremendous pressure and heat totally within the planet or star itself. Mineral analysis of the content of other planets in our solar system, other stars, and planets of those stars, whether they share various minerals, will add greatly to this knowledge.

There are many terms in Particle Science that are related, similar in meaning and concept. All are names for science study in subatomic particles. This is a realm of physics, new within the mid-20th century, and differs from Newtonian or Einsteinian physic of matter:

- Particle Science
- Particle Physics
- Subatomic Particles
- The Quantum

- Quantum Mechanics
- Quantum Theory
- Quantum Objects
- Quantum Field Theory
- Subatomic Physics

An additional, unsolved query about Black Holes:

When does a Black Hole end? Does ejection (i.e., Big Bang) cause the end of a Black Hole, or does the Black Hole continue on, evolving further in attracting, by gravitation, and to lead to further ejection of continuous Big Bangs?

As an analogy, what happens to a tornado when the apex tip touches the ground? Does the tornado then lose energy and dissipate, or does it continue on in its whirlwind, energetic, and energy-dissipating system?

I believe both sequences have been observed of the tornado expiring once the energy of the tornado has been dissipated, but at other times, the same tornado will again touch down to dissipate more energy in a different location.

By analogy then, are some Big Bangs, and consequently births of galaxies, both single and multiple? Are perhaps spiral galaxies a single Big Bang, and other galaxies, more complex in shape, the result of multiple Big Bangs in different, yet close, locations in space that give the appearance of one complex galaxy? (For an analysis of the Black Hole and Big Bang cosmography theories, please see U. S. News And World Report. July 20, 1998, *What Came Before Creation?)*

The world of antimatter, reason will tell us, may also be subject to celestial and physical forces, as we in the world of matter are. More knowledge, research, and exploration in the world of antimatter would need to be undertaken in order for mortals to progress in knowledge and understanding, to better exist in this sister world to matter, the world of antimatter.

Perhaps there is a real heaven to scientists, to pursue their loved field of study, in the world of antimatter after death.

Perhaps following their own death, even novices will be engaged in explorations of reason in order to understand their new-to-them world of the soul. Their new knowledge and information resulting from research and exploration, however, would not come from libraries of physical publications and books or even computers, but would need to come from some telepathic phenomena of universal knowledge not involving the workings of a brain, which would have been lost at death.

It would follow that intellectual activity does exist also in other creations, and further, that intellectual activity would exist for all souls and spirits.

If God is an energy and an intellect, and souls are a part of the God-Substance, which the author maintains, it would follow that souls also have an intellect, a curiosity, and a desire to find answers and to take action. Each soul would have an independence of pursuit in intellectual matters within the confines of his (or her) new world of antimatter.

The natural form of existence, that existed in Unification before the Big Bang, is antimatter. There was no such thing as "matter" prior to Unification and Big Bang. When energy is applied, matter, with its base of electrons derived from proton annihilation, is created. This creation of matter is expressed in Albert Einstein's formula $E = MC^2$, where E is energy, M is mass, and C is the speed of light in a vacuum, which is squared in the formula.

Energy is derived from matter, and matter is derived from energy. (A theory developed by Albert Einstein) Therefore, when energy is applied, such as occurred in the Big Bang, matter is created; when matter was created, energy (which had been cosmic energy) was utilized in proportion to the formula. This creation seemed to be from near nothingness, (which was the Unification), through electron-proton annihilation, and through creation of positrons (positively charged electrons), from which antimatter was created.

It is often asked, "How did living organisms come about when there were only inanimate, inorganic elements before?

Originally, in the period following the "Big Bang", the cosmos consisted only of helium and pure hydrogen. In multiple gravitational contractions of gases, and resulting buildups of pressure and heat, followed by subsequent expansions and contractions, heavier elements and metals were formed, resulting in new gases, stars, and eventually even planets, moons, comets, and all other celestial bodies that are experienced or may be found in galaxies.

In terms of physics and chemistry, two hydrogen atoms united to form one helium atom. Every time a helium atom was created, photons were forged by gamma rays, a form of light having very high energy. Other and subsequent elements that we know today were also forged in much the same process.

The primordial soup that developed later consisted of hydrogen, helium, nitrogen, oxygen, phosphorus, sulfur, iron, and traces of a few other basic elements. Even when certain basic elements combined to make other molecules, such as hydrogen and oxygen combining to make water, or when sulfur, oxygen, and hydrogen combined to make sulfur dioxide, or a variation which is sulfuric acid, or a wide variety of other acids and bases developed, how did these evolve into a substance that would grow, divide, replicate, and specialize?

Based on research and writings by eminent scientists, well respected in their academic communities, an answer is proposed. Accepted research holds that inorganic elements combined to form the "basic building blocks of life", and combined with a variety of enzymes, phosphates, esters, peptides, thios (the element, sulfur, replaced oxygen in the atom), alcohols, proteins, carbohydrates, chlorophyll, and other compounds, forming molecules.

First life on this earth may very likely have started from action of volcanoes. At the very start of solidification of the earth 4 1/2 billion years ago, there was nothing but rock, both solid and some still in various stages of molten, and ever present lava.

This period was even before the presence of moisture, the chemical combination of hydrogen and oxygen, and before the existence of water, vapor, clouds, and lightning. Without lightning from clouds, there was little source of high temperatures to facilitate chemical combination from anything except volcanic action.

From this first stimulus of chemical combinations, algae plants were first created.

First land masses supported archaic grasses and trees, which decayed from oxidation and formed the first organic basis of soil, which then supported successive plants, decaying to more soil, etc. for billions of years.

The basic building blocks of life are compounds of molecules, which are made up of atoms of the various basic elements. The four building blocks, or nucleotides, are compounds called adenine, guanine, cytosine, and thymine, all of which occur and match other proteins in various combinations. These building blocks are all found in RNA and DNA of the genetic code. (Source: <u>Biological Science</u>. W. T. Keeton, Norton & Co. Publishers.)

First cells were relatively simple, consisting of a nucleus and having a single purpose. These are known as Prokaryote cells ("pro" meaning first); as of this writing (November 1996) earliest Prokaryotic life has been discovered at 3.85 billion years ago. Some Prokaryote cells exist even today as yeast, algae, and amoeba.

At about 3 billion years BCE, and after about 1.5 billion years of life with only Prokaryote cells, a new, supercell, called the Eukaryote cell, developed, which devoured and incorporated various types of Prokaryote cells, each having their own unique, special purpose and qualities.

With this evolution the Eukaryote cell developed to have multiple, symbiotic qualities, which allowed multiple functions of predation (predatory behavior), invasion, ingestion, digestion, excretion, energy storage, RNA, DNA, growth, and division, all encased within a "working" cell wall, that allowed absorption and envelopment of substances from outside the cell wall for nourishment.

The ingestion, by Eukaryote cells, of Prokaryote cells, each having unique "operational" qualities, might be the first of the mantra held by dietitians of today, *"you are what you eat"*.

The "eating" is accomplished by a process called phagocytosis, which is that of physically engulfing an exterior object. We can think of the similarity in process of spreading a covering of sawdust over an oil spot on a garage floor to "swallow up" the oil.

The operations of biochemistry are fraught with technical terminology that describes a wide variety of processes involved in the Eukaryote cell. This writing is intended as portrayal of a schematic possibility, based on the writings of various learned researchers in their respective fields of study, and not as a college text in biochemistry.

However a good explanation of the biochemistry processes is set forth in the book, *Vital Dust,* authored by a Nobel Laureate, Christian de Duve (Basic Books Division of Harper Collins Publishers. NY, NY, 1995), and also in *The Birth of Complex Cells* by the same author, in Scientific American magazine, April, 1996.

Nature's building of the Eukaryote cell strikes me as similar to the accomplishment of constructing the first automobile. The rudiments, or separate components of that machine, all existed prior to that time when components were all organized to make the original invention of a self-propelled vehicle. The internal combustion engine had already been invented, certainly gears had been designed, with variations to accomplish certain engineering objectives, and wheels and carriage had been in existence for centuries.

Likewise with development of the Eukaryote cell. The components all existed previously and it was only when the components were each brought within the cell walls of the larger, Eukaryote cell, one by one, that the complete and functional unit of cell was able to "operate" as we know it today.

Again, we can see an analogy in the development in operation of the internal combustion engine. All components were in existence prior to this invention, of gasoline, air, spark, and mechanics (cylinder, piston, connecting rod, crankshaft, etc.) from usage in the steam engine. It was only when the right combination and sequence of these factors were developed that the energy of the internal combustion engine could be harnessed.

Just as Eukaryote cells were collections within a cell wall of various individual Prokaryotic cells having different specialties, so did the animal forerunners of fish and mammals consist of collections of various specialized organisms. These specialized organisms later amalgamated the plans and structures for light sensitivity (later eyes), circulation (later heart which developed arteries, veins, and capillaries), cleansing operations (later kidneys), oxygen/carbon dioxide exchange (later lungs), nutrient digestion (later viscera), as well as spleen, sexual organs of male and female, skin, hearing mechanisms, and other organs of our complex bodies.

Animals developed from plants by formation from two dimensional algae and amoeba into three dimensional tubes and worms, having an alimentary canal for nutrient intake, digestion, and excretion.

There later evolved an interdependency and synergy of insects, animals, bacteria, fish, and plants.

First beat of a heart was generated from a periodic exchange of ions between points within the heart, causing contractions and release within the heart muscle and a pumping action for an elementary blood circulation system.

So too, did the "right" combination of chemistry in biological cells evolve over millions and millions of years to form the first, and then a wide variety of Prokaryote cells, which would eventually be components of the more complex Eukaryote cells known to us today.

Scientific research has provided, as we turn to the second millennium, facts that are a far cry from the biblical account stated in the Book of Genesis. The need for blind faith has been superseded by the gain in knowledge of over 2,600 years.

Recent findings in microbial development present an example of how microbes can exist in seemingly impossible situations.

In the 1920s it was first hinted that microorganisms lived in the deep subsurface, hundreds to thousands of meters below ground. The idea did not gain favor until 1987 when several deep boreholes in South Carolina near the Savannah River Nuclear Materials Processing Facility were drilled.

Scientists learned that diverse types of microorganisms lived at depths extending at least 500 meters beneath the surface, at temperatures as high as 167 degrees Fahrenheit, and from depths of 1.7 miles below the surface.

Diverse bacterial communities thrive in most sedimentary rocks, which commonly contain a rich supply of organic compounds to nourish microorganism. These nutrients were originally produced by plants at the earth's surface before the loose sands, silts, or clays that constitute most sedimentary formations were buried and consolidated into solid rock, as long as nutrients remained available.

Microorganisms living within the pores of the sediment can continue to thrive and grow. Sedimentary rocks also supply oxidized forms of sulfur, iron and manganese that can provide the energy these microbes need.

Bacterial communities have also been found in basalt rock. The bacterial communities living there include autotrophs *, or organisms that synthesize organic compounds from inorganic sources. The autotrophs living in these basalts use hydrogen gas for energy and derive carbon from inorganic carbon dioxide. The compounds then excrete simple organic compounds that other bacteria can in turn consume.

Some subsurface microbial communities, surviving because essential nutrients are constantly renewed from ground water, must be at least several million years old, with a very slow metabolic rate, and cell division that may be once a century or less.

Autotrophs are organisms that synthesize organic compounds (proteins, fats, and other biological molecules rich in carbon) from inorganic sources. Many types of autotrophic bacteria capture energy from inorganic chemical reactions involving iron or sulfur. Autotrophs living in basalts derive carbon from inorganic carbon dioxide. These "acetones" then excrete simple organic compounds that other bacteria can in turn consume. In basalts the hydrogen gas is produced by the reaction of oxygen-poor water with iron-bearing minerals.

Such environments are called "SLIME", which means, subsurface lithoautotrophic microbial ecosystems. SLIME microorganisms can persist indefinitely without any supply of carbon from the surface. (Source: Scientific American magazine, Earth From the Inside Out, Year 2000, Microbes Deep Inside the Earth, pages 10-15.)

At a time approximately 250 to 150 million years ago, the ancient super-continent Pangaea split into sections, one called Laurasia, which moved north, and Gondwana which remained in the south hemisphere of the earth. The movement and division of continental plates, and further subdivision and movements upon the globe of earth, is studied by analyzing likenesses and differences, at different locations of earth, in archaeological finds of ancient fossils of dinosaurs, studies of geology continuums in different continents, likenesses and differences between continents of mammals and even birds.

Even with continental separation, land bridges and shallow seas between Laurasia and Gondwana, various species could intermix on the same land masses 100 million and 10 million years ago. (Source: Scientific American magazine, August, 1996, Page 24)

It is true that paleoecologists have shown, that at one time, there were clearly only two masses of land and water on the earth. The single continent of Pangaea was the source of our present seven continents. (Perhaps some aspects in the creation story of the Bible do go back to a time of God's existence millions of years ago.)

Early in the chemical and geologic creation of earth, sea water rose as a tremendous sink of hydrogen and oxygen combined to form water over the previous barren rock of earth. Rock itself rose as the crust of earth heaved and swelled, showing even higher elevations than the increasing seas.

There are recent findings that land emerging from the falling levels of the seas and later division of lands occurred even before Pangaea. *(In Times of Ur,* Discovery magazine, January, 1997, Pages 18-19)

About three billion years ago a single craton (the ancient core of a continent), that has been named Ur, appeared in the single ocean of the world. Later, at two billion years ago, three other cratons formed: Arctica (which would later become Canada, Greenland, and a large part of Siberia), Baltica (later becoming most of Western Europe), and Atlantica (later eastern South America and western Africa).

These four cratons combined at about two billion years ago to form a single land mass of Rodina, the predecessor land mass of Pangaea and Gondwana. Remnants of the original craton of Ur are found today in South Africa, Madagascar, Southern India, and Australia.

The concept that RNA and DNA were purposely manipulated by intelligent beings, specifically souls working at the direction of God, provides credence to a possible answer for a basic question concerning evolution.

One argument advanced among anthropologists holds that all humanity, all Cro-Magnon man, originated in one spot on earth, Africa, and branched out, somehow, throughout the known world.

Through biological and cultural isolation over thousands of years, the different races, Caucasian, Negroid, Mongolian, Oriental, Indo-European, and all variations of these races, developed and created their own separate lineage of racial, biological and anatomical qualities.

Another concept, that I favor, and this could have happened only with intelligent direction, holds that evolution, with its many mutations, happened simultaneously in more than one location of the world. How else could earth have produced evidence, through fossil remains, of man's existence in primitive times at such diverse locations as Africa, the Orient, Tierra del Fuego, New Mexico in the United States, England, Europe, and possibly the Mid East and central Asia. The distance alone is prohibiting.

The same steps in evolution took place repeatedly, by individual cells forming two dimensional plants, similar to what we call algae today. The flat algae later folded within itself and formed into three dimensional tubes, having one end for nourishment intake, digestion occurring between, and excretion happening through the opposite end of this tube animal. Specialization took place within the tubes to form living worms having specialized parts that later evolved into neural system, brain, heart, digestive system, lungs, and limbs, as well as all other organs and systems of animals that developed over time.

These changes in direction of evolution were all mutations. Each mutation could well have evolved into a direction different than what indeed happened. It is apparent that some force "directed" these parallel mutations.

It is important to grasp this concept that development in evolution, even when, by so-called chance, turned out to be generally the same (allowing only for subtle differences in the various races), regardless of where the organism developed.

An initial happening, and successive happenings, in another separate location could well have taken a completely different direction if left independently to its own chaotic choices.

However, and only with intelligent direction, evolution occurring in different locations on earth could have been coordinated and directed by some higher, intelligent power, that we call God, acting through angels, to manipulate genes of evolving animals in a parallel fashion, wherever the evolving animal might be on earth.

It occurs to us once again that God is the greatest of all scientists.

About 550 million years ago, or even further back in time, a gene called Distal-less evolved that regulates expression of other genes during the process of limb formation in living organisms. From this a basic configuration of vertebrates evolved, the basic anatomy found in fish, reptiles, and mammals.

From this turning point in evolution, other forms of life evolved having limbs, fins, or wings, with related components comparable to knees, ankles, toes, and similar skeletal features. These parallel evolutions in different locations on earth would have needed to be coordinated by some intelligent power to avoid a ridiculous, chaotic variation in life forms.

As primates and Homo sapiens further evolved, some species, perhaps oriented to climate in different locations of earth, developed certain subtle changes in anatomical qualities, including different pigmentation in their skin, as well as relative strengths and weaknesses in other systems within their respective bodies.

The above explanation is a way, and the only way, that I can visualize, that variance occurred in race, anatomical structure, brain capacity, tooth formation, glandular systems, robustness, height, and other qualities unique to the various types of humans on earth that exist today, and yet provide a basic uniformity between races in anatomy and biology.

I believe in evolution, but I also believe that nature is too planned and systematic to have evolved strictly by accident and by mutation. Left to pure chance, mutations would have produced many grotesque changes indeed in humans, mammals, fish, insects, animals and plants. Unfortunately, such are seen today in grotesque birth defects, but also may be observed in organisms of deep sea life, unique in their biological independence.

The phenomena of butterflies, with the protective design on their wings, and the unique coloration and system of a myriad of insects, provide perfect examples of camouflage for protection in nature's system.

Some force of intelligence played a part in the evolutionary development of natures creatures, including primates and Homo sapiens.

I believe this force was a superior intelligence, that we call God, and became operational for changes on earth through angels and souls acting as subjects of God, for making changes in evolution upon life on earth.

Genetic change in Homo specimens, as Homo was developing from hominids, and which we theorize was brought about by spiritual genetic engineering, could result in the thinking and reasoning ability, allowed by the convolutions, or folding, in the cerebral cortex (the 1/8th inch thick layer that covers the brain of some mammals and other animal life forms).

This convolution in the brain of Homo, that does not exist in brain of other life forms, may be the difference in biological engineering of Homo that allows spirituality, and could be a caused mutation, the same type (as theorized here) that caused the mutations by spiritual forces that controlled evolution of one complex life form after another, leading to primates, and thence to Homo and modern man (Cro-Magnon).

It is not the basic intelligence that varies from one person to another (and possibly even from one mammal to another) but the ability to think and reason that varies. The ability to think and reason is the result of the convolutions in the cerebral cortex of the brain. For further information, see Discovery magazine, June 1997, page 32.

Instead of holding that life forms that eventually evolved to Homo sapiens developed only in Africa, consider that perhaps elemental hominid life forms evolved somewhat simultaneously in many parts of earth, perhaps as thick as fleas on a dog.

Most of these diverse forms were not able to continue existence because of climate, weather conditions, dryness, lack of necessary available nutrients, and a variety of other conditions not conducive to sustained life.

Of the many locations in which parallel elemental life may have existed, it seems that only those in the hot equatorial belt of Africa had continuing conditions that allowed sustained development.

There is geologic evidence that earth experienced a shift of magnetic poles at some time in its history, probably over 15 million years ago. It is possible that the African location on earth's equator happened to be the one site on earth that was geographically common as the equator when the axis of earth shifted, therefore allowing undisturbed continued evolution. The tilting of the earth caused radical change in localized climate at many of the other sites theretofore populated by emerging life forms, extinguishing further development of hominid life in many locations.

Just as directed evolution, as advocated in this book, joined the primitive body and the conscious soul together to form man (Homo erectus and Homo sapiens), parallel activity took place to join different species of Homo sapiens to the conscious soul. In such theory this was done at least seven times to form the various races of Caucasian,

Mideastern, Asian, Mongolian, Indian, Negroid, and American Indian, all with commonalty of also having souls.

The various races of man were thereby created by joining the one universal soul to many species of hominids (Homo sapiens). We are all equal in soul, but have different appearance in anatomy, skin color, facial characteristics, and biological makeup.

In another theory, the long line and dead ends in the evolutionary history of human ancestry, began when the first line of hominids came out of the African trees and began to walk upright on two legs—perhaps as far back as 4 to 5 million years ago.

Scientists try to piece together the prehistory of the human species. They have been puzzled again and again by the appearance as far from Africa as Indonesia of fossil bones (Java Man—1.8 million years ago) that bear hints of similarities to fossils of early African toolmakers.

Primitive stone tools known as Olduwan types, and fossils of skulls, found together in Russian Georgia, are typical of many used by early hominids as far back as 2.4 million years ago. The tools and skull fossils were dated by radioactive carbon and paleomagnetic measurements at age of about 1.7 million years ago. These archaic people migrating from Africa to Asia were of the species Homo erectus (relating to and called Homo ergaster by some) and spread to Asia, Middle East, and Europe, as well as toward India, Java, and China. Early human type beings turned up in Spain about 800,000 years ago.

Fossil of an early African hominid boy was discovered in Kenya reliably dated at 1.8 to 1.6 million years old.

The find in Russian Georgia and the find in Kenya are nearly identical, making the first known event of African-looking hominids in Asia.

This shows migration of early human ancestors from Africa. A glacial period was receding then, the environment was changing, and so were the animals that could provide the migrants with a regular supply of meat for protein.

The human genome is contained in 23 chromosomes, which are contained in the nucleus of every cell in the body. Each chromosome consists of a DNA double helix that is wrapped around spool-like proteins called histones. The DNA-histone complexes are then coiled and double-coiled to comprise the complete chromosomes.

Within each chromosome, the DNA helix and sequence has the ability to reproduce itself in a new cell with a compatible sequence of four specific amino acids. The four building blocks, or nucleotides, are compounds called adenine, guanine, cytosine, and thymine, all of which occur and match each other proteins in various combinations. This DNA sequence determines, in total, the function and quality of the new cell, an exact reproduction of its parent cell.

The DNA sequence will determine whether the protein that is encoded shall become, say, part of a heart muscle, a fingernail, a certain bone or joint, eye, hair, etc., and determine physical characteristics of hair, skin, and eye color, height, skeletal mass, immune system abilities, susceptibility to certain diseases, and all other characteristics, together with possibly personality and emotional traits.

In understanding DNA (Deoxyribonucleic Acid) and RNA (Ribonuclei Acid), DNA sequences could be compared with the specifics of design, specifications, quality, and uniformity of the individual components of a living organism that come together, as in the details required in making a complete automobile. Each assembled unit of a given automobile model will be essentially identical. (In all humans 99.9% of DNA are common to all other humans).

The RNA is the messenger factor, like an outline of the general method, or manufacturing system and communication necessary that will be employed to result in the assembly process.

You might say the DNA controls the "what?" and RNA determines the "how?" of fabrication.

However, in the manufacture of automobiles there will be differences in color, appointments, extra equipment, and quality of the individual parts.

In quality and wear, some parts will fail simply because they are not in perfect unison with another part after assembly. (Engine parts will gradually wear or fail, due simply to aging, continued exposure to operating or explosive forces within the engine, necessary to make the automobile run.)

So too with the body; certain organs and body components will deteriorate from stress, aging, and outside factors, and may suddenly, or eventually, fail.

In the case of nature's organisms, including humans, the mere process of living causes a preference to change some aspect of their biological or botanical makeup in order to avoid hardship in its life. This preference then prompts the need for a mutation and change in the DNA of that organism, and successive hereditary offspring of that organism.

The need for change, and manipulation of DNA to effect these changes, is a prime subject of this book as a directed goal in evolution of organisms.

The nucleus of each atom, and consequently each cell and molecule of an organism, contains many particles, including neutrons, protons, macrophage, and chromosomes. Electrons that define the atom qualities are located outside the nucleus in the electron rings.

As stated, in each cell, of each human being, there are 23 pairs of chromosomes. (Other mammals and plants have the same, more, or less number of chromosomes than those of a human.) Each chromosome contains a mixture of four different proteins, or bases, named Adenine, Thymine, Cytosine, and Guanine. These bases pair up within the DNA double helix strand in certain orders: Adenine always matches in a "ladder rung" effect with Thymine; likewise, Cystosine always matches with Guanine.

These linear strings of bases join to form a double-sided helix. The ladders within the double helix DNA strand becomes a nucleotide base. There are many (estimated at 3 million) nucleotide bases or combinations of human DNA, each arranged in a definite sequence, that determine a like number of qualities, traits, and characteristics of the organism.

The DNA sequence determines the proteins and enzymes that will be formed at various locations, and at various time sequences in the body. The enzymes might be likened to RNA, the vehicle that facilitates actions to happen, or to carry out the biochemical reactions of life.

Each nucleotide determines the physical, biological, anatomical, and perhaps emotional and psychological, attributes of the individual person. (This applies also to nonhuman animals and plants.)

The proteins making up the various body components are comprised of molecules of amino acids. The determining factors, the nucleotides, are linked together in a long string. Each string folds in a way that determines the timing of predominance and function of a protein. The order of the amino acids is set by the DNA base sequence of the gene that encodes (determines) a given protein, through the intermediaries called RNA.

The nucleotides control the composition of cells that make up the various parts and organs of the body. Occasionally (perhaps once in 1,000 nucleotides) there is variation from absolute conformity in the matching that forms the nucleotides. Such variation in an organism may cause what is called a mutation. (In engineering and manufacturing terminology this could be called an "engineering change".)

The chromosomes thus control the features of each person, animal, or plant. The chromosomes contain the specific blueprint that will determine the exact composition of each living creature and plant. The estimated six million bases (the genes) of the human genome encode approximately 100,000 proteins. The average human's DNA code has 3.1 billion letters. (Source: U.S. News & World Report. Oct. 23, 2000, pg. 58)

Absolute identicalness from one person to another occurs about 99.9 percent of the time. The 1/10th of 1

Do We Live In Two Worlds?
PART II - Creation

DNA And RNA

percent in deviations account for and causes variations from one person to another in adult height, skeletal structure, color of hair, skin and eyes, length of toes and fingers, a weakness to combat certain diseases, and a myriad of other personal features.

Before the existence of DNA and RNA (in the early Archeozoic and Proterozoic eras on earth of Prokaryotes) each plant organism (there probably weren't yet any animal organisms) and then each offspring was an exact duplicate of its progenitor (parent). Each cell was an exact duplicate of each other.

With the advent of RNA and DNA (scientists are not sure which came first) there developed the ability of change. The new RNA and DNA could take on the inherited features and abilities of its female parent AND male parent, often blended in characteristics of both parent; male and female. This was the first sexual reproduction.

Mutation would follow in which even this two-possibility variation might branch into other unlimited possibilities of variation in the offspring from its parents.

From this, evolution in biology and botany developed (if it hadn't already developed through advent of the RNA/DNA change). Cells multiplied and changed in the never-ending variations that formed then both existing and extinct variations in plant, animal, insect and bacteria organisms.

Within 50 years, medical science expects comprehensive genomics-based health care to be the norm in the U.S. We will understand the molecular foundation of diseases, be able to prevent them in many cases, and design accurate, individual therapies for illnesses. The average life span will reach 90 to 95 years or more.

The Human Genome Project seeks not just to elucidate all the proteins produced within a body, but also to comprehend how the genes that encode the proteins are expressed.

Molecular genetic scientists have thought that all persons of today's human population originated from a common female that they call "Eve", about 3 1/2 million years ago. Some anthropologists theorize that "Eve" lived in Africa, placing origin there for this phenomena.

The DNA sequence is thought by some scientists to have started about 3 1/2 million years ago, and by others at a much earlier time, at the outset of life.

The "common thread" of the lineage is a component of cellular structures called mitochondria DNA. Mitochondria DNA is carried only through the female of the human species.

Molecular sequences have been indispensable tools since the 1960s for drawing taxonomies. DNA sequence data have already exposed the record of 3 1/2 million years of evolution, sorting things into three domains: Archaea (single-celled organisms of ancient origins), Bacteria, and Eukarya (organisms whose cells have a nucleus and revealing the branching patterns of hundreds of kingdoms and divisions of life.) Perhaps from this we might conclude:

1. The spirit or soul of humans, which have evolved to today's state, was first unified by God into this original "Adam and Eve" if that in fact happened, and

2. Mitochondria DNA is the vehicle for transferring physical, biological, and perhaps emotional and psychological qualities of the organism, in a linear sense, through the many generations to the present day.

It is the author's contention, frankly without academically recognized scientific expertise, that DNA regulates and determines one's personality traits, as well as biological and physical features. DNA determines personality features such as humor, aggressiveness, determination, leadership qualities, loyalty, propensity to be moral, and a host of other personality traits.

The author is aware and cautious not to confuse personality traits learned by nurture (acquired by learning or association) from those traits that are inherent and biologically inherited. Many traits are acquired simply by association and family living.

But some unique traits of individuals would surface even if the child offspring were to leave the family circle, as often happened in the 19th and early 20th centuries when "excess" children of large families were sent off to be raised by relatives or friends, or even complete strangers, who wished for a child (or a family worker) of their own.

Psychological studies of siblings who were separated at, or shortly after birth and reared in different family cultures, meeting perhaps by chance in later life, possessed many of the same basic personality traits.

In studying ancestors, and those ancestors who have "made their mark" in accomplishments to some personal extent, often through wealth accumulation, politics, administrative or leadership ability, creativity, natural propensity in social or science areas, or other factors for which certain ancestors might have been known, the question is often asked, "So what does that make me?" The answer is usually heard as "Nothing".

But the true answer has a source in the genes. For example, if your own ancestors possessed the genes that allowed certain accomplishments, there is a good chance that those unique genes also exist, at least to some extent, in your own biochemistry makeup. The genes within you might be only lacking the opportunity to be expressed by you.

These personality traits, that are encoded in your genes, tend also to evolve, to be strengthened or weakened in successive generations, just as the shape of bills on birds change in each generation depending upon the environmental needs (per Darwin's studies).

Traits may also be blended by acquisitions from the genetic inheritance of the two parents which will strengthen or weaken each personality trait of their mate-derived offspring.

For centuries a saying has been common, *"Like father, like son"*, or the same with mother and daughter, or even cross sex comparisons. This is at least partial evidence that personality traits are genetically inherited to an extent beyond what would derive simply through acquisitions from nurture or familiarity.

The author anticipates that future study of genes and genetic inheritance will reveal more in this regard.

A. Within the human body many organs exist.

B. Within each organ many cells exist.

C. Within each cell a nucleus exists.

D. Within each nucleus many chromosomes exist.

E. Within each chromosome (humans have 23) many genes exist.

F. Within each gene many nucleotides exist. It is estimated that approximately six million bases (genes) exist within the average person.

G. Within each nucleotide many building blocks exist, bonded together in sequence. Each nucleotide is composed of three still smaller constituent parts: A phosphate group, a 5-carbon sugar called deoxyribose, and an organic nitrogen-containing base.

H. Within each nucleotide exists a nitrogen-containing base compound of atoms, each one of which is either:

- A—Adenine (single ring)
- T—Thymine (single ring)
- C—Cytosine (double ring)
- G—Guanine (double ring)
- Adenine combines with Thymine and
- Cytosine combines with Guanine

In each double helix a nitrogen containing base combines at each "side" with either a phosphate group or deoxyribose to form a "ladder rung" of nucleotide bases. "Ladder sides" are composed of strings of phosphate group and deoxyribose.

In cell division, nucleotides construct their own image for replication in each new cell.

Structure	State	Code (See text)

 Nitrogen-containing base compounds of atoms: G,H
Adenine, Thymine. Cysteine, Guanine:

a) phosphate group
b) 5-carbon group (called deoxyribonucleic acid),
c) nitrogen-containing base

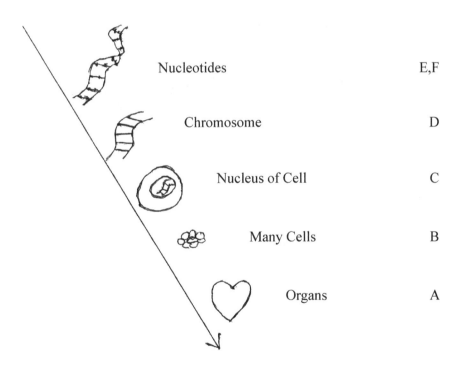

Nucleotides	E,F
Chromosome	D
Nucleus of Cell	C
Many Cells	B
Organs	A

Each building block is a prueine (single—ring structure) or a pryrimidine (double ring structure) derivative of an organic nitrogenous base that will form uric acid upon oxidation. Match of either phosphate or deoxyribose with a nitrogen containing base determines composition that in turn determines trait of each gene. It is estimated that there are about 3.3 billion building blocks within the average person, each controlling the trait of its respective biological cell.

The complete genome is a part of all body cells. Each chromosome contains the determinants for all cells of the entire body. Activation or change of only one or a few nucleotides determine the quality of respective cells in the body accounting for physical features, health, and probably talents and thoughts.

As indicated in this book, the author believes there are two worlds in which we live; the one consisting of matter that incorporates the human body, and second, a world of antimatter, that incorporates the mind, the soul, the spirit of God, angels, and the hereafter. The two worlds exist within the human body, in tandem with each other, and are inseparable in secular life.

In evolution of secular life there are obvious signs that intelligence has guided change throughout millions of years. Without intelligence and a guided pattern, creatures of the world, fish, plants, and insects would develop in total chaos, without logical functions in their development.

A reasonable man observing the complex, creative, systematic, and logical being of specific reproduction and worldly existence, must conclude that a guiding hand has been applied to development and evolution from the start of life. This book contends that, the guiding hand has been planned and exerted by God, and carried out by his messenger angels and souls, through manipulation of factors that control development, by DNA and RNA complexities, in the form of successive mutations.

From time to time there are events that the author has termed "crossover", whereby fleeting experience of the spiritual world become manifested in the universe of matter. By crossover, I mean a relationship where effect is felt, but the evidence of the spiritual world, and our world of matter, are not tangibly intermixed.

I think of my forced air furnace in which burning gas heats a barrel-like structure (the heat exchanger) from a flame inside. The house air, being forced by a fan around the heat exchanger, acquires heat from the heat exchanger to warm the rooms of the house. There is a crossover, or transfer of energy, of caloric heat, without the source of heat (the flame) intermixing with the passing air.

Crossover is evident too in our ability to smell extraneous sensations, and for the body to convert that stimulus into biological transactions that identify, say, a rose from that of putrid meat. This transference, or crossover, takes place within the olfactory sense of the nose, and is identified by a process of the brain.

Another example of "crossover" is when oxygen that we breathe is transferred within our lungs and kidneys to become part of our purified blood, which, in turn, purifies and feeds the various tissues and organs of our body. There is an ion exchange from oxygen taken in from the breath, through the pulmonary and renal systems, that will affect quality of the blood, without actual intermixing of the two, incoming and outgoing, sources.

Also, a phenomenon happens in life experiences that we can associate and call "crossover". There are experiences, often referred to as parapsychology, that are most difficult to document as evidence, but enough sincerity in reporting and documentation occurs to give credence that the phenomenon exists.

-Out of body experiences have been reported many times, whereby individuals recall viewing their own body, such as on a bed or on a hospital operating table, and events surrounding their body, as seen from a viewpoint away from their body location.

-Deep concentration, such as in meditation, has resulted in magnificent overview and at least quasi-spiritual contact between our physical brain and our spiritual mind.

-Near Death Experiences (NDE) are examples of "crossover". There are reports from persons who have undergone symptoms of impending death in accidents or surgery in a hospital operating room. NDE could be dismissed as dreams or "mind tricks", except for the sameness of the experiences reported by various persons. Those persons who have experienced NDE commonly report a strange type of travel, often through some sort of tunnel, at rapid speed, towards an intense light source at the end. The person's experiencing and reporting NDE recover their health, at least temporarily, and live to tell the story.

-Certain individuals, such as Jean Dixon and Edgar Casey, have exhibited evidence of foretelling future events, and transmigration of thought over many miles to "view" circumstances, as if they were physically present.

-Reports of ghosts, specters, and apparitions have been reported thousands of times in present and past years over many centuries. Firm evidence to corroborate such events is scarce, but individuals who have experienced this phenomena are usually firm in their beliefs in recalling the event.

-Magnificent religious experiences are also parallel to this same phenomena, whereby individuals are confident in their mind of the realism of an experienced event.

-The facts surrounding so-called "flying saucers" are still not firmly evidenced. However, the individuals who claim to have experienced these encounters, seem adamant in their beliefs and reporting of their experiences. Are "flying saucers" perhaps a visitation from a parallel universe—perhaps a universe of antimatter? Such parallel universe concepts could explain the reported erratic and disappearing movements of these travelers. Do qualities of our Earth atmosphere foment visibility of such space visitors?

The skeptic might dismiss these reports of phenomena and parapsychology, out of body experiences, meditation, near death experiences, foretelling, ghosts, magnificent religious experiences, and "flying saucers" as so much bunk. But those who vouch for the authenticity of their own experience are numerous, most are reasonable people, often are qualified observers (airline pilots, law enforcement officers, respected citizens), reporting from widespread geographic areas, over a considerable span of time, often one report validating another report. Reports cannot be dismissed as unproven any more than they can be proven. We can only say for fact that the reports exist, and would seem possible.

Are radio waves a means of transference between the world of antimatter and the world of matter? Gamma rays are the most energetic type of electromagnetic radiation. One source of Gamma rays is radiation from Black Holes, quasars, galaxies, exploding stars, electromagnetic forces, and other exotic astronomical bodies and occurrences. Gamma rays could be the means that allows transference from an antimatter state to a state of matter, and vice versa.

Werner Heisenberg was a 1932 winner of the Nobel Prize for Physics. He formulated a principle that an object cannot exist in a certain location and be in motion at the same moment.

The saying that *"Everyone has to be someplace"* may not apply to objects in the antimatter universe and in particle science. Here, objects without form of matter that would be based on conventional electron presence in atoms and with proton and neutron presence in an atom nucleus, could exist as somewhat of a plasma.

In a gas or plasma state, objects or molecules would diversify over an area. A mirror twin of itself in matter would exist and perhaps even appear to be in more than one location at the same time, simply because of the identicalness of certain matter and its identically opposite (like a view in a mirror) antimatter. A molecule in matter and a molecule composed of anti-particles (the exact opposite of particles in matter) could appear to be the same, although clearly two different substances.

As an illustration of identical but separate molecules; identical molecules of matter presently exist in widely dispersed locations within the rarefied stratosphere, and in open, deep space. Rare molecules of oxygen, say, numbering perhaps only one molecule in a cubic mile of stratosphere, would be found to be identical to its distant neighbor oxygen molecule. Clearly, each molecule is in a different location, but for all practical purposes, they are identical and can be considered to be in different locations because they are interchangeable in appearance.

Distinct, but identical molecules, such as would exist in matter and its mirror image existing in antimatter, could conceivably appear to be in two (or more) locations at the same moment.

This philosophical theory might appear to dispute Werner Heisenberg's formulation that an object cannot exist in more than one location at the same moment of time.

But identical objects can appear (emphasis on "appear") to be in different places at a given moment in time, giving the impression that one object is in different locations at the same time.

In studies of atomic particles and particle science, it may be only academic whether the particles observed in two locations are actually different, or merely identical.

Could illusion and perception be a breakthrough to travel into different dimensions of space and/or time, or into another universe, and return?

Could this principle be applied to "crossover" where, upon death, a person's observable essence changes from matter to antimatter from a secular body to an opposite charged soul?

It has long been a question in anthropology about:
1. whether man evolved from primates, and
2. if man did evolve from primates, did he evolve from; a) monkey, b) chimpanzee, c) ape, d) gorilla, or e) some other form of life?

Modern man today has many features that are in common with each of the several primates. Our eyes face forward to provide depth perception. We have ears that project outward, better to catch sound waves for better hearing. We walk upright and have a significant brain cavity and brain ability. We have a tail bone, save it is generally useless today. Our skeletal features are generally the same as those of primates. We are generally social in living style, and have the ability to correct for certain diseases.

There are examples in evolution where anatomy and features of two or more species, in both animals and plants, have both branched and later merged in a form of parallel evolution.

Various breeds of dogs have been crossbred to create progressively new breeds, and this has also been accomplished in horses, felines, and other animals. We, as humans, create a blending of traits every time a child is born from father and mother.

It is popular theory that today's wide variety of birds evolved through untold generations, from prehistoric dinosaurs that were in the form of both reptiles and mammals. Snakes evolved from lizards having limbs.

PART II - Creation

Whales once utilized what are now anatomical remnants of limbs, and lived for a considerable period of time on land before returning to the seas. Many examples exist of evolutionary change, in stages of both division and union.

The origin of man has never been agreed to by all anthropologists nor by all theologians. However it is agreed that nearly all persons of the world today are deemed to be of the genus Homo sapiens or Modern Man, regardless of their race or culture. We are all genetically within about 99.9% of being identical to each other.

Identicalness within our genus includes the Aborigines of northern Australia, inhabitants of rarely visited islands of the Pacific, Eskimos, or Inuit Indians of the northern polar regions, Indians of South America, (theorized to have originated from southeastern Asia, Polynesian islands, and/or migrated from north, south, or from the old world to southern Brazil, Paraguay and the Amazon basin which was once, in past geologic ages, an inland sea), American Indians, (who reportedly traversed an ancient land bridge from present Russia, and of Mongolian ancestry), brown, and ruddy-complexion persons of North Africa, the mid-east and India, Orientals, or Caucasians with ancestry from Europe and western Asia. The Homo-sapiens genus is thought to have started about 100,000 BC, although the specific period has not been determined.

Another genus, Homo neanderthalis, commonly called Neanderthal, existed prior to and during the time of Homo sapiens. Their existence dated from about 250,000 BC and expired as a known genus at about 35,000 BC. (Recollections of some traits of Neanderthal Man are shown by some Basque people in the Pyrenees Mountains region between France and Spain.) There was an overlap of about 65,000 years when these two (at least) species of humans, all existed on earth.

Neanderthals had unique skeletal features such as relatively short length of leg and arm bones, cranium features of smaller-than-today brain cavity size, bone protrusions at the eyebrows, sharpness in figuration of the forehead, and other features unique to their specie. These all are direct variance in anatomy, with indication of different appearance and probably living routines, from that of Homo sapiens.

A predecessor of Neanderthal, or possibly coexistent with them, were Homo erectus, and prior to them Homo ergaster, Homo habilis, and Homo rudofensis, all living at about 2 million years ago.

The first known form of mankind, living at about 3 1/2 million years ago in Africa was a four foot tall representative, named by anthropologists as "Lucy", of a specie called Australopithecus Afarensis.

Prior to the advent of recognizable forms of man there existed a variety of primates. Remnants of these ancient mammal forms exist today as gorilla, chimpanzee, baboon, monkey (both Old World and New World species), orangutan, and a variety of other species, both living and extinct. (An important difference from non-mammals is that mammals normally birth their young as opposed to laying eggs to hatch externally.)

Did gorilla, chimpanzee, ape, monkey, and perhaps other species, which had evolved from a single primate, perhaps a Lemur or some other elementary mammal, recombine in their parallel evolutionary path to form one new evolving specie, a humanoid, that eventually formed Homo erectus, later to evolve to Modern Man?

Predecessors of the primates were varieties of four-footed mammals known as Lemur, Tarsier, and earlier life forms. In March, 2,000 a new find in anthropology was announced in the journals <u>Nature</u> and <u>The Journal of Human Evolution</u>. With sharp teeth and frenetic nocturnal foraging, these fossils are of a thumb-size primate which has been named "Eosimias". This primate weighed only a third as much as the diminutive Mouse Lemur of Madagascar. The fossil was found in a Chinese limestone quarry, having lived prior to 45 million years ago. Humans clearly inherited the rotating arms and hand-eye coordination of early primates.

"A five inch long fossil proves that placental mammals thrived among dinosaurs far longer than anyone knew. Eomaia (dawn mother), also found in a fossil bed of northeastern China, is a 125 million year-old mouse like animal. Minute patterns in the teeth, bones, and fur, exquisitely preserved by the fine shale at this site, clearly identify the creature as an early member of Eutheria, the group of placentals that includes people as well as almost all modern mammals. Eomaia, the earliest known placental mammal, had two layers of fur—an undercoat covered by longer guard hairs—just like that of many modern dogs.

"A placenta allows a fetus to grow a longer time in the womb, which is critical for the better development of brains and other structures that allowed Eutherians to

diversify so successfully after the dinosaurs disappeared 65 million years ago.

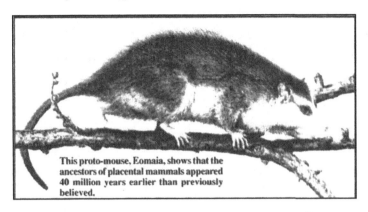

This proto-mouse, Eomaia, shows that the ancestors of placental mammals appeared 40 million years earlier than previously believed.

"Eomaia's anatomy hints at what mammalian life was like back in the Mesozoic Era. The long, curved fingers and sharp claws suggest the Eomaia was highly skilled at climbing trees and shrubs, an adaptive development that most scientist thought happened tens of millions of years later. The new fossils belie the popular image of scarce mammals hiding from marauding velociraptors. Eomaia probably climbed not just to avoid predators, the team leader, Zhexi Luo, a paleontologist at the Carnegie Museum in Pittsburgh says, but to escape competition from its fellow fur-covered cousins."

—Jocelyn Selim, <u>Discover Magazine</u>. August 2002.

Mammals evolved from reptiles, or at least from the same core creature which evolved plant, fish and sea life. Earlier life were ancestors of nematodes (worms), algae, virus, Prokaryote single-cell organisms, and later complex Eukaryote cells. The author calls this "Divergent Evolution", in which new genus and species are created.

At an earlier, elementary stage of life on earth, perhaps 3 1/2 billion years ago, various simple Prokaryote cells existed. Later, different Prokaryotic cells were ingested into a larger cell and consolidated their traits in a symbiotic relationship to form, over time, a new, complex, multi-component, Eukaryote cell. (Prokaryotic cells continue to exist today in the form of amoeba and yeast.)

This specie consolidation is an example of what the author calls "Consolidation Evolution". (See: <u>Scientific American</u>. *Earth From The Inside Out, 2000, "The Birth Of Complex Cells",* by Christian de Duve.)

Later divergence in creatures took place in a need to meet newly emerging complexities of life, caused by meeting new environmental conditions, and the need to exhibit variation in physical qualities and traits. Numerous other moments of diversification occurred to form new genera and species as needs of more complex life progressed. This division into new species was an example of "Divergent Evolution".

It is the author's theory that some branches of the primates continued their evolution, but other branches of these same primate species evolved in a new, reverse or return path of evolution, merging with others of the close, divergent species, in a crossbreeding process that still exists today. Various species resulting from divergent evolution, still living in close proximity with each other, and having similar foraging methods and association with one another, some, not all, of the divergent species crossbred with other species, which had also been created in divergent evolution, creating still another specie having consolidated features in the newly joined creature.

This seeming reversal of diverse evolution is an example of "consolidated evolution" whereby traits of different species are consolidated to form a new specie.

In botany this propagation is known as "grafting" one variety of plant onto another plant variety, and this can then be done progressively in the resulting seeds, thereby propagating a whole new variety in successive generations.

From a "stem" creature, divergent evolution manifested a division in gene development that would form specie Primate A. Further evolution resulted in species of Primate B, Primate C, and so on.

One by one the various primate species rejoined to form a new "stem specie" with consolidation of all their desirable traits ("Consolidation Evolution"), forming creation of a new manlike creature, the first hominid.

Graphically, diverse evolutionary lines would resemble a rosebud, with the various petals (representing species) originating from one source, spreading and reforming into new species, like the concave shaped petals of the rosebud. These lines would thus form, first "divergent evolution", and then subsequently reuniting into a single path, once again to form a new specie in "Consolidation Evolution".

Let it not be said by naysayers that cross breeding between species is impossible. It has been done in the past, cite the various Kingdoms, families, genera, and species that are outgrowths of single, core creatures. Crossbreeding between species of mice and rats has also recently been accomplished in the laboratory. (See Appendix: *Making the Sperm of Others*)

The process of divergent and consolidated evolution continued over time to produce a primate having consolidated features that would lead to, and later become, the first hominid, and later the genus Australopithecus afarensis, and "Lucy".

Features leading to upright walking, more mobile skeletal joints, larger brain case size, loss of need for tail, shorter arm length, change to a more carnivorous diet (that would provide needed protein for energy and organ growth not found in eating green plants), and other changes developed variation in skeletal makeup, biological features and life style, intelligence, and creativity. From this new genus, early forms of mankind leading to forms of humans evolved, through "Lucy", and various stages of Homo to Modern Man which we are today.

Anthropologists have identified various examples of reverse evolution. All life originally stemmed from the seas as plants, and later animals. Insects, bacteria (animals) and virus (plants) may have originally been products of the wetlands. Even now they thrive in a moist environment after hatching (or other method of reproduction such as metamorphosis), but can exist well and migrate in a dry culture out of water as well, but returning to water for breeding, e.g., the mosquito and mayfly family.

Lepidoptera, that includes a wide variety of butterflies and moths, experience metamorphosis, progressing through stages of egg, worm, larvae, changing to mature butterfly or moth, and which consequently lay eggs to create a new generation and cycle of life.

Amphibians, such as crocodiles and alligators can presently live on either land or in water. This may be evidence of a current stage in evolution of fish progressing to reptile, or an example of progress in a transition from reptile to mammal.

The genera of equine and bovine, that contain the families of common horses and cattle, are derivative in the mammal class. Mammals normally have a complex bone structure in the femur, knee, ankle, and many bones of the foot itself. Skeletons of both horse and cattle indicate various bones of mammal have been merged with unneeded specific skeletal components. Bones and joints had become melded into a more simple anatomical structure, with the calcium-rich hoof pertaining to the toenail of humans, and the ankle and foot bones of horses and cattle grown together to form a nearly indistinguishable skeletal feature. Elbow joints of equine and bovine are reversed from that of primates and humans in order to flex downward for support of weight, rather than upward in primates and humans to perform a lifting action.

In the years following the last glacial recession the Woolly Mammoth and Mastodon evolved out of existence, helped perhaps by the food hunting activity of our ancestor Homo sapiens and Neanderthal. The common elephant (Asian and African), now mostly hairless, is an outgrowth of these extinct pachyderms.

Some dinosaurs were apparently much the same in appearance, differing only in their telltale fossil skeletons that indicate whether they were reptile or mammal.

Passenger pigeons in Michigan, said to be once *"thick as to blot out the sun"* have been hunted to extinction, as numerous other animals, plants, bacteria, viruses, and insects have become extinct.

There are species whose evolutionary paths have progressed outward from a central source, and subsequently changed their "nature" (read changes in the DNA and RNA genome) to become a new creature in life's variety of creation.

The Time Line chart (see Appendix) presents the prehistory and early-time evolution of the cosmos, the gaseous cloud forming our solar system, and subsequently Earth. Evolving chemistry lead to first forms of one-cell animals and developing life.

Sea life, land plants, flora as an ecological system, reptiles, mammals, primates, and man forms developed and evolved through various human forms, to Neanderthal, hence to Homo sapiens and Modern Man. Momentous changes in geology took place simultaneously all during this time concurrent with both divergent evolution and consolidation evolution of life.

Such evolution could very well have occurred naturally, chaotic as it might have been, but would have been greatly enhanced by an evolution path that had been planned. Such programmed evolution, the author proposes, would be directed by God (and therefore created by God), carried out by His angels and souls, and be implemented mystically by manipulation of the DNA and RNA genome within the various organisms affecting evolutionary change.

Much of this theory conflicts with standard church doctrines, but there are few simple answers to most deep spiritual questions.

A time line (see Appendix) presents the author's prediction of existence on Earth after an eventual catastrophic demise of the physical, human form of mankind, probably some thousands of years into the future. Life would not cease on Earth but would be in the form of non-physical souls, as the realm of God is presently. Civilization, at that time, will truly experience Heaven on Earth.

A ROSEBUD THEORY OF DIVERGENT
AND CONSOLIDATED EVOLUTION

"Just as all life may have originated from the first algae and amoeba on this earth, which was created by the chemical union of specific proteins, and perhaps 'welded' together by high voltage electrical discharge of lightning, all primates later originated from one source, and diverged to each become their own specie. One later source, or specie, was the recently discovered features of Eosimas or 'Dawn Monkey' living before a time when higher primates like monkeys, apes, and humans split from Lemur, some 45 million years ago.

"The discovery of Eosimas (detailed in the March, 2000 journal, <u>Nature</u> and <u>The Journal of Human Evolution</u>), illuminates a 20 million-year period in primal evolution heretofore bereft of fossil evidence and suggests that monkeys first appeared in Asia, not Africa. It redefines the base of the evolution-branching tree.

"For a 'missing link', Eosimas and its kin seem impossibly small. The Mouse Lemurs of Madagascar, the smallest primates alive today, weigh three times as much as Eosimas. These primitive primates were probably 'mainlining' sugary nectars and devouring insects constantly just to stay alive."

"Acid-like etchings on the offal remains suggest that owls ate a great many, But humans clearly inherited the survivor's rotating arms and hand-eye coordination."

Source: <u>U.S. News & World Report</u>. March, 2000.

Robert Greenough

PART II - Creation

A Rosebud Theory Of Divergent And Consolidated Evolution

A second article—

"Nature wastes no time at turning one specie into two when a specie is exposed to a new environment, according to research that examined wild sockeye salmon stocked in a Washington lake in the 1930s?

The finding, reported in the current issue of <u>Science</u>, adds important insight into the laws that govern nature and its species-making machinery, experts say.

The most valuable contribution of the study . . . is the first conclusive evidence that animals of the same species:

- - Can quickly develop new traits under the pressures of a new environment.
- - Become less likely to interbreed in a short period of time as they fill different ecological niches.
- - Rapidly begin diverging into different species as a direct result of the ecological pressures."

"Within 70 years (12 generations), the male river salmon developed slender bodies adapted to swimming against currents, while the male lake salmon, which do not have to struggle against currents, had the luxury of developing large, fatter bodies—a distinct edge in selecting mates.

"The river females, meanwhile, developed larger bodies capable of digging deeper nests that provide protection from fluctuating river levels. But lake females developed smaller bodies, all they needed for digging shallow shore nests.

135

"Surprisingly, a third, smaller group was found to be living in the river but spawning on the beach. This group is the least successful of the salmon in terms of reproduction and is likely to disappear eventually.

"Similar rapid evolutionary changes were discovered in a separate study of male fruit flies. After only nine generations, the males of the first species had altered their pheromones to match those of males in the second species. Scientists now believe they have had their first view of those slow changes in progress."

Source: USA Today. October 23, 2000, pg. 100

And a third article—

"New fossil analysis shows that some ancestors of humans had wrist structures similar to those found in gorillas and chimpanzees, providing evidence that humans evolved directly from an ancestor that walked around on its knuckles.

"Gorillas and chimpanzees have a wrist mechanism that locks in place to support the weight of knuckle walking. This fossil trait was also found in the ancient species, Australopithecus afarensis—known as 'Lucy'. Both walked upright but they lived at least a million years after the evolutionary split from apes.

"This discovery shows that the ancestor that gave rise to upright walkers and humans was a knuckle walker. That means it's shared between ancestors of humans, chimpanzees, and gorillas.

"The newly analyzed fossils belong to Australopithecus anamensis and Australopithecus afarensis, the latter

known as 'Lucy'. Both lived in Africa between 4.1 million and 3 million years ago—at least a million years after the evolutionary split from apes!'

Source: The journal, <u>Nature</u>

The author of this book proposes a new theory of evolutionary development. First divergent, and then consolidated evolution of primates resulted when DNA joined and caused a specific phase of evolution.

This happened when the creature, Australopithecus afarensis, the scientifically-reasoned focal source of all Mitochondria DNA, developed from the merged characteristics of the various species of ape, chimpanzees, monkeys, and other primate species.

The merged characteristics, resulting from the expanded DNA, caused evolution into a new creature named "Lucy" by anthropologists. Mitochondria DNA is traceable through the female of species back through past evolutionary development. The trace stopped at "Lucy".

As species originally split in evolution into ape, gorilla, chimpanzee, monkey (and probably other species now extinct), they became and developed separately into their own notable traits.

Through systematic gene engineering, that the author believes was planned by God, and carried out by His angels (a continuation of early bioengineering), DNA and RNA were manipulated to bring about mutations which would also join all primate species into one humanoid body structure. The complex cells of today, with all characteristics of the merged cells incorporated within the cell wall was the result.

This mystical process is somewhat of a repeat of an earlier primal time when Eukaryote cells resulted from a grand merging of various Prokaryote cells, each having their own characteristics.

This manipulation and gene engineering for evolution involved animals as well as possibly plants and insects in a God-planned developing world.

Like a polymer chemist today can modify one element in a chemical structure to create a different compound and a different product, genes could be "tweaked", or mutated, to produce changes in characteristics for completely new living organisms and would create new species of Hominids. Various forms of Hominid evolved from "Lucy".

Graphically this would appear as perhaps a rosebud emerging from a single stem. That single stem would have contained all DNA determinants for characteristics and qualities of the rose. This "stem", or evolutionary line, incorporated features of many species into one bud, and eventual petals of the flower, analogous to different species of Hominid.

Each petal represented a new specie (divergent evolution) of the newly-formed core species (consolidation evolution) of manlike creatures.

In like manner, the traits of the various incorporated primate species produced one new specie that scientists have labeled "Lucy". Originating from "Lucy", various future forms of Hominid developed.

Even today, a mother can produce two or more daughters who are nearly the same in a macro way, but differ specifically in appearance, anatomy, brain capacity, and biological features. Identical genes are in both daughters, differing only in certain mutations of chromosomes that caused different characteristics in each daughter and their following offspring. "Lucy" could have given birth to two or more children who each, by mutation, turned out to be forerunners of new species.

The DNA of each petal, or line, possessing features of all the primate species which had been incorporated to form the new specie, were "tweaked" to evolve new species of man. From "Lucy", then, both Homo sapiens and Neanderthal Man or their equivalents, evolved (such as represented in each petal of the rose).

With this new specie (Lucy), or with some later specie of man, soul was incarnated (and later reincarnated) into Homo sapiens (and perhaps other beings), leading to the evolutionary path resulting in today's Modern Man.

Illustration of Divergent and Consolidation Evolution

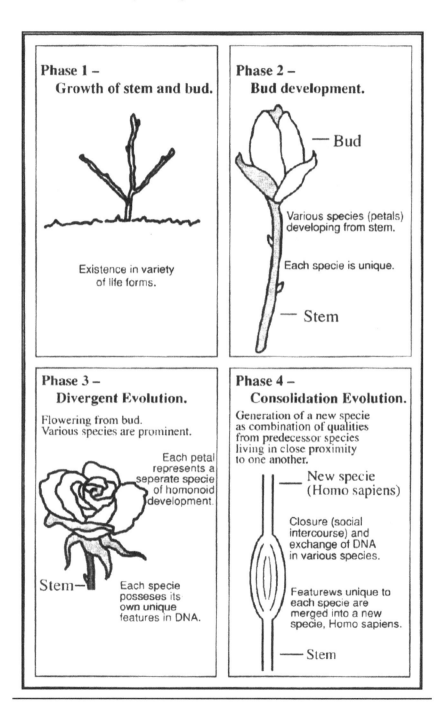

Phase 1 –
Growth of stem and bud.

Existence in variety
of life forms.

Phase 2 –
Bud development.

— Bud

Various species (petals)
developing from stem.

Each specie is unique.

— Stem

Phase 3 –
Divergent Evolution.

Flowering from bud.
Various species are prominent.

Each petal
represents a
seperate specie
of homonoid
development.

Stem—

Each specie
posseses its
own unique
features in DNA.

Phase 4 –
Consolidation Evolution.

Generation of a new specie
as combination of qualities
from predecessor species
living in close proximity
to one another.

New specie
(Homo sapiens)

Closure (social
intercourse) and
exchange of DNA
in various species.

Featurews unique to
each specie are
merged into a new
specie, Homo sapiens.

— Stem

PART III
THE COSMOS

- Thoughts And Questions Of An Amateur Cosmologist
- Today's View Of The Cosmos

Note: *In the three articles of Part III the author has included observations and several questions he has found perplexing concerning bodies in space other than our earth. Written here are perceived dynamics of the "Big Bang", "Black Holes", galaxies, evolution, structure of the cosmos, time, photons, and the growth of the universe. The articles perhaps have little to do with man and mind. They serve to illustrate the science which is basic to our understanding a relationship that exists throughout our cosmos. If there is a system outside of chaos, we may someday, through constant pursuit of knowledge and understanding, arrive at an answer to why and how this cosmos and we human beings exist.*

I

It is not only the force of expansion (explosion) of the "Big Bang" that causes elements of matter (stars, galaxies, planets, asteroids, etc.) to be propelled through space. Another force, inherent in those elements of matter, must exist that, by itself, provides an additional force that excites movement through space, but in the vectors described by the Big Bang expansion. Cosmologists use the term to describe this as "The Great Attractor" The effect of this continued expansion is like a fish swimming excitedly away from some disturbance, far away, and farther away than would thought to be needed or reasonable, from the disturbance that caused the fish to be excited in the first place. The question arises, why did the fish swim so far away?

I have no idea what this inherent force in the cosmos might be, unless it might be gravitational pull from some cosmic structures existing beyond our observable cosmos. Observed rate of recession increases (decreasing would seem to be more logical) with distance from Earth. Are objects being pulled at a logarithmic-increasing speed by some gravitation force beyond our telescopic view?

Another possible propellant force might be the expansion itself of the various components of the cosmos, following as result of the Big Bang and inflationary theory. The expansion of a cosmic structure such as matter at extreme of the universe might exert an opposing force that promotes propulsion, upon "Dark Matter", or photons existing in the cosmos, much like a water jet engine "pushes" on the water to propel the engine forward.

II

Could it be that each "Black Hole" does not give birth to a whole galaxy or to the entire universe, which is popular theory, but instead gives birth to only one star or one galaxy? Do stars and galaxies come from many Black Holes?

Under this theory a galaxy represents the birth and existence of several stars, each independent from another, but localized in one area of space, and held together in a system by an orbital gravitation of the universe.

Each galaxy, or group of stars, may likewise be the result of numerous, separate Black Hole actions occurring in different areas of space.

The galaxy would grow over time in the number of stars that attracted to the galaxy by orbital gravitation, thus leaving vast voids in space between galaxies. Each star existing separately, outside of a "nearby" galaxy, would eventually be attracted to that galaxy, and become a part of the swirling mass of the galaxy.

Dark matter and cosmic gases would also be localized into the star or galaxy mass, thus clearing out the celestial space between stars and adding to the black void of space.

Perhaps Our Big Bang didn't create the entire cosmos but merely created our own "Milky Way" galaxy, sun and planets, comets, asteroids, and dark matter, forged in our solar system. The creation of other suns, stars, galaxies, or universe in this theory, was left to separate Big Bang events.

Perhaps the source of the various independent and separate Big Bangs was a universe that preceded our own "in a time before time".

This theory could account for the varying size, make up, and physical (or quantum physical) qualities of each star or galaxy system. Each star is alike, but chemically different. This parallelism is similar to existence of the various children of parents, as we observe in human families, each having similarities, yet differences.

III

Are superclusters of galaxies lying at (and perhaps beyond) the extent of the observable limits of our viewing (within 186,000 miles per second, multiplied by the number of seconds that have occurred since the start of our time of 10 to 20 billion years ago) the evidence of existence of a cosmos in a previous era, that spawned a Black Hole, consequently and eventually creating the singularity or unification, a Big Bang of our present cosmos?

Our present universe may be a spin-off from a previously existing cosmos, existing prior to our Big Bang.

Thought: God, intelligence, and consciousness, requiring no physical existence, could have existed in such previous eras.

IV

The cosmos, including our sun, planets and earth, occurred and developed by laws of physics and mathematics. But the biological life, including the animal person of Homo sapiens, did not develop by rule of physics and mathematics. There is a distinction between organic and inorganic matter, in the laws under which each was originated and developed.

The orderliness of physical laws is reversible and repeatable, and could be run either forward or backward in evolution or geology with predictable and regular results. In contrast, the disorder, or chaos, of biological development are not predictable and repeatable. It would be impossible to repeat the steps in the evolution of man, but it might be possible to repeat, in some laboratory, the evolution of our cosmos.

V

Physicists have recently derived the illogical conclusion that some stars are actually older than the universe itself. This could be interpreted that some stars were in existence, and had been in existence, for sometime before the moment of our Big Bang that formed "our" universe.

This could also be reasoned that these preexistent stars were remnants of a previous universe that existed, was partially swallowed into a Black Hole, heated, and exploded into our present concept of the "Big Bang".

VI

Time is circular. Time is never perfectly straight for an infinite distance, but is continually being "bent" by gravity. Time is space and light, and light is matter, defined by photons. The photons are affected by gravity. Albert Einstein showed that light rays are bent by gravity. It is theoretically possible that time can "lap" itself, form a complete circle, repeat itself or form a parallel "time ring".

Milliseconds after the moment of unification and the Big Bang, space and time were still infinitesimally small, and light and time would bend quickly into a circle, to create time warps, very rapidly and short at the start, and becoming increasingly longer in length and time span as the universe expanded.

Complete "time rings" would have been more readily formed in the first milliseconds following a Big Bang. Travel in time could theoretically be experienced through such time warps. Travel in time could therefore be experienced without a comparable travel in distance, but by "jumping" to a concentric "time ring".

Because time is relative directly to distance, time lapse was relative to age. Time was near zero in terms of distance in space traveled immediately following the Big Bang. But time is graduated differently as it is dependent upon the age of the cosmos, expanding to time as it is defined today. Time gradation, or definition of a unit of time was relatively "short" following a Big Bang, but became "longer" as the universe expanded, and will be extended as the future evolves.

VII

PHOTONS: As we sit in our room, or outside, or elsewhere in the world, or in space, and look away to see what is there, we may see bookshelves on the opposite wall, or trees, or the distant horizon. We see these because of photons. We note that when astronauts are in space, they do not see an object that may be just outside their window, except to the extent of seeing reflected light.

In areas in which we can see, such as in our room, we are bathed in a sea of photons. It is like we have an ability to live underwater—in a sea of water—the "water" being actually zillions of separate particles that are grouped to form a body of water. So too, the photons surrounding us like water would not be unlike water surrounding us when we are submerged. As the light of day, or illumination by a light bulb, occurs, so does the quantity of light in which we theoretically sit, exist (e.g., we are "under water"), or, in darkness, does not exist (e.g., we are like "on dry land"), or as in deep space. We are constantly in light, in shades of light, or in total darkness depending upon the extent of illumination of the photons.

Photons are matter, albeit minuscule, but do manifest presence where there is light, and expires where there is no light (darkness). Photons have infinitesimally small masses.

Because they are matter, photons are subject to gravitational pull, with a phenomenon that light can be bent, both on earth by a prism, or in outer space by observing the light of obscured stars being bent around our sun during periods of eclipse.

Photons are dark in traveling through space, from our sun or stars, or reflected by the moon, but illuminated when they intersect an object like earth, or the far walls of our room, our body, or anything that we "see".

(Question in logic: Do we actually exist in the dark, and exist only when we can see those objects that are reflecting light, e.g., matter intersecting photons? This is similar to the philosophical query, *"does a falling tree make sound when there is no one there to hear it.* Again, we are confronted with the paradox of Werner Heisenberg's mind experiment with a cat, that appears when observed and is nonexistent when it is not observed.)

On a moonless night, when there is no source of light, we see nothing or, as often said, *". . . couldn't see my hand in front of my face"*. There are, in this scenario, no photons reflected from the light source of the moon to be excited when they strike matter.

When we look at a distant star, through the black void of space, we are actually looking head-on at a path of photons coming directly towards us, and we "see" a disc of photons that meets our eye.

Photons probably exist in all of space. They certainly exist on all surfaces of earth, whether it be daylight or nighttime. We do not see them to any great extent at night because they are not being energized by a light source, such as the sun, moon, stars, or flashlight.

Could photons be the lost dark matter that scientific theory states exists, the 90 percent of matter that is not accounted for by earth, planets, sun, stars, and galaxies?

I was not yet born in 1923 when Edwin Hubble discovered that galaxies are moving away from each other, and the rate of movement, Hubble's Constant, launched the modern era of cosmology. Hubble's calculations showed that we (our own solar system) were part of a uniformly expanding universe.

His observations and calculations showed that a galaxy, say, three times further away from our own galaxy than a reference galaxy, was moving away three times faster than did the reference galaxy. Everything in the universe was in motion.

"Seventy years ago galaxies were thought by many to be simple fuzzy smudges floating in the Milky Way. We are living in the golden age of cosmic discovery." (Neil de Grasse Tyson, Astrophysicist, Natural History Magazine. November, 1996 *Outward Bound)*

We are intrigued by the photographs of the cosmos taken through the Hubble Telescope. I am further intrigued by the patterns in the sky made by the relative location of stars and galaxies. (See *Appendix)*

It seems that one could easily connect the dots of stars in a line, much like connect-the-dots drawings we all did as youngsters. Skywatchers since ancient time have "connected the dots" to show pictures in the sky of crabs, archers, fish, men, etc. in the various constellations.

A few isolated situations can be assimilated to form a possible scenario on how and why certain stars and galaxies are where they are:

Do We Live In Two Worlds?
PART III - The Cosmos

Today's View Of The Cosmos

First, I have previously theorized that there have been more than one, perhaps several, "Big Bangs", each evolving from a previous "Black Hole". In this theory, each star or galaxy would have been created separately as "Small Bangs" occurred, each occupying a certain location in the cosmos.

Second, we think of the various islands of the Hawaiian Archipelago. Each of these islands was created over thousands of years by volcanic action when each island was located, like on a moving belt, over a fixed "hot spot" on the earth, the location of each volcanic activity changing as the continental plate moved eastward. The oldest volcanic activity of this sort occurred on the eastern most islands of the Hawaiian Archipelago. Thus the islands form an organized row of surfaced volcanoes, since worn down by erosion and other ecological action.

Could it be that the location of the various stars and galaxies was also determined by some form of relative movement in the cosmos that provided an organized relationship in "Small Bang" activity. The galaxies that we can now view back to the earliest five percent of entire time, may be aligned in curved, or even somewhat straight line locations.

These stars look very much like the first stars in the process of forming—they looked so old that they must be from the first few million years of the cosmos. Through the Hubble Telescope we have found objects that are very distant and therefore very far back in time and very possibly the first generation of stars forming. Scientists do not yet agree on how old the universe is, but some think it is anywhere between 9 and 17 billion years old.

The reader may refer to the *"Appendix"* for further information about the Hubble Telescope.

PART IV
THE SOUL

155

The soul, in its primitive form, existed parallel with the animal body at or soon after the advent of the first living organism. The purpose of that soul was to "engineer" development of the evolving animal bodies acting as the intermediary, or functionary, directing changes or mutations in development. Change in the genome were effected by changing the DNA and RNA arrangements, thereby causing mutations of biologic, anatomical, and neural change.

Another important difference is that of logic, which may reflect to qualities of the mind. Many males have been frustrated by what, for lack of a better term, I will call "female logic". Of course, the reverse is true, with females not always understanding the workings of the male mind and that thinking process.

Female logic is not evident in all females, nor is the reverse found in all males. Many females rise to a position of leadership in society, government, business, and personal existence through their ability to be logical and to obtain agreement with others in negotiation and compromise.

Persons, male and female, who are biologically "female-oriented" excel in certain activities such as artistic expression, where demonstration of logic is secondary. This is often observed in art, decorating, and various "soft" subjects.

It may be that this attraction of differences is a factor in productive mating, and of sexual attraction of male and female in various species, another system in nature

Do We Live In Two Worlds?
PART IV - The Soul

Soul—An Overview

providing checks and balances and in advantageous gene sharing.

At some point in time, perhaps at time of "Lucy" around 3.7 million years ago, the scope of soul changed to reflect in the animal body an intelligence and consciousness, a microcosm of the entity from a superior being from which soul had originally derived. This provided the developing Homo australopithicus to posses qualities of empathy, affection, emotion, love, judgment, introspection, and other qualities we realize exist in Homo sapiens today.

For lack of better terms the author refers to the souls of the two periods before and after existence of intelligence and consciousness as Soul I and Soul II.

The author struggled for some time with the concept of one soul existing from initial commencement of soul to that of modern-day existence. The author questions, for example, did dinosaurs have a soul? There was no reason to expect that dinosaurs and other creatures of the period, possessed soul of the same qualities presently recognized in Modern Man.

A logical answer to the question would be "no". However, initial reasoning dictated that either soul existed, or it did not. The author concluded that prior to advent of Soul II, there existed only Soul I, devoted to evolution in refining the animal biologic sophistication. Soul II would follow at a later period leading to Modern Man.

The Superior Being is one entity, regardless of the name assigned by various cultural and religious entities. Judeo-Christian cultures called their entities "Yahweh", "God", or other such name. Native American cultures termed the entity as "The Great Spirit". Muslim cultures refer to "Allah". Other names were unique to various cultures throughout the world. Most cultures independently recognized that some superior entity does exist.

In our present state of technological development of understanding the world we live in, and how we may capitalize on the sources available to us, we create materials and systems for our own worldly use. Civilization, like a tremendous Tsunami wave arriving at land, creates a condition where the force at the moment of action (now) is overpowering in comparison to the residual state afterwards. A new way of life, a new culture, often evolves after the initial impact and when the Tsunami is gone.

Likewise is the wave of knowledge that has enveloped us as we turn to the 21st Century. Our knowledge of science has overpowered our understanding of ourselves as individuals, where the individual relates in society, and the mystical through studies in metaphysics.

The individual human is more than another animal populating the earth. In the entire "Noah's Ark" of the world, humans alone are unique in that we possess a, so far unexplained inner self that, at least most other animals do not have. (Qualified in respect to the various Animalism religions of the world that believe the soul returns to earth in the embodiment of many forms besides humans.)

We have a soul that allow humans to live in two worlds. A soul allows the human mind to operate in a dimension far in excess of the computerlike myriad of communication networks that we call our brain.

Like a computer, the hardware and systems are in place at time of birth and programming with data input taking place continually, perhaps even soon after the moment of conception, that the combined genome determines the capability and the formation of the human brain.

But that brain is limited against manipulation of intangibles known as emotion, vision, insight, understanding of outside values of energy, love, attraction, and similar phenomena. These intangibles are outside the capabilities of the biological mechanism of our brain, much like computer chips and wiring diagrams of our modern-day electronic marvel of computers cannot calculate the qualitative values of these phenomena.

The brain operates by millions of transmitters and synapses or "connections" in nerves, with communication lines that put AT & T to shame. These communication lines in turn connect with a vast, complex system for interactions correlating with other vast, complex systems existing within our brain. The result is a transference of fabulous complex brain messages resulting in thought or muscular action.

But like a computer cannot, at least presently, exert force on these intangible phenomena, the brain is also limited. We come to the shore, the dividing line between one concept and another, the division between brain and mind.

Beyond the shore is a different world. We will experience the ocean world when we place a boat on the surface and travel around in two dimensions. We are only recently starting to explore other dimensions of oceans such as depth, chemistry, life within, the system and organization, and the factors that effect that organization.

So too, we can delve into understanding the world, perhaps the universe, of the mind, a second world that is there to be explored and understood, that will allow a more comprehensive understanding of our existence, and where we as individuals and as a society fit into "the general scheme of things".

Modern day science provides for the existence of souls. This book attempts to explain how souls came into existence, what their function is in regard to causing human evolution, and their existence in afterlife.

Many physicists and medical doctors, noted in their respective fields, are quick to acknowledge that unexplained events happen that are beyond knowledge in the current state of achievement in their studies. Despite thousands of years of scientific advancement, there is still a void of explainable events that we have called miracles and mystical.

God is a supersoul. When the Bible states that *"God created man in His own image"*, it does NOT mean that He created the human body of man, but that He created the soul, which was in the image of God.

The soul exists within the body of man, and uses the body as a medium for its own development towards a oneness with God, that is, towards itself being a supersoul, a part of God, or at least nearly so.

The development to perfection of the soul is a slow, progressive path requiring the lifetimes of many physical bodies. Some sources and religions state that a soul may even "fall backwards" in its development by taking the body of a lower-than-human existence, such as some animal, or even an inanimate object, such as a tree, stone, plant, etc., as told in ancient religions of India, and in the animism of Native American Indian religions.

In this development through evolution, the soul is struggling towards perfection to attain an eternal existence in Paradise. Spirit life is an enigma, (or indefinite and difficult to describe in its existence).

A "job" of souls in the antimatter world, was, in the past and is presently, to oversee the development of evolution in secular organisms. The soul would be instrumental to "redesign" skeletons, skin, organs, etc. as conditions changed on earth. The mechanism of change was through control of the RNA and DNA, and through mutations between generations of these organisms.

Souls, in their limitless travel through time, are much like a young child playing on an elevator of a tall apartment building, traveling to, and stopping at, whichever floor suits his fancy. The soul too might meander in time to different time periods, both before the present time, and in the future, to live in the life of bodies of the respective time periods.

My analogy, of course, is that each time period throughout the endless life of a soul is comparable to an individual floor of a limitlessly tall skyscraper, and the elevator represents his travel up and down to the future, and backward through time.

Is observable time real, or is it illusory, with all of time existing at one instant, are we all traveling, so to speak, vertically like the elevator in a building? Or need we continue to think of time as linear and horizontal, as cars driving on a bridge?

Perhaps souls evolved over time, dating from the "Big Bang". Under this theory, at first the makings of souls was no more than positrons, or positive charged electrons. Their evolutionary development was guided directly by God, and quickly became complex forces of energy having a purpose in their existence.

These forces of energy, now called souls, served God in guiding and planning the evolution of various forms of matter from Prokaryotic cells, to amoeba, and Eukaryotic cells, worms, polyps, simple functioning animals, fish, reptiles, mammals, and eventually to primates and various forms of man.

The tool of changing life forms was manipulation of the RNA and DNA systems in the nucleus of cells. Manipulation is accomplished by bio-electricity changing genome, that affect enzymes, that determine and control the life form.

Development of plants, animals, insects, microbes and bacteria kingdoms progressed through nearly all imaginable forms and processes of secular life over nearly 4.5 billion years on earth, to the present existence of these kingdoms.

Today, and ever since the existence of Homo sapiens, (also called Cro-Magnon man), man and souls, and perhaps other life forms too (as proposed in certain Animist religions), have coexisted in a worldly body during that being's secular lifetime.

The Biblical Adam and Eve, prior to the events at the Garden of Eden, were existing souls in the realm of God. They were, in fact, at a state of perfect innocence before as souls, and original sin occurred after they became incarnated to hominoid bodies.

The fact stated in the Bible that Satan (in the form of a snake) existed in the Garden of Eden, (and also that many souls also are mentioned as existing at the "Creation" of Adam and Eve) indicates that a realm of souls was in existence prior to the time of the events related in the Garden of Eden and concerning the creation of Adam and Eve.

In a concept that God was in existence at time of the "Big Bang", a survivor of a previous cosmos, then God did in fact "create" the heaven and the earth, creating the world out of nothing, which particle scientists today have dubbed the "Singularity".

All living creatures have souls. Souls are the tie between God and life on earth. The Bible states in Genesis that God granted dominion *"over the fish of the sea, and over the*

---

birds of the air, and over the cattle, and over all the wild animals of the earth."

The soul evolves much like secular animals evolve and mature. Souls change from basic atoms of positrons, as in the beginning, to the being that they exhibit today as complex images with wonderful abilities. This compares with man's evolution from prehistoric algae, amoebae, and bacteria to the exhibit of man today, 4.5 billion years later.

One can believe in and follow the theory of evolution, but have extreme trouble in believing that all modifications happened by accident and by mutations.

There must have been a plan. To illustrate, a purposeful machine would never be built by monkeys rummaging in a junkyard. Yet, a mechanic-minded man, rummaging in that same yard with a concept of function and what two elements or parts put together could do in operation, could assemble and create a functional machine.

This same principle would apply in evolution. Without an intelligence and a plan, either preexisting, or spontaneous with each new "find", no functional, biologic change is possible. There is required to be an intelligence and a plan.

The mechanics for the change in evolutionary development is in the manipulation of the RNA and DNA code of the various living organisms. This was the "blueprint" to reproduce what existed, and in modern-day industrial language, the "engineering change" blueprint that detailed what the new modification would be, and exactly how it would work in the plan.

My interpretation to what force performed the planning and the operations is theological. I contend that the planning was done by energy of God, and that the operation aspects of physically (or biologically) affecting the changes were performed by God's angels, manipulating the RNA and DNA of algae, amoeba, microbes, insects, and subsequent higher complexes in living organisms.

This concept may appear strange, but the idea could answer a lot of questions that arise in theology and science.

A predecessor of Homo sapiens, Homo erectus, lacked the ability of speech. However, Homo sapiens, known also as Modern Man, Cro-Magnon or "Thinking Man", did have this ability.

A biological change or addition in anatomy, biologically "engineered" by RNA and DNA coding, allowed this radical change in human form that was developing from simian form, to take place.

The ability of speech, through a larynx, allowed Homo sapiens to communicate in meaningful sounds, and to construct a meaningful sequence of sounds to communicate an idea. This was a necessary first step to develop a civilization as we know it.

From this first speech, talk and two-way conversation developed, to be followed with written communication by pictures, and later by interchangeable pictographs and hieroglyphics, words, sentences, stories, and eventually an alphabet, numbers, record keeping, historical writing, and beyond.

I

Can a person, or a spirit, "will" his soul into another body? What would happen to the soul that is already in that body?

Can a person, somewhat consciously, carry with him in an "inter-generational transfer", qualities of consciousness such as values, acquired knowledge, emotions, memories, forgetfulness, inspiration, tact, how to choose, what and how to divine, will, intelligence, and direction in which that intelligence will be applied, conviction, strength of devotion, patterns of behavior, awareness, purpose and desire of the present soul/mind, thoughts, sensations, emotions, inspiration, feeling, perception, and other similar qualities?

Is there evidence of a physical process that would influence the memory contents of another brain in a later, successive life? Yoga is purported to be a method to permit transmigration, not only within one species, but between species. How can a soul and mind make a choice on the proper action, if the living person has no recollection of where he has been before in another life?

II

This book advances the theory that: God existed and souls were created at time of the Big Bang 12 to 20 billion years ago, with first habitation of the earth by algae and microbic life at approximately 4 1/2 billion years ago. The period from 4 1/2 billion years saw evolution of algae, amoeba, microbes, arthropods, insects, fish, reptiles, and some mammals. Dinosaurs came upon the earth scene about 220 million years ago. Dinosaur extinction and the growth of mammal population occurred at about 65 million years ago. Manlike forms did not exist before 4-5 million years ago, with culture of Modern Man (language and designed tools) starting at about 10,000 BC.

Did dinosaurs have souls? It would follow that God and souls were in existence at the time of the dinosaurs, approximately 220 to 65 million years ago.

What was the earthly body manifestation of souls during this 4 1/2 billion year interim period, or was there no earthly manifestation at all?

This book theorizes that manlike features were evolved through God-designed evolution that caused the present day Homo sapiens to evolve and to receive the soul from the antimatter world for soul-body existence on this earth.

We should not be so egotistical to believe that souls were paired only with manlike creatures over these eons, during the age of dinosaurs. In the Triassic and Jurassic periods of 220 to 135 million years ago, these creatures may also be the earthly vehicles for souls and evolution to have physical existence on earth.

Do chimpanzees and apes, the closest primate relatives to humans in the tree of life, have a soul, or did souls merely act externally of these primates in manipulating DNA? Is the existence of soul one of the primary differences between Homo sapiens and nonhuman but humanlike mammals? Are chimpanzees, apes, and monkeys the latest evolutionary division in the tree of life? The lowly swine has body parts, (kidney) that modern medical science

Do We Live In Two Worlds?
PART IV - The Soul

Comments Regarding The Soul

states are interchangeable with that of humans. How could we possibly define a soul and determine whether it exists in a certain mammal (perhaps in certain people) or not?

Some persons are convinced that certain animals have souls, such as dogs, cats, and certain other animals, both domesticated and wild. Hindus believe the Brahma cow is sacred. Native American Indians speak of the soul in wild animals, and even in inanimate objects such as stones, the earth, trees, winds, birds, sun, and moon. Many owners of pet dogs and cats argue extensively that qualities of soul exist within their pet. These qualities of soul have been reported as existing also in wildlife, especially in the canine and feline family of animals.

III

Man exists in two parts: First is the animal body, developed by evolution, and guided in that evolution by the wisdom of God, and through the genes and DNA to become what he is today, and will become in the future through further evolution. Secondly is an intelligence, as an integral part of the body, but separate and separable. Incarnation is an immaculate joining of body and soul.

The intelligence and an energy, not the body as we have parroted from the Bible since our childhood, was created in the image of God. Again, from our childhood learning, Eve ate in the Garden of Eden from the "Tree of Knowledge". This is merely a symbolism that the eating was an action directed to gaining intelligence and to gain worldly insight, and was not a physical eating merely to gain calories or enjoyment from an apple.

Prior to the Garden of Eden, man was more like animal, although nearing the human form of Cro-Magnon (thinking man), and emerging from Australopithecus, a forerunner of Homo sapiens (humans). This was the locale (theologically, if not geographically) where soul and body were merged.

My personal view of the location of the Garden of Eden, if that place in fact did exist, is that it is probably now at the bottom of the Persian Gulf, or near the Straits of Hormuz. The author reasons that an earthquake may have opened this geologic mountain formation, still visible on either side of the Straits, allowing waters of the present Indian Ocean to flood in and form the Persian Gulf.

The "overwash" into the Euphrates valley, later, could well have been the flood at the time of Noah, with an eventual resolve of the water into the present Persian Gulf. All life in the path of those floodwaters would have been suddenly destroyed by the extremely deep flood waters, happening concurrent with cycles of deluge rain, evaporation, and more deluge rain, continuing for an extended time.

The Biblical account that rain would account for several tens of feet of flood waters would seem illogical and unequaled in modern weather recordings. The existence of a tremendous and lasting rain period coinciding with the "Great Flood" might well have been the essence of the oral history reported in the Book of Genesis.

This suggested location of a Garden of Eden would not be far from the ancient city of Ur, located in the Tigris and Euphrates River valley, the reputed oldest city in

Mesopotamia, and possibly the site of the oldest grouping of civilized people in the Mideast. However, older communities did exist in Egypt, China, and the Americas, as fossils indicating civilizations there have been found by anthropologists.

The quest by the souls of Eve and Adam, for insightful knowledge of good and evil beyond that afforded by God, is what raised the ire of God and is recognized as the first sin committed by man.

Since the pairing of intelligence and animal, man has had the facility to develop and prove his soul. Souls, like physical beings, physical structures, the cosmos, machines on earth, and virtually all things, are "born" with, and may develop, imperfections. The lifetimes of humans is for the purpose that imperfections can be "worked out" in a path leading to perfection in which the soul of each of us will hopefully become a unity with God.

Numerous cycles, or human lifetimes through successive reincarnations, may be necessary to attain this perfection. Some souls will attain perfection sooner than others.

Jesus Christ may be an example of a soul that has attained perfection. This theory would be reconciliation of whether Jesus Christ is God, is the Son of God incarnate, or is the Spirit of God. As a perfected soul, He would be all three.

Doers of heinous crimes, which we read about in today's newspapers and in history books, represent souls, if indeed those persons have one, that are far from perfect, and will require further "refinement", perhaps in another life on earth. The latter may also represent the relative position in the "tug of war" of souls between God and Satan. So many times, it seems, that evil men do not live a long life.

In recognition of this thought and philosophy, that the human body is only a vehicle for the soul, one can rightly cast away his body upon death, retaining the soul to continue on in eternal life.

The body can be used to help mankind by donation to others of its usable parts upon death, depending upon one's own thoughts and reverence for his body, and the ultimate balance of good that would be derived.

IV

By the definition of mind equals soul, organisms other than humans also have soul, such as certain primates of great ape, chimpanzee, orangutan, gorilla, macaque, gibbon, and marmoset, other animals, mammals, reptiles, sea life and plants. These primates have evidenced having qualities of mind which, at least in part, are common with certain qualities of the human mind. This definition of mind would apply to water mammals such as the porpoise and whale.

V

No one knows, of course, but the author has the feeling, reinforced by reason and logic, that the world of God is, in its own way, somewhat rational and systematic. Nevertheless, it seems to us to be irrational and unsystematic in viewing Heaven from our secular set of values and expectations.

But Heaven is of a different universe, so to speak, if not in actuality. We can better understand the differences between ourselves and other existences by observing nature.

We are amazed and perplexed about the culture, routines, and capabilities of ants, bees, migrating birds and insects, of the wild animals, and bacteria. Theirs is different from our own behavior, yet we can observe and somewhat understand what and why they perform as they do.

Likewise in understanding the ways of the soul, spirit world, and Heaven we must appreciate that things are done reasonably and for a purpose. There is creation, existence, and passage, all with a system and rationality within.

VI

The Temple of Petra, in the former Transjordan, is not constructed but is instead sculpted out of solid rock. Its facade is intricately fashioned in precise detail. Inside is a larger room, plain in design. On each of three sides is a small chamber for the reception of the dead.

Could the "temple to nowhere" be a passageway, built well before the days of Christ, from the mortal and physical world of man to the immortal and spiritual world, where physical presence of rock is not a barrier to passage into the world of God and souls?

VII

The author believes the number of souls in the universe is finite. There is a definite maximum number of souls that do or will exist. Whether that maximum is the present number of living people on earth, some larger number, or possibly some lesser number is hard to say. Some religions, especially Hindu and North American Indians, propose that souls return to relatively minor forms of existence other than human, such as to inorganic forms like Earth, winds, rock, etc. Because of this maximum number, reincarnation is necessary, for among other reasons, an infinite number is improbable and without reason or purpose.

The present population of earth (in the year 2001) is somewhere between 4 and 6 billion people. We can assume that each living person possesses a soul of one sort or another. This does not even consider those souls that Animists believe to exist in nonhuman forms.

With an arbitrary average population of the earth at any one time over the past 1,000 generations, without reincarnation or recycling of souls, there would, by quick arithmetic, mean that there are and were 1,000,000,000,000, or 1 trillion, souls in existence today. The author feels this population of souls is not reasonable (If souls exist in non-human forms, population of souls might well be reasonable.) and would have little purpose in God's scheme of existence. But on the other hand, what difference would it make if the soul population were a trillion or merely a million.

What was the stature of persons with souls in a previously reincarnated life? Two of the most well-known persons of modern times who claim a previous life are General George Patton of World War II fame, and Shirley McClain of Hollywood acclaim. General Patton felt and

Do We Live In Two Worlds?
PART IV - The Soul

Comments Regarding The Soul

stated that he was a Roman general in a previous life. Was Shirley McClain, currently an entertainment principal, of a significant social status in a previous life? And were their no reincarnated souls of what were merely the "common man" in a previous existence? Surely there were!

Many persons would have been the common man or woman, perhaps a serf or other person not in a social leadership capacity. Are persons reincarnated within their own blood line family? Are persons who possessed a "bad" or inferior soul in a previous life reincarnated now into a "good" or worthy and to-be-proven soul in their current life? Were, as Animists believe, even a human soul at all as their reincarnated soul recycled through the series of reincarnation over the past 1,000 or more generations?

Fifty years ago the world population was somewhere less—perhaps only 4 billion. Fifty years before the population was even less, and so forth, tracing back into the generations of 1,000 or more since souls, even a single soul, came into existence. Certain biblical historians would have us believe that there was the first generation of souls in the Garden of Eden in the year 4004 BC, although there is support that souls existed even before the time of Adam and Eve.

Some of us, in fact most of us, must have been reincarnated from persons who were classed as "common people". Abraham Lincoln is credited as saying, *"The Good Lord must have loved the common people very much because he made so many of us."*

VIII

Eugenics, Selective Breeding, Abortion, and Execution:

The pros and cons of continuing or discontinuing a human life for reasons that are arguable from a social goal have been debated widely for decades. Is it wrong to eliminate the life of a fetus that, if born, will be pitied because of physical or mental deficiencies, imbecile or feeblemindedness, incapacity to ever live independently, a constant drain on the efforts of parents and society, unloved, even despised? Should a child, born of rape, be forced to be born to an unaccepting and rejecting mother? Should a convicted serial killer be continued in life at the expense of his or her fellow people, and with little productivity or purpose in the continuing life? The author believes that principles advocated in this book can be of assistance in deciding individual questions.

In this concept that we live in two worlds, we live in a biological world and we also live in a spiritual world. If we can sort, in our own minds, the unity and the difference between the two, a decision becomes somehow easier.

The concept of the spiritual world recognizes that we each possess a nonphysical being of mind and soul. This soul can be, and eventually at time of death will be, divided from the physical body. It is possible to think of the nonphysical being as separate from the physical being.

Once separated into the two categories, we can make decisions based on disposition of the physical, biological body that does not necessarily involve a decision regarding the soul of the person. Discontinuance of the physical body does not necessarily mean discontinuance of the soul.

Do We Live In Two Worlds?
PART IV - The Soul

Comments Regarding The Soul

The soul of stillborn infant or fetus will be "reassigned" to another body. The soul of an executed murderer may continue on in afterlife and has not been terminated with the deceased body. It is discontinuance of the physical body, not of the soul, that is the question.

With this division in mind, we are not "playing God" by consenting to abortion or to capital punishment. We are merely, although it is a momentous decision, deciding on the "total good" of discontinuing the biological body. We are not discontinuing the soul.

Eugenics (selective breeding) needs to be based on individual decision. In the past where eugenics has run counter to rational or emotional judgment, such as in the Nazi death camps of World War II, it has been where decisions were placed at the discretion of the state, rather than at the discretion of the individuals involved.

IX

Reincarnation within blood lines: Do ghosts, spirits, and souls appear to, or reincarnate within, the same family blood lines? The following observation is made simply as a comment, without an attempt in persuasion of whether return of souls to earth by reincarnation stay within biologic family and blood lines of past generations in family.

There is some indication that souls retain their blood family association. An Egyptologist, in discovering the burial of an ancient, mummified Egyptian family, unwittingly separated the individual mummies of the family to different locations. He noticed a flaking of paint on some of the mummy cases and was haunted by lack of sleep and thoughts that bothered him. By chance, he realized the separation of family that he had caused. He relocated mummies of the family to be together again. The flaking of the paint and his haunting thoughts stopped. These events could be coincidental, environmental or psychological, or they could be meaningful.

Reports of individuals over decades and centuries of souls returning to visit persons on earth, that chose to associate with an earthly person, sometimes involves a family relationship with one another.

Assuming reincarnation, and when reincarnation does occur, this may sometimes occur within the biological blood lines of a family.

Is your soul the soul of some of your own ancestors, continuing now in some dynasty of your family? Do you possess some characteristic of either physical or a personality type, of one of your ancestors?

This hypothesis needs considerable study to draw any conclusions, but may be a viable question in the study of reincarnation.

Upon death, the human body, of course, ceases to function. The person is declared legally dead, the funeral is held, and the body is disposed of by burial, cremation, or perhaps by some exotic means such as cryogenic entombment. Within three days, it is said, the soul leaves that animal body and becomes a resident of Heaven. Death is a part of life.

I visualize three scenarios in the then existence of the soul, recently separated from the deceased body.

I

The first scenario might be termed the classic. This is the reward for leading a good life on earth that has been communicated by the churches and philosophers from the time of Christian advocates, and before, in a time going back at least to the philosophers, Socrates, Plato, and Aristotle.

In this classic view, the deceased will meet again, in Heaven, all of his or her deceased loved ones, parents, plus the various saints, prophets, Jesus, and perhaps God Himself. I suppose the deceased would also meet up with souls of persons he or she knew in life and had hoped would never see again.

It is undefined just what will occupy the time of this soul for the next millennium, and what earthly pleasures might be allowed, or disallowed, in Heaven.

On the Day of Reckoning, biblical fundamentalists tell us, the long since dusty bones of the deceased animal body will somehow be reconstituted and arise out of the grave or cremation urn. Somehow this scenario does not ring true to my way of thinking.

II

A second scenario abandons the promise of bodily resurrection on the Day of Judgment, but does provide for the existence of souls in Heaven. The soul exists in some form of nothingness, perhaps like a cloud or mist.

The soul has an ability to transfer to, and intermix with, the earthly world of mortal human existence, as well as communication within Heaven, wherever that might be, with other souls, and with the administrative hierarchy of infinity. The soul, in a mist or cloud form, would exhibit no unique appearance or personality, except as by its own will, such as in making earthly presentations.

Instead of existing in nothingness for at least a millennium of years, the soul is classified and directed for reassignment, or reincarnation, either perhaps to a newborn child, or to some living person of unfortunate being whose soul and life has been misdirected in pathetic circumstance.

III

The third scenario I would like to elaborate on in some detail. This is when, upon the death of the human, the soul becomes united with the substance of God, becoming as undivided from God as a drop of water on water, which, upon contact, becomes absorbed into a larger body of the same substance. I propose that it was from this God-body that the soul evolved, from the identical substance as God Himself.

The records of the Old Testament had said that Man was created in God's own image, and it is now reasoned this did not mean anatomically, as theologians and fundamentalists have, for tens of hundreds of years, interpreted the Bible, but that man was created spiritually, in God's own image. The soul of man is the same substance as the soul of God. God and soul, as one, is a consciousness, an intelligence, without physical being or limitation.

This creation of God and the potential of soul has existed since the era of the first appearance of Cro-Magnon man, since the era of universal and interstellar star dust, since the moment of particle unification, since the moment of zero time, and perhaps even before time, in the era of Black Hole accumulation, and perhaps before that, into some prior cosmos.

It is soul and God, serving as one, that has operated the intricacies of life on earth since the very beginning, and will continue forever more in a merging of soul, in the image of God, conjoined with the animal body of the evolved Homo sapiens.

It is this Godly wonderment that allows a transcendence of time and minds, evidenced through the phenomena and psychic powers of deja vu, mental telepathy, thought transference, premonition, intuition, foretelling, love, conscience, and insight, that is often experienced by mortal men.

Other "uncomputerlike" phenomena that mankind experiences include the exercise of free will, intentions, consciousness, awareness, intuitive direction, morality, ethics, belief, faith, emotion, feelings, recognition of summum bonum (a supreme or highest good), and visions. These mystic phenomena are recognized as opposed to those functions of the brain-thought processes.

These are all operations outside the electro-functioning of the brain, with its complex, biological neural system and its millions of neurons, axons, and synapses. The thinking processes of the brain, that "computational", "computerlike" electromechanical and wonderful sense transference of our neural center, is different than that of the "mind", defined in the phenomena stated in the previous two scenarios.

1.

We live our mortal life in two worlds. Biologists' study and research has made an excellent case for the scenario of how the human body has evolved over millions of years, from marine algae to Homo sapiens. But biologists will also be the first to recognize that there are some aspects of human life that their studies cannot explain.

2.

We have to believe that Heaven exists right here on earth. It is not in the clouds, as church dogma has taught for thousand of years. God and souls are existing among us in a world (parallel universe) that we cannot see, feel, or comprehend. We know that a mystical world exists because of the unexplainable happenings that we try to explain away as ghosts, visions, angels, and a living God. Heaven is both at our side, and an infinity away.

Do We Live In Two Worlds?
PART IV - The Soul

Three Scenarios In Heaven

Hell may be simply the universe of souls, supposedly then, assigned to the realm of Lucifer or Satan, that have been denied rejoining the desirable God-substance. Those souls would be joined into the substance of Satan, or worse, be left as an individual soul, unassigned to contemplate for eternity his, or her, errors when on earth. Hell is also believed to be located on the surface of Earth, but also in a dimension different from that of "acceptable" souls in Heaven. (See later Chapter, "Hell".)

God punishes or rewards, at the time of death, by determining the continuity of soul (i.e., acceptance back into the God-substance). It would be tantamount to an existence in Hell to not have the potential for continuation of soul, to be later conjoined, or united to, the human body in a God-supporting way.

By the same token, if Satan and a Hell do exist, this too must be located on the surface of our planet, and not in the depths of the earth as portrayed in the essay of the mortal Dante in the *Divine Comedy,* written in the 14th century frame of theological reference.

Perhaps this is support for the multiple universe theories that are revealing themselves to the present-day state of humanity's advancing knowledge, whereby different states, or universes, exist, side by side, each not experienced and unbeknown to the others.

3.

God, and souls in man, are of the same substance. A difference between God and soul in man, it can be reasoned, is that man currently expresses only a small percentage of his potential.

Even Albert Einstein, one of the most renowned and respected thinkers of our time, and others in comparable scope in reasoning, psychologists tell us, utilized only a small percent of his actual mental ability. If this is so, if his astounding ability were to be multiplied by some factor, his accomplishments and demonstrated ability could not be comparable to that of God.

It may be true that there is a little bit of God in each of us, and that God is, indeed, everywhere.

The best, the most accomplished of the human brains in Cro-Magnon man, are at present, vastly incapable of presently maintaining pace, in any sense of the word, with the potential of the soul, which is of the substance of God.

Spirit beings may inhabit the earth, perhaps when the living of humans on earth is physically impossible through some future ecological or cosmic accident.

Perhaps at some millennium in the future, another transition will be made, as Neanderthal man transcended on this world to Homo sapiens, Homo sapiens (Cro-Magnon) man will be displaced by some more advanced type of intelligence.

"And the meek shall inherit the earth."

4.

What will be the criteria for acceptance back into the substance of God? Surprisingly, I don't think it will necessarily be in the conventional thought of "religious". The concept of "religious" in a large part of the earth's population is oriented to belief in Judeo-Christian concepts. The existence of God, however, transcends all and every form of "religion" as visualized by mankind from the year one.

It logically follows that God's criterion would encompass a requirement that all forms of humanity must live by. This may or may not be summarized in the Judeo-Christian Ten Commandments, The Golden Rule, and the commandment given by Jesus Christ of *"Love One Another"*, but that might be a good place to start.

I propose that God is a societal, and individual-oriented being. He would like all of His "particles" to be able to exist in harmony with one another. I also propose that He would require that each particle exert a respect for, a reflection in existence of, that God-substance from which we came, and hopefully will return. This would include all of the qualities that we each might associate with those of our God, and those phenomena that were previously suggested as qualities of the soul in association with a human body.

(From here definition of God becomes very difficult and I leave it to the reader to define God in his, or her, own particular way, but please see "Empire of God" in a later chapter.)

5.

What would existence in Heaven be like? One philosopher has reasoned a likeness in Heaven of our experience in dreams, or in a state of living in a world of thought alone, in a purely intellectual and emotional activity.

Souls would exist without form, without physical being, and without bodily senses or thinking by brain processes. Thought would consist only of those mind phenomena experienced previously. There would be no concept in passage of time, again much like we experience in a dream. This phenomena of mind alone would be the qualities left after the physical body, senses, and brain had been left in the earthly grave.

6.

I reason that one would not need to have led an outwardly religious, or "churchy" life in order to warrant being considered "good" at the time of judgment. Many persons act and behave in a "good" manner, even though their professed thoughts, and even beliefs, are not considered, in the popular sense, religious. After all, God was judging the quality of souls long before the present array of religions in the world were conceived.

The Judeo-Christian, and other religions too, present a story that individuals may or may not adopt in totality. From the standpoint of judgment of the soul's future, it is reasonable that adherence to the concept of Godliness would be most important in determining the immortality of the soul.

Like observing bubbles rising in soda water, we cannot always see the action that causes effervescence, but we can observe the results of that cause by the path of bubbles that result. People can lead a good life even without following a religious life, but the person's acts will parallel those acts expected of a religious person.

Do We Live In Two Worlds?
PART IV - The Soul

Three Scenarios In Heaven

7.

We are faced here with a choice in selecting which will be our preferred theory of soul continuation. Are souls returning from human life fully amalgamated into the main God-body substance, or does the soul instead remain outside the God-body, and retain its individuality? Dogma of the Catholic church provides for Purgatory, or an evaluation time following human death and acceptance into Heaven.

If the first instance occurs, full return and consolidation into the God-body, all individuality would be lost for any rebirth. There would probably be no retention of individuality of the soul once it had become a part of the whole.

On the other hand, if the souls were to not be amalgamated into the God-body, then individuality could be maintained for continuity in the future. This individuality could be manifest in a purpose for a program of soul improvement through continuing reincarnation into successive human lives.

This latter theory would also account for the phenomena of recognizing a preexistence that are claimed by such persons as General George Patton and actress, Shirley McClain, who claim they were, in fact, a definite person in another life, hundreds of years prior in history. These are claims that are unsupported by evidence, but I am sure are very real to those, and other persons, who feel the phenomenon of a preexistence.

Perhaps the proposed theories are both true. Reasonably, a soul would need to be absolutely perfect to be accepted for return to the God-body. Until that state of perfection is attained, the soul would be held outside the God-body, and be reincarnated successively over eons of time until perfection had been achieved, only then to be returned to the God-body.

This latter view would also give support for the beliefs of Animists, beliefs which we must respect even if it is not in one's own personal philosophy, that all living things, and perhaps certain inanimate objects, contain a soul, and perhaps the soul is improved as it progresses upwards in refinement and perfection through the soul's transcendence through various forms of life.

This story of animism is expressed in the religious theories of some Native Americans, Ancients of India, Hindus, Buddhists, and persons of certain other religions throughout the world. Who is to say which is correct or incorrect?

8.

A miracle is defined as a violation of laws of nature. If nature could conceivably, within any realm of probability, account for the happening of the act, then there is question whether this event has been a true miracle. The occurrence will be called by many, with some basis in fact, as merely a coincidence.

It could be said that miracles can happen only when a person has a sincere belief that the event has no possibility of happening, that it is impossible.

A second type of miracle is that deemed so incredible in its violation of laws of nature, that it would be determined by nearly all observers as an absolute impossibility. One philosopher has called these S (strong sense)—miracles. These might be as preposterous as the sun reversing its path in the sky, or of a person physically being in two places at the same instant. That same philosopher states that "S-miracles" might be possible, but there is no record that they ever have.

Miracles then must be considered in the light that there is no degree of possibility or coincidence in the event logically happening.

9.

Angels and saints are the "administrative staff" in Heaven. They are chosen representatives of God and exist to carry out the will of God. Angels are the messengers between Heaven and earthbound humans.

Angels have been elevated to a supernatural state and had to pass through a period of probation before being admitted to the beatific vision of God. It is considered that every man on earth, even though he is not baptized and a sinner or infidel, has his guardian angel.

Saints are designated, by various levels of sainthood, to "administrate" different functions, and each of different scope. In the Old Testament, angels are variously called "messengers", "sons of God", "spirits", "holy ones", "watchers", "host of the Lord", and "host of Heaven". Their functions are to praise God and to attend upon His throne, to execute His commands on earth, to protect the faithful, to punish the wicked, and to drive away evil spirits. They manifest themselves in assumed or apparent bodies in humans. (Source: Encyclopedia Britannica. 1959, Vol. I, *Angel,* with Bible citations)

Three angels were revealed in the Old Testament: Gabriel, Michael, and Raphael, each of different rank. Many saints have also been designated by earthly religions, Saint Peter and Saint Paul being only two of a myriad of saints designated in a wide variety of churches. Saints Anthony, Augustine, Barnabas, Christopher, Gregory, Ignatius, Jerome, Olaf, and Zeno are only a few of well over 100 saints declared by various churches as possessing the qualities of sainthood.

Theologians have divided angels into nine orders, differing in rank. In the Book of Isaiah, the attendants upon the divine throne are called Seraphim. Cherubim are said to be the guardians of paradise. In organization, functional officers in the earthly Vatican and the Swiss Guard come to mind here as having a parallel form of hierarchy as Seraphim and Cherubim in Heaven.

Other ranks of angels, in descending order, are Thrones, Dominations, Virtues, Powers, Principalities, Angels, and Archangels. The various officers of a church might parallel these ranks of angels such as Cardinals, Bishops, Priests, Ministers, and Laymen.

10.

Do We Live In Two Worlds?
PART IV - The Soul

Three Scenarios In Heaven

Souls in Heaven will possess certain ethereal qualities that were once an integral part of their recognized human existence.

These ethereal qualities are beyond the purely maintenance operations necessary for the basic animalistic functioning of the human body to maintain life on earth.

They include such qualities as an ability to manifest love and affection, to imagine and plan, to project wisdom, grace, sensitivity, empathy and insight, to demonstrate free will, intention, faith, morality, ethics and shame, and to appreciate a Summum Bonum as a supreme or highest good. (See chapter, "Functions In Life")

Souls would also have the surfaced ability to project and receive exterior thought impulses and to view forward and back into time, because there is no dimension of time or space in after life.

11.

The world of God in Heaven will be found to have purpose and organization. It is the apparent nature of God not to have haphazard existence. In evidence, there is nothing haphazard about a system that arranges the existence and match up of a soul to the physical being of man, to exist with, and to compliment, the abilities of a person's mentality. What a wonder in mystical science!

There is purpose to an existence that provides for return of souls of deceased persons to earth in the form of visions, or invisible beings, that give guidance and motivation in the form of visions or thought to earth-bound humans.

For those who believe that the human anatomy is the creation of God and not simply the result of a series of successive steps in complex evolution over millions of years, the human existence is a marvel in design of purpose and organization. Could even the greatest of our most technologically advanced engineers and scientists produce a working model that would function in the total, complex system of the human brain and body, and grow from sperm and egg, through birth, infancy, adolescence, and maturity.

And those who hold that the world of living trees and plants, the weather and air, the earth of soil and stone, including historical geologic rock formations was the creation of God, again, could any one force except that of God have created such a marvel as our ecosystem. What other way could our sun, the planets, stars and cosmos have been not only created but assembled in a scientific way?

I prefer to think that physical things were created in a scientific way, and the mystical things are the word of God. *"Render unto Caesar that which is Caesar's and to God that which is God's"*.

There is purpose and organization in the decision of acceptance into God's substance, and in the hierarchy of angels and saints.

There was purpose in God sending to earth the souls of various prophets and of Jesus Christ to communicate and inform for productive liaison between beings of earth and existence in Heaven. Death is truly, after all, a part of living.

12.

The view stated in this book that the soul of Jesus Christ was of the same substance and part of God, will go far in reconciling the historic question of whether Jesus was God, was the Son of God, or was the Spirit of God. Acceptance of the theory that souls of all persons are a part of God, the answer to the question would be that Jesus Christ was all, God, Soul, and Spirit.

13.

At death, and in the beginning of entrance to Heaven (or Afterlife), when a soul is being integrated into the proper category, there is no meeting with God. Such meeting will be saved for a future moment.

At the immediate beginning, a soul is considered in a state of probation, or as the Catholics religion terms it, as Purgatory. A soul meeting with the existence of God would likely follow extended proving the quality of soul for entrance to God's inner kingdom.

Scientists have shown that there are certain biological changes that take place in humans, and some other mammals, that are common to emotions. The emotion of pleasure in mammals, for example, is associated with a rise in body temperature and heart rate. To a less precise measure of feelings, behavior and body language are associated with certain emotions. It may therefore be scientifically possible to validate the rise of an emotion by measuring biological changes.

Some scientists believe that consciousness arose when animals began to experience physical pleasure and displeasure, and evolved further along this line, with other emotions developing later.

The processes in the total functioning of the human being can be divided into two categories. The first will encompass those body and neural processes that are common to all animals, most fish, and some insects, generally the notochord and chordate families of life. These processes are devoted primarily to sustaining life and are basic to existence.

The second are qualities of a deeper and individualistic nature. They are qualities of the mind, more complex, variable, and are unique to the individual organism expressing these qualities. They go beyond functions of organs and systems that serve only to sustain life.

Examples of the functions to maintain life and qualities of the soul are given on the following pages.

To illustrate, one can think of a draft horse, or some other farm animal, as a fair example of a pure division

Do We Live In Two Worlds?
PART IV - The Soul

Qualities Of The Soul

between these and the more complete qualities of the human "animal". These are functions purely of the body and brain, and are absent of the functions of the mind.

As far as we know, we see no qualities in these animals such as love, vision, mental telepathy, creativity, empathy, consciousness, intuition, morality, emotion, or recognition of a supreme good, although it could be argued that "man's best friend", dogs, cats, and certain other pets and wild animals do exhibit various qualities and degrees of affection, planning, cunningness, emotion, creativity, and even thought transference.

The second category involves functioning and processes beyond the electro-mechanical-chemical-muscular-neural system functioning of the brain and body, They involve sensations that are wholly intangible and not reproducible by some rote, computerlike communications process.

Some qualities are required to maintain the animal body to function in maintaining life. Other qualities are found that maintain the essence of soul in a human body.

Two lists of many of these qualities is presented. I suggest that among these are the qualities of the soul, and are retained by the soul after physical death of the body has taken place. These are qualities of the souls in Heaven. Perhaps they too, are the qualities of the God-substance, and God himself.

When the animal (man or other) expresses these qualities it is expressing the presence of Soul. Perhaps the degree of development (maturity) of the soul is defined as the extent that these qualities are present.

Basic Functions of the Body and Brain

These qualities require only molecular systems that will keep an animal alive and functional. These mechanisms build tissue, power the body, assist in form and motion, have memory, elementary analytical ability, and mount defense against threats such as viruses.

The molecular mechanisms might be viewed as near mechanical-like, with an observable cause and effect, or perhaps viewed like a computer that will have predicable results from specific stimuli. The organisms will lack esoteric qualities of the mind that are detailed at *Qualities Purely Of The Mind.*

Communication ability (hearing and doing)
Nervous system (sensing and reaction)
Motivation and sensing to muscles: Voluntary and involuntary
Sensory and nerve impulse transference to the brain:
    Sight
    Hearing
    Taste
    Touch
    Smell

Mental computation and analysis
Maintenance:
    Digestion (intake, nourishment and excretion)
    Cell replacement and organ health retention
    Blood and circulation
    Respiratory and pulmonary functioning

Nervous, neural system, and reflexes
Functioning of other organs and systems

Guttural Sound and voice
Motor abilities (muscle movement)
Knowledge accumulation, storage and processing
States of mind (chemically altered or stimulated)
Thoughtless muscular reflexes
Cognitive thought
Persistence

Qualities Purely Of The Mind (Consciousness)

The qualities listed here are those of the mind and are beyond functions of organs and systems that serve only to sustain life. The qualities are ehtereal in that they are intangible, personal, unpredictable, and mystical. Many are untaught. None of these qualities found in humans would be found, say, in a computer, robot, or dumb animal (save certain members of canine, feline, and primate families:

Abstract reasoning and planning
   (creative, theoretical, aesthetic,
   visionary, metaphysical)
Appreciation of aesthetics
Artistic appreciation
Awareness of others
Awe
Beauty, appreciation of
   Community concern
Conscience (intuitive direction)
Consciousness (awareness)
Creativity, Reflection
Deceit

Embarrassment
Emotion, Feelings, Sensations
Expression of art, Nostalgia
Fear
Foretelling (prediction)
Grace,
Poise, Honesty valuations
Inspiration
Intuition Joy, Cheer, Triumph,
Elation, Love
Mental telepathy
Mercy
Parental responsibility

Functions In Life

Sorrow, Grief
Sympathy, Spontaneity
Thought transference
Vision (to imagine)
Affection, Societal
Altruism (unselfish concern for
   others)
Anger
Approximate (estimate)
Awareness, Anticipation
Astonishment, Righteous indignation
   (audacity) Compassion,
Generosity,
Kindness, Cooperation
Curiosity, Wonder, Suspense
Deja vu (experienced before)

Empathy (feeling for others)
Envy, Faith (trust), Hope, Peace,
Bliss
Free will (belief, choice)
Guilt, Sense of justice, Insight
Intention and Planning
Introspection Judgment (whether
   to extend or adhere to tolerance
   limits)
Morality, Ethics (knowing right from
   wrong)
Personality
Spirit communication
Think metaphorically
Visions (to experience scenes)
Wisdom (best judgment)

Findings in science, and those in metaphysical existence in theology, comprise an undivided wholeness. A relationship exists between thought and "feeling", which is a deeper level of consciousness. Thought is an electro-biological operation of the brain in processing impulses to actuate a response. That response will be modified by judgment, which might also be a learned electro-biological operation of the brain, or it might be modified by a feeling that is associated with our deeper consciousness, or intelligence.

Feelings, on the other hand, are an ehtereal and non-systematic impulse that is different from the mere thought process of the brain. True love is an example.

It will take considerable scientific effort to prove this relationship in a scientific method that requires validity and reliability.

A definition of consciousness, which includes feeling, is: The ability and performance to think, to analyze, to visualize, to show concept of self to other beings, to plan ahead.

The expert gardener seems to constantly experiment, cross breed his plant varieties, cultivate, weed out, stimulate, and develop more healthy strains, many times by trial and error. Some unsuccessful varieties wither and become discontinued, while other varieties will "catch on" and even become the base from which other varieties later develop.

John Burroughs was a research and developmental gardener who experimented in cross-fertilization of plants to develop new and better, or at least different, strains of plants. His activity in this research field is legendary in the annals of plant botany.

Like some millennium-aged John Burroughs, I contend that souls of God performed similar "gardening", experimenting with the very biological life forms that have existed over the past billions of years. The essence for the souls of God, the God-substance, was created in the world of antimatter at time of the "Big Bang". The souls' "job" since that time has been to develop (plan) different and better strains of biological life on earth.

Souls of God, I contend, are particles of God that exist to perform the works of God. They are the souls who also come to inhabit the human, and perhaps animal, plant, and even insect, reptile, and inanimate forms on earth, as some mystical religions hold.

The souls of God are as much like God as a drop of water from the pail of water is like the whole of the water in the pail. The analogy of course is that the whole of the pail of water is like God and each drop of water is a portion of God Himself. Souls in humans come from God, and return to God.

I have wondered, what, since the creation of souls during the "Big Bang" (which is my theory), have souls done over the period of 4 1/2 billion years.

We assume in our egotism that souls exist for the purpose of matching with a human body, or in the event of reincarnation, into several bodies over centuries. But what about that time before humans existed?

Some activities on earth over the eons seem to have aspects of mystical development. Were these activities, and are they now, directed and purposeful activities of the souls? Some queries and observations concerning development of life and mind are presented.

I

What caused the atmosphere of earth to change in oxygen content from stages of zero oxygen, to one of highly excessive sulphur, murderous proportions in the atmosphere, and to the present, delicately controlled proportion that allows life today?

It has been proposed that the first gases of earth were hydrogen and nitrogen. However, hydrogen and nitrogen are prone to leave the gravitational confines of earth.

After millions of years of the earth having zero gases, volcanic action presented the surface of earth with carbon dioxide. Through conversion by plant life of carbon dioxide to oxygen, the oxygen was gradually instituted into the atmosphere of earth. However, the extremely high concentration, more than exists today in our atmosphere, was deadly to most of the increasing number of elementary early life forms on the surface of earth.

II

What caused change in cells from the early existence of amoeba and green algae that has no cellular wall (Prokaryote cells), to the later existence of cells consisting of wall, nucleus, mitochondrion DNA, RNA, and other features (Eukaryote cells) still not fully understood in today's science.

What caused the first mutation from the initial life form on earth? What caused further mutations to form species from plant and animal families in evolution?

The human and animal heart is truly an amazing creation in itself. It beats continuously for our lifetime, which an increasing number of us can expect to be 80 to 100 years. Within the past century lifetimes upwards of 125 and 140 years have been recorded. Biblical statements report lifetimes of Noah, Methuselah, and others of 1,000 years.

The heart is self-powered by the continual exchange of ions occurring between two groups of cells located within the heart that serve as alternating positive and negative electrodes for ion exchange. This causes the pumping action of the heart, with the four chambers (in humans) contracting and releasing, causing circulation throughout the body, including the brain, lungs, kidneys, arms, legs, and all other parts of the anatomy.

The heart muscle, with its ingenious self-powering method, pumping, and circulation system, must have been one of the first organs developed in protozoic worms, the first elementary animal life on earth, 4.3 billion years ago.

III

What caused the development of primordial life forms to sprout from the first element contents existing on the earth 2 to 3 billion years ago? (See previous chapter, "From Mineral to Life".)

IV

What causes mutations to happen in development of biological bodies? Science holds that nothing happens without a cause—that there are no accidents in science. What causes these seeming "accidents" in planning, evolutionary development, and to happen with a seeming direction?

V

What caused different strains of manlike creatures, including our own Homo sapiens strain, to develop and to wither away, over the past 1 to 2 million years? Are we, Homo sapiens, the end product, or merely a transitional stage in development of some different type of "human"?

Are we, Homo sapiens, the "Peace Rose", the most beautiful rose development of its day, that has since been overshadowed by roses of better strain?

VI

Is there an element of truth in the existence of Greek and Roman mythology gods, as well as in the powers of prophets related in the Bible?

There seems to be just enough realism in the writing and reporting of the Ancients that make one wonder if this could have been fact? Zeus, Athena, Mars, Apollo, Mercury, etc. conceivably might have been manifestations of souls of God, experimentally placed on the earth.

VII

What empowered certain characters as reported in the Old Testament and in later occurrences, to have communication with God and angels of God? Communication with God is reported for Adam, Abraham, Elisha, Jesus, Mohammed, Joseph Smith (of the Mormon religion), and others.

VIII

One particularly interesting period in development of life forms on earth is the age of dinosaurs, starting at about 220 to 280 million years ago. Archeologists have assembled, over the past 200 years, much evidence of a complex array of reptiles, mammals, amphibians, fish, and birds, some with a genetic, identifiable progression, and others similar, but following from completely different genetic history, such as dinosaurs that would appear to be the same, but of both mammalian and reptilian types in their biology.

IX

Do We Live In Two Worlds?
PART IV - The Soul

Earth's Garden In Development

Has ruddiness in skin color of Egyptian and North African nationalities resulted from a cross breeding of black Nubians (Ethiopians), originating in the upper White Nile River region, now Ethiopia, and a white, (Caucasian) race coming from the north and east, Mesopotamia lands, of a Semite or Hittite race?

It would be logical that ancient man from Mesopotamia, say in the 10,000 to 8,000 BC period, would follow the sun westward, as if the sun were beckoning to a questioning and seeking Homo sapiens, that he and his people should follow the sun as it disappeared into the western horizon in a death that would allow "him" to be born the next morning in the east. With this change in venue, cross breeding with Nubians from the south would evolve a new race of people on the southern shore of the Mediterranean Sea.

X

One can visualize John Burrows cross breeding various flowers in pollination to create completely new, or dynamically different strains. The vehicle for change in biological and botanical evolution is mutation.

Is mutation, existing in genes in subsequent generations, purely accident, or is an act of mutation a planned activity of these souls of God? Have angels manipulated and guided evolution through changes in RNA and DNA over eons of time?

XI

The **"normal" formation** of the appendages, that we now call our arms and legs, were, historically, quite short, such as we see today in vertebrates of fish fins, turtle legs, whale flippers, beaver, opossum, and other animals of the wild.

In the course of evolution, the primate family developed a life existing in trees, and a mode of movement by grasping and swinging from limb to limb.

In doing such swinging, the forearms became stretched, and it was advantageous to have longer arms. Gene engineering of evolution facilitated the needed change in length of arms.

Extension of leg bones followed in a like manner, and in parallel development, that allowed the primate family to stand erect and walk.

Variations of this development are seen in the feline and canine families, where each of the four legs are approximately the same length. However the rear legs, sometimes being slightly longer than the forelegs, provide mobility that is often by successive movement of either the paired same side, diagonally paired legs, or of paired front and rear legs.

Certain dinosaurs had long leg bones, useful for self-transportation, but relatively short arm bones, useful mainly to facilitate food gathering and eating.

Living organisms upon earth become mobile in a number of ways. Ray fish undulate their flexible, broad flat body with winglike pectoral fins and long slender tail through water in waves to propel their body forward. The octopus literally crawls upon its food source but can also travel rapidly by bringing all of its eight arms quickly into

Do We Live In Two Worlds?
PART IV - The Soul

Earth's Garden In Development

a bullet-like position to propel forward. Worms transmit muscular energy laterally along their sectional tubular body, pushing forward as other anterior sections hold fast to a surface. Slugs and caterpillars have multiple legs that work in unison to transport its body forward. Insects move their multiple wing sections hundreds of cycles each second to fly through air. Fish swim, and turtles are amphibious. Sea Nettles and Man-O-War are mushroom-shaped creatures that propel water jets for mobility. These are all variations seen in the general anatomy of living organisms.

This is an example of how evolution has directed formation of various animal, reptile, fish, plant and insect life over eons of that being's existence.

Angels are defined in the Christian religion to determine a being endowed with intellect and free will, specifically distinct from and superior in man but essentially inferior to God. In the Old Testament they are variously called "messengers", "sons of God", "spirits", "holy ones", "watchers", "host of the Lord", and "host of Heaven". Their number is a myriad. (Daniel vii, 10).

In the Jewish literature, the Book of Enoch cites the names of 150 angels, with names of three angels revealed as Gabriel, Michael, and Raphael. Michael is the prince of the Jewish people; other nations and cultures have their guardian angels also. Not all angels are equal in rank, for Michael is one of the chief princes. In some passages the "Angel of the Lord" seems to be identified with the Lord Himself. The existence of angels was denied by the Sadducee of Biblical times (Acts xxiii, 8).

"Their functions are to praise God and to attend upon His throne." (Psalms xxix, 1)," *To execute His commands here on earth."* (Genesis xxii, 11; xxviii, 12), *"To protect the faithful."* (Psalms xci, 11), *"To punish the wicked."* (II Kings xix, 35), *"And to drive away evil spirits."* (Tobias viii, 3). *"They are of their nature invisible to man; they manifest themselves in assumed or apparent bodies."* (Tobias xii, 19).

The New Testament confirms and supplements the teaching of the Old. *"The angels were created by God in vast numbers and in diverse classes."* (Colossians i, 16; Revelation v, 11). *"They are devoid of human flesh and blood."* (Hebrews i, 14; Ephesians vi, 12). *"Some of*

Do We Live In Two Worlds?
PART IV - The Soul

Angels

them sinned and were cast into Hell." (Jude 6, II Peter ii, 4). *"Those who remain faithful enjoy eternal beatitude."* (Matthew xviii, 10; Hebrews xiii, 22). *"They enjoy Jesus Christ who is their Head."* (Ephesians i, 21; Philippians ii, 10). *"Their duties with regard to men are to manifest and execute the divine will."* (Matthew i, 20 ff; ii, 13, 20; Luke 11, 2), *"To offer up the prayers of the faithful and intercede for them."* (Revelation viii, 3), *"To incite men to good."* (Acts viii, 26), *"And to save them in peril."* (Acts xii, 7 ff). *"Each child has its own guardian angel."* (Matthew xviii, 10).

Angels were the intermediaries of the Mosaic revelation as taught by St. Paul (Galatians iii, 19; Hebrews ii, 2).

In Isaiah the attendants upon the divine throne are called Seraphim (vi, I); they are reported in biblical literature and lore to have six wings but appear to have a human figure in other respects. Cherubim are said to be the guardians of paradise (Genesis iii, 24); in the visions of Ezekiel living beings called Cherubim, with four wings and four faces, are beneath the divine throne (i, 3 ff.; x, 1 ff). Whether the Seraphim and Cherubim form distinct classes of angels is not clear from the Old Testament. Their representations are purely symbolic and are not indicative of their real nature. Some of the Church Fathers ascribed subtle or ethereal bodies to the angels, but it is now considered theologically certain that they are pure spirits.

Satan, who in the Old Testament is a malevolent, superhuman being, distinct from the angels in the New Testament, is the chief of the fallen angels or demons

(Matthew ix, 34). He is also called "the Devil" and Christians also speak of his demons as devils.

The teaching of the Roman Catholic Church is based on the scriptural data. It is defined that the angels were created in time; it is commonly held that they were created together with the material universe. (Compare with the author's reasoning that the source of antimatter and souls was at the moment of the Big Bang.)

Theologians teach that the angels were elevated to a supernatural state and that they had to pass through a period of probation before being admitted to the beatific vision of God. Some, how many is not known, sinned grievously during this period and were eternally damned. This is an article of faith. Their sin is generally thought to have been one of pride.

It is considered that every man, even though he be not baptized and a sinner or infidel, has his guardian angel.

The angels of Islam are derived from Jewish and Christian sources. (Source: Encyclopedia Britannica. 1959, Vol. 1, *Angel).*

I frankly am guessing regarding the subject of angels. I do believe they exist and that they are messengers from God and from Heaven. I believe they are the actual communicants with earth and secular life.

They are the force that make things happen. I can react only from observation and reasoning. Perhaps when we pray to God, the deliverance is actually by angels.

Church and religious art through the ages portray angels and cherubim as having wings growing from their bodies. I suppose this was a liberty taken by artists of the

Dark and Middle Ages, and that has been carried forward to the modern day.

Consistent with the author's stated concept of God, angel, and soul that physical being does not exist in Heaven, it is illogical that angels and cherubim have wings because there is no physical body to consider. They exist in a parallel universe, outside of secular matter, without weight of body, and would have no need for wings.

People speak of miracles. I believe "miracles" are rational events, the specifics of which have been orchestrated, perhaps by angels, to provide a certain result.

When a person is cured of an "incurable" disease, events, including changes in the person's biology and anatomy, have conceivably been manipulated to allow a normal and rational change to take place, once a certain modification has been made.

Manipulation is attained when change in protein is affected by change in enzymes that is affected by the protein of DNA.

Events occurring that are absolutely contrary to physical laws, such as the sun stopping (the earth stopping in its orbit), or going backward in the sky, or turning black, are wholly unsubstantiated. When miraculous events have taken place, there has been change in the conditions that allow the event to come about, although the manipulation may be miraculous.

Miraculous change implies that events of life are programmed for the future, and are therefore subject to change or manipulation. This concept of programmed future is highly controversial in theology and philosophy.

When change of a person's activity in a human or social setting takes place, perhaps where a person decides not to commit suicide, or some similar change, where the gun fails to fire, or whatever, a manipulating force has come into play. These supernatural actions might well be programmed by angels.

Angels are advocated in many occurrences and in many religions. The Mormon religion is based on belief that the angel, Moroni, led Joseph Smith to find a golden tray, from which the entire faith of Mormonism has grown.

Numerous citations of visualizing the Virgin Mary (or possibly a similar appearing angel) have been authenticated by the Catholic Church.

Mohammed, in about the year 616 AD, founded the Moslem religion, that today embraces 10 to 15 percent of the world's population, reportedly upon receiving a communication from either God or an angel.

Native American Indians report communication with non-secular personalities, as do many other cultures and religions of the world.

Many individuals have testified that they have witnessed angels coming into their own presence, and which gave instructions or guidance, through communication or change in conditions.

Reverend Billy Graham, Jean Dixon, other modern-era people, and many Biblical personalities have vouched for the existence of angels.

As a businessman, having some sense and need for project work organization, I have often wondered how one force, God, can listen to and act upon the concerns of over

Do We Live In Two Worlds?
PART IV - The Soul

Angels

four billion humans on the earth at any given time. Perhaps this "span of control" in organization is accomplished through angels.

A minister told from the pulpit what he interpreted as a set of miracles surrounding the first organization of the church Bible school. Many governmental obstructions prevented the first class from happening, but one by one, those governmental obstructions for building code enforcement, food service regulations, parking requirements, and a multitude of other problems vanished. Perhaps here are examples of acts by angels that allowed the miracles the minister spoke of to happen by the angels manipulating certain events necessary to accomplish the desired end.

Thomas Aquinas, (1225-1274) stated that there were seven levels of angels. The Bible mentions three angels, Gabriel, Michael, and Raphael.

Theologians commonly divide the angels into nine orders differing in rank. They are Seraphim, Cherubim, Thrones, Dominations, Virtues, Powers, Principalities, Archangels, and Angels.

It is possible that angels, and even humans, can perform rational acts that are commonly viewed as miracles. We think of the person, Helen Keller. Helen Keller was born blind, deaf, and unable to speak. She rose in her life to overcome these handicaps to become legendary in her lifetime by her accomplishments, despite the limitation and what persons other than herself would term impossibilities. She did this by manipulating the various aspects of her life.

Angels too can manipulate aspects of one's life in a way that will allow that person to accomplish seemingly impossible tasks.

I do not preclude that Helen Keller had the assistance of her own guardian angel in overcoming her limitations and accomplishing the humanitarian acts which she performed in her life. I merely wish to illustrate a specific, modern day example, of a person who has performed a "miracle" by manipulating her own life and circumstances.

Are "miracles" accomplished by acts of the person, or by acts of angels? Perhaps there is element of both. *"The Lord helps him who helps himself.*

Much has been said over hundreds of years that a person has a personal guardian angel. The guardian angel is recognized when events occur that could very well have resulted in disaster, but did not, supposedly because the person's guardian angel manipulated events to prevent or counteract events leading to the disastrous event.

Research studies at Dartmouth Medical School and the National Institute for Healthcare Research, a private Maryland based organization, reported that patients with strong religious commitment recovered faster, lived longer, and coped better with chronic illness. The religious patients were less prone to depression, suicide, and addictions, and had lower rates of major illness, including cancer and heart disease.

"A study that has been ongoing for 30 years at the University of California, Berkley reports that people who go to church once a week or more have 25 to 30 percent lower mortality rate from all causes of disease than non-churchgoers." (Source: The Cleveland Clinic. *Heart Advisor,* September, 1998.)

Nearly a quarter of the medical schools offer courses on religions and spiritual issues. It is difficult to document evidence of guardian angels and the direct effects on activities of persons and activities, but those who vouch for their presence are unshaken in their belief.

Is a guardian angel any different than any other angel? Angels would have many functions in earth activities, not all of them personal. Some angels have a very personal and direct association with a particular human individual. It is easy to associate an act of good fortune with the oversight actions of a personal guardian angel.

Recently, and for the first time in my life, I believe I experienced the presence of a guardian angel. There may have been the presence at earlier times, but this was the first that a presence was felt.

It was in the early hours of Monday, March 12, 2001. I had been admitted to a major hospital the previous Friday for a medical stress test concerning an angina "flare-up". Three years earlier I had had an angioplasty with a stent placement and thought this would be merely a repeat of that experience. I was prepared to accept this.

The stress test and following heart catherization on Friday revealed more. It showed that my heart had several locations of oxygen blockage and that bypass surgery was required. The cardiovascular surgeon who would perform the surgery, my wife, and I had a frank discussion on Sunday so that I had a pretty good idea of what lay ahead. At age 74 I realized the possible risks. It turned out to be a 5-way coronary bypass surgery.

I felt independently strong preparing for the bypass surgery that would take place on that Monday, but I did have a brief period of emotional weakness, perhaps about 7:00 A.M. Tears had come to my eyes and I felt that control was out of my hands. I had said a silent prayer for guidance in the upcoming surgery. The event had met my definition of the third level of prayer.

As a bed patient since the previous Friday, I had become familiar with the various nurses, patient care technicians, and other staff that performed different procedures of

Do We Live In Two Worlds?
PART IV - The Soul

Guardian Angels

ERG, TPR, and the like. One nurse in particular, Dena, impressed me as sweet and compassionate. She had been on duty Sunday morning, and again on the 11 P.M. to 7:00 A.M. shift on Monday.

Dena came into my room on that Monday morning, stating that she wanted to wish me well before she ended her shift. She stated that she thought I was a nice man, a view that I was always glad to hear.

Dena exhibited a "bedside manner" that was uncommon. She seemed especially empathetic, soft-spoken, and compassionate. She stated that she had lost her own father when he was age 54. 1 accepted a bond with her that perhaps I was an image of her father and that she had a special relationship to me. I remember voicing that I felt she was my guardian angel. At this, she merely smiled, not a convincing argument to a critical observer, but adequate in my mind that my personal care was being overseen by a power greater than that of secular medical people.

The surgery was successful. I write this experience as related to my other observations regarding guardian angels.

Isaiah tells of his message given by God, *"Behold my servant, whom I uphold; mine elect in whom my soul delights. I have put my spirit upon him."*

This is a clarification of the difference between soul and spirit. Soul is an entity possessed by all, including God. It is the aspect of personality and being of an individual that is beyond any basic animal qualities.

Spirit is a concept, a belief, an image that is given out, like a memory of one's ancestors, or the reputation of a present entity, or a nationalism.

Recognition of soul within nonhuman animal bodies is cited in families of feline, bovine, and canine. Egyptology is rich in the glorification of cats as holy entities possessing a godliness akin to that believed existing with humans.

Religions of India recognize a holiness of the Brahma cow.

An intelligence and near-humanness in comprehension and empathy is related in folklore worldwide of both domesticated and wild forms of canines in nearly all species of wolves, foxes, and dogs, both wild and pet.

Pet lovers will attest to a communication between themselves and their pets that is often eerie.

I have often wondered and been entranced by the fact that, at certain times in history, and at certain locations in the world, there seems to be concentrations of persons having unique skills and personal attributes. I have wondered, why this?, why then? and why there?

We can see this phenomena in the age of Renaissance between 1300 and 1600 AD, with great figures of history in advancement and creation of art and mechanics, occurring in the geographic location of Florence, Venice, southern France, Spain, and elsewhere in Europe.

We can see it in ancient Greece of the 500 to 200 BC period, with the many persons advancing knowledge in mathematics and philosophy.

We see it in the 1500s to 1900s with the great age of exploration, although exploration activity was continuous to a limited extent at nearly all times.

The 18th, 19th, and 20th Centuries have produced men who made great advances in science, culminating perhaps in today's advancements in space exploration, and ironically, the very opposite in scope of particle physics knowledge of subatomic particles and Quantum Mechanics.

Why were there these specific concentrations of human ability at certain times, at certain places, and in different fields of knowledge? Perhaps men of genius may have grouped because there was a ferment of thought which can draw original ideas from secondary talents of men.

Perhaps one reason is that the minds of certain individuals were selected and honed by some certain power, with inspiration that came through powers of their minds, and that inspiration was directed by a force acting upon the minds of men.

One possibility is that this directed force was that of God, or of His messengers, angels, acting at the direction of God.

It is a basic concept of Christianity that the spirit of God was in Jesus Christ. Also, the Bible relates that certain God-given powers, and the spirit of God, was within prophets, and was given to certain other personalities mentioned in the Bible. Cannot this transmutation be extended to each of us, or at least to certain God-selected persons?

Perhaps each of us is provided a directed action in our mind activity by some external force. Men from all cultures call upon forces through prayers or rituals to assist their human activity or to give guidance, whether it is to guide their spears in some upcoming animal hunt, as portrayed in ancient cave paintings, or to provide psychological or spiritual guidance on some personal problem similar to these that we all encounter from time to time.

We are all, perhaps, guided by angels of God. The angels sometime act in unison, or in a directed program to formulate some directed action.

I compare this phenomena with that of a high school athletic coach who sends out the call for all interested students to try out for the school athletic team. Students of various talents respond, and the coach selects the certain ones that seem to best qualify for the positions available.

With those selected persons, the coach and his staff then provide special training, knowledge, inspiration, and sense of teamwork, all directed towards advancing the goals of the team, and all that surround this goal. Constant presence of mind is required during competition to orchestrate the specific movements and plays on a continuing basis. So too with the angels servicing the world under the direction of God.

We are all, then, orchestrated in our mind activity to act in certain ways and in certain directions. We are not entirely individual minds acting in totally independent ways.

Perhaps Heaven is, in some sense, very much like earth in its operations, adding another dimension to antimatter, antiprotons, antiquarks, etc. Perhaps there exists an antiearth or antiworld, the same, but opposite, of our known secular world.

Exploring spiritualism, in some ways, is like the saying about the weather: *"Everyone talks about the weather, but no one does anything about it".*

Christians seem to piously wring their hands, if only figuratively, when discussing Heaven, talking about their "great reward", and to greet their kin folk and loved ones who have previously died, and even meeting God.

We talk about living in a world with no problems, but beyond this there seems a dearth of any concept of what Heaven is like, why it exists, where it exists, how it functions, how it came into existence, the nature and purpose of its inhabitants (souls), or what lies in the future for those inhabitants.

We see no relationship between the world of Heaven and this secular world outside of a belief that our admittance is dependent upon how we behave in this world. Commonly, when the subject of spiritualism, spirits, ghosts, afterlife, extra sensory perception (ESP), reincarnation, evolution, and other ethereal subjects are proposed, we seem to "pooh-pooh" the ideas as something beyond rational thought. Outside of a few church philosophers, few have come forward to explore, even theoretically, the details of what afterlife might be like.

Persons who do not believe in Heaven, or who question its existence, discard any interest they might have in the concept, and often as a result, also refuse any openness to accept a religion for themselves. With this refusal they often lose a firm personal grasp or program of ethics and morality that are associated with most religions. The seesaw like battle between good and evil, between brilliance and darkness, ebbs toward the ungodly.

Perhaps this exploration will provide a closer familiarity with a previously unexplored area, similar to our lack of knowledge of the African Congo, and then our gain of insight with the exploration of that culture by Dr. Livingston in the late 1800s.

Of necessity, this exploration is theoretical, rather than tangible and physical. The theory is based upon thoughts, writings, and beliefs of philosophical thought, worldwide, of many religions and cultures.

It ties together knowledge in science with concepts in spiritualism, with each supporting the other. It brings together in a continuum a comprehensive and encompassing, though elementary, view of God and afterlife, or as we might conceive, of a "prelife".

Here follows the highlights of this comprehensive concept of spiritualism:

- **Souls, not physical man,** were created in God's own image. "God's Image" has nothing to do with the physical features of biological man. The Christian world has been deluded for 2,000 years somehow into a belief of a concept that one's personal body takes on qualities described for a soul, including existence in heaven, resurrection, and recognition of earthly acquaintances in an afterlife, and more. Reason, and evidence arising from space travel, hold that there's no entity in the sky that might be evidence of Heaven. Deceased, but now living, physical bodies do not exist in either the world of matter or, conceivably, antimatter, on this earth or in the atmosphere.

- **Souls are as old as the Creation.** God may have existed prior to the theoretical "Big Bang", in a previous cosmos. Matter was cycled through one or more "Black Holes", but with the energy and intelligence of God, being a non-physical entity, would have been a constant in the bridge from a previous cosmos. Souls are a fractional part of God, just as a child is a fractional part of the parent, and are created from God.

- **God and souls are of antimatter. Antimatter is proven** and described in the study of physics as having all the elements of matter, but possessing the exact opposite qualities of matter. For example, in antimatter, electrons are replaced by protons and protons are replaced by electrons. Positrons are negatively charged protons. Quarks are the most elementary and smallest known components of electrons but have an equivalent in antimatter as antiquarks. Other particles and qualities of matter are known in the world of antimatter by their qualities that are opposite to their counterparts in matter.

- **Certain souls, designated as Angels**, acting for God, nurtured evolution, through manipulation of genes in the chromosomes of the first cells and life forms, progressing through eons to a present-day state of physical life.

- **Souls merged with biological man** at a time between 100,000 and 10,000 BC with advent of Cro-Magnon (thinking man). Functioning of souls and mind is at a consciousness level above that merely of brain and thought manipulation.

- **The mind, that functioning entity** that cannot be likened to the cause and effect operation of a neural network somewhat like that of computer operation, can be identified by its variety of ethereal qualities, e.g. insight, judgment, emotion, faith, love, etc.

- **Each person has a soul.** The direction taken by a soul at any given time may also be influenced by an energy of Satan, which is also a superior, near-God energy and intelligence. (Satan was once a Prince of God.)

- **Perhaps other elements and substances** also have souls, a philosophy followed by Animistic religions and cultures of the world. Souls may have existed in various mammals, creatures, and objects throughout history.

- **All of the religions and cultures** of the world that recognize a supreme power are, in actuality, recognizing the same God, but by a different name and concept of how their "Great Spirit" should be honored. It is really no different than in the Judeo-Christian-Moslem world where Jews, Catholics, Protestants, and Moslems vary in their dogma and rituals, but not in their basic belief in the existence of God.

• **Souls return at death to Heaven,** an existence which may very well be positioned upon earth, but in another universe, invisible to our conventionally-known universe. (There is, in knowledgeable fields of science and philosophy, a developing concept of multiple universes, or existences in parallel time completely separate from our conventional concept of existence.)

• **Perfected souls may, in afterlife,** merge with and become part of the "God-substance" for eternal existence with, or even as a part of God. Certain souls in afterlife, either perfected or unperfected, may maintain their own individualism for later reincarnation and pursuit of soul perfection.

There are various personifications of perfected souls: Jesus Christ, John the Baptist, Adam, Moses, Paul of Tarsus, Mohammed, Buddha, Krishna (Hindi), Great Spirit (Native American), gods of black magic (primitive cultures), and others:

• **Unperfected souls are reincarnated** to life forms (or other elements, as Animists believe), striving for perfection and eternal life.

This Comprehensive Concept Of Spiritualism, In A Nutshell

- **Eventually, say 50,000 years or so** in the future, all human life forms on earth will become extinct, leaving only souls to occupy earth. *("And the meek shall inherit the earth")*. This transition will be comparable to the anthropologic change from Neanderthal Man to Homo sapiens, and to the earlier changes from primates to various forms of pre-man.

- **Heaven is on earth presently** as a physical location, but in another universe, and will remain here.

- **A new form of science** is rapidly developing, dating from the early to mid 1900s-Particle Physics, that has evidence of the basic particles that make up atoms, such as quarks, and the qualities and behaviors of those particles. The science also recognizes antimatter, which is the exact opposite of the tangible matter around which we live as humans.

This knowledge of particle science is a breakthrough in understanding the underlying or parallel existence of another universe, one being that of antimatter.

This new knowledge supplements the level of knowing in scientific mechanics and Neutonian physics that has existed and developed gradually since the first use by man of tools and the later start of civilization.

- **The author believes there exists** a direct interrelationship of antimatter and souls that parallels the recognized relationship of matter and biological humans.

- **Further inroads of spiritual understanding** will develop from future scientific knowledge of time and time lapse. The space-value of time has changed from the zero-time condition existing at the moment of unification prior to the "Big Bang", to the present space-value of time,(Albert Einstein theorized that time equals space: therefore, as space expands, time-values change), with a continuum developing since that initial moment, of the numeric values of space-time.

We do not easily recognize this changing value of space-time because we are "like on the surface of an expanding balloon" unable to comprehend the continuing change.

- **We will also find in the future** the concept and existence of multiple universes, with a relationship to the existence, qualities, and acts of soul.

This new knowledge of antimatter, time, multi-universes, and more, may be the actual meaning of the Biblical "Second Coming of Christ", which may actually be a coming of our civilization to God.

- **An increasingly large body** of information and evidence has been found through architectural finds and logic that support historical statements in the Bible.

On the other hand, deviations from Biblical portrayals have also been found. Deviations in doctrine have occurred over the past 2,000 years that differ from commonly recognized, modern-day church doctrine and ritual. This has resulted from compromises and interpretations among various religious sects over uncounted centuries concerning the actual happenings and facts.

- **The Biblical portrayal of Creation** may differ as results of findings in archaeology, especially over the past 200 years.

The dating of the Garden of Eden with Adam and Eve, and of the Great Flood, might be dated back through the Exodus from Egypt, back through Moses, Abraham, and all the "begats" given in the Bible, back through Noah and Adam, to approximately 6,000-8,000 BCE. (One historic authority dated the precise time of creation at 4004 BC)

- **Evidence of civilization in Egypt** has been found dating to 8,000 to10,000 years ago, from people possibly emanating from once lush lands of the present northern Sahara Desert.

- **The Jewish calendar** was the method of recording years prior to the Roman calendar, and later the Gregorian calendar which is in common use today. The Jewish calendar, based upon the lunar month, predates the Roman calendar which was instituted about the time of Christ and is based on solar orbits, by about 4,758 years, that is, Year 1 AD of the Roman calendar relates to Year

4,758 of the Jewish calendar, and Year 1983 is Year 5,743 of the Jewish calendar, the difference of year calculation lying in how the unit of "year" was determined.

The Gregorian calendar, adopted in the year 1582, made a further change in the periods specified by the Roman calendar in recognizing the solar year at 3651/2 days and that the lunar cycle and the solar cycle equate every 19 years.

- **One must remember** that there were events, as evidenced by findings in archaeology and scientific dating, that occurred on earth in civilizations prior to Year 1 of the Hebrew calendar.

- **Archaeological findings of the existence** of some form of man had been found at earlier times in Africa (4.8 million years ago), in Southwest United States (Sandia Cave in central New Mexico, carbon dated at 15,000 to 33,000 BCE), at Clovis, New Mexico, (10,000-11,000 years BCE), at new, and as yet not substantiated dating, of 40,000 to 55,000 years ago at Pendejo Cave in the southwest U.S., at Tierra Del Fuego in the southern tip of South America (about 20,000 years ago), and supposedly Asia before that time.

- **This book reconciles these facts** by interpreting the Biblical Creation as the moment that the spirit of God was incarnated into the mammalian and primate form of Paleo-man. In this context Man was created by God and in God's own image, e.g. as a soul. Also, in this context of gene adjustments to biological and botanical beings, God created all life on earth, and . . . like a Design Engineer of industry in like manner has developed and controls all life on earth.

God in His rightful place—A premise of this presentation is that God is not a physical person alike to human beings on earth, but is instead an existence of energy, intelligence, and consciousness. Further, God also exists not in our recognized universe of matter, but is existent in a parallel universe characterized by predominance of protons rather than electrons in its atomic structure, or in a universe of antimatter.

Nevertheless, Biblical and historical reporting tells of the physical presence of God on earth. First, God spoke to Adam in the Biblical story of creation (Genesis 2-3). This would be entirely possible in that communication of soul (God) to soul (Adam) occurred, without a physical presence of God. The author contends that the creation of man (Adam) from clay, and his mate (Eve) from the rib of Adam did not happen as reported in Genesis. This can be dismissed as folklore. Instead, a variety of manlike specie (perhaps Homo erectus) was incarnated with soul to create the Modern Man or Homo sapiens. From this, soul to soul communication (God to Adam/Eve) did exist.

Secondly Moses, in Biblical reporting, met God on Mount Sinai, where, according to the Bible, God created the Ten Commandments on stone (Exodus 34). Aside from the irrationality of the story, it could have occurred, but in a slightly different context. God could have communicated with Moses, again on a soul to soul basis, from which

Moses actually engraved the messages on stone himself as directed by God, or as suggested earlier, perhaps the message was not engraved on stone but was instead written, in the language known to Moses, on papyrus scrolls. Papyrus scrolls would have been much easier to transport in the Ark of the Covenant and also account for why the alleged Ten Commandment stones have never been found.

A third event is reported in *The Complete Dead Sea Scrolls In English* (Penguin Press. 1997, *The Temple Scroll).* In this documentation the reporter, writing as if he were God, is verbose in describing over several pages (scrolls) numerous required sacrifices of several sheep, goats, and oxen. Sacrifices of the extent described, and on a daily basis, would have quickly depleted the livestock holdings of the tribes. The author believes that a God would not require such physical sacrifices to honor His existence.

The author believes that in the accounts of the Dead Sea Scrolls a later high priest or Moses himself voiced what he interpreted the message of what God had communicated to Moses. The high priest took liberties to embellish the communications from God. Unfortunately, the high priest or Moses did so in an irrational manner and extent. The voracity and credence given to such a high authority was apparently not questioned at that time. If Moses stated that he was speaking the word of God, this was accepted as fact.

This explanation of the three events cited here are more in keeping with rationality. They reconcile the occurrence of the events with a reasonable account of how the reported communications may have actually taken place.

At least for persons who follow the Judeo-Christian cultures, and the various religions associated with these cultures, there can be little doubt of the existence of souls. Most other religions also teach of the existence of an inner self that traverses beyond earthly life. Many also believe in the existence of Angels, with documentation in the Bible of this existence, support by various philosophical and theological leaders over many centuries, and testimonials by religious followers over many years.

Transmigration from earthly life to a supernatural life, and return, is practiced by shamans in a variety of religions, including certain cultures of Native American Indians. We are taught that after our worldly death there will be continuation of our souls in existence in Heaven or Hell.

It is obvious that our body does not make the transition from this earthly world to life in the hereafter. Our deceased body remains in the grave, crypt, or cremated ashes as physical evidence of the presence of our former tangible existence. That evidence remains until nature's way finally turns the body remains to dust.

The continuing existence, then, is that of a soul that continues on for our reward or penalty in Heaven or Hell. The existence of soul is believed by most cultures of the world to be a definite.

Church doctrine has been vague on defining just what the soul is. There are beliefs of the transmigration of the soul, leaving the deceased body and entering the hereafter. There is even instruction that we will recognize the bodily features of family and friends in Heaven that have died in the past. This illogical instruction is given even though the bodily remains of deceased persons have been deposited in their death back on earth.

There are beliefs, and even testimonials, of the return of souls to earth that affect persons living on earth.

Souls have a quality and ability unique from life as we know it. That quality and ability of the soul has been largely undefined heretofore in psychological and theological reasoning.

We can speculate on the purpose and abilities in the afterlife of each soul. It is reasonable to expect that souls have unlimited abilities, being a part and unit of whatever each culture chooses to call the Supreme Power, which the Judeo-Christian cultures, and some others, call God.

It is not unreasonable to believe that among those unlimited abilities of souls is the wherewithal to affect changes within living persons through the mystical manipulation of the chromosomes, individual genes, and the DNA specifics only now becoming known to science. These changes then result in mystical and magnificent changes, which some people refer to as miracles, within the biological and mind components of a living body.

Such manipulations of DNA (science of today calls this "genetic engineering") within one person and perhaps within others associating tangentially to that person, allows the body to produce effects that allow change in appearance, health, attitude, reasoning, and events.

The change in specific genes within the chromosomes is the factor that prompts mutations, resulting in subtle

Do We Live In Two Worlds?
PART IV - The Soul

Souls And Miracles

changes of the configuration in the beak of birds, their plumage, the variety of trees, or the presence or absence of hair on humans. What we have called evolution is actually a series of changes in the markers of DNA within the chromosomes of the various living species and the changes have been passed down to subsequent generations by heredity.

As in the system of some corporate complex, actions from prayers to God, like communications to the corporate president, are often relegated to subordinates, in this instance souls, as a corporate president often relegates to unit managers, which have the ability and power to effect change.

Many believe that each individual person on earth has a guardian angel that will affect our earthly livelihood through mystical and magnificent changes. The author proposes that such actions in oversight occur through manipulations as outlined here.

Through advancements in science during the last half of the second millennium, and particularly during the 20th Century, we realize that there is a reason and cause for everything.

Even chaos has now been studied and identified as a mathematical system. It is evident that there is a specific, physical cause for each action that we have called miracles.

There are estimated to be about 3 billion individual markers in the nucleotides, within the now discovered double helix, that are components of the chromosomes, within the nucleus of each cell, of a living animal or plant. Each marker determines composition of a specific cell, or group of cells, in the organism. The many cells make up a living organism, whether it be fauna or flora, including the human body.

It is estimated that a 6 foot tall person has about 100 trillion cells in his body, whereas a 5 footer has only about 60 trillion, each cell containing a full complement of markers on the nucleotides. Change in only one of these markers, or genes, will result in change of the biology and physical features or mind of a human being, animal, plant, virus, or bacteria. Charles Darwin outlined the result of changes occurring in various species of nature over time.

Each cell is programmed in biology to be unique and will form one function in a specific organ of the body, thus forming, for example, an organized finger, skin, fingernail, fingerprint, bone, joint, cartilage, blood, artery, vein, muscle, etc. as components of that finger, ad infinitum throughout all organs of the body and brain. The organ of the brain may be considered, in part, as a tool of the mind that will implement desires of the mind.

Not that actions and "miracles" are not induced by God and by souls or angels. The question has now come forth of what specifically, from a biological, physical, mental, or psychological viewpoint, changed in fact to bring about the turning point within the body or associated event.

Prayers can be answered and will be implemented in a specific, eventually-known-to-science, and understandable way. The continuing advancements in the study of DNA, the genetic code, and genetic engineering, will go far in explaining exactly how changes in body and mind will be effected and will bring about "miracles".

Do We Live In Two Worlds?
PART IV - The Soul

Souls And Miracles

Thus, what seems like a miracle in the creation of a human body, animal body, a tree, stalk of grain, and other growing things in the world, is explained by a series of what 20th Century industry calls "production specifications". In biology these "engineering changes" happen within the specific nucleotides, that are within the DNA double helix, that make up the many chromosomes, in each cell, of an organic body.

A master production engineer employed in the automobile industry is familiar with the detail and specifications of the thousands of various parts and assembly processes involved in the manufacture of today's automobiles. This is a microcosm of the system found in spiritual existence for creation, care, and evolution.

In the process of industry, steel, rubber, chemicals, and glass are manipulated into various characteristics and forms to be assembled into an automobile. For example, steel becomes sheet metal for body skin, cast metal for engine parts, stock for various screws, nuts, and bolts, and intricate shapes for a variety of special applications. One screw in the assembly of the automobile may determine the proper functioning of the assembled part, with the quality, presence, or absence of the specific part critical to the proper functioning of the whole.

Likewise, proteins and amino acids are utilized in different ways within the human body, depending upon the need and the body organ of which it is a part. One nucleotide might control, say, the shape, functioning, quality, and health of a certain valve in the heart within an individual.

There have been differences in philosophy of religion and findings in science for centuries. These differences, in retrospect, are unnecessary. Differences are reduced, or even eliminated, in reconciling not-evidenced religious reporting with new advances in science, including studies in particle physics and in antimatter, augmented by recent findings in cosmology, biology, neurological science, medicine, social sciences, and other disciplines of study.

For us who are secularly bound to earth life, it is impossible to fully understand the world of souls. Our language, experiences, and comprehension are not of a scope that allows us to understand this strange universe.

It is like the turtle who might try to explain to a fish that he had taken a walk. The fish would not have a basis for understanding what would be commonplace in the world of the turtle.

So, we in this self-oriented, worldly life cannot fully comprehend the acts in existence of an afterlife. We can only hope to understand, based upon the projections of others, in the words common to both, much like a world traveler might try to describe to a listener, the various worlds existing in Tibet, deepest Africa, the Arctic, the Amazon region, or other exotic areas or cultures of the earth.

Existence in afterlife will be as different as the worlds of the fish and the turtle.

Buddha, in the 6th century BC, used the words *"Here (Absolute Truth) the four elements of solidity, fluidity, heat, and motion have no place"; the notions of length and breadth, the subtle and the gross, good and evil, name and form are altogether destroyed; neither this world nor the other, nor coming, going or standing, neither death nor birth, nor sense objects are to be found."*

I wish to present here some thoughts on the philosophy of Buddhism. The Buddha, whose personal name was Siddattha (Siddhartha in Sanskrit), and family name Gotama, lived in north India in the 6th century, BC. His father was the ruler of the kingdom of the Sakyas (in modern Nepal). His mother was Queen Maya. According to the custom of his time, he was married quite young, at the age of sixteen, to a beautiful and devoted young Princess named Yasodhara. The young Prince lived in his palace with every luxury at his command. Confronted with the reality of life and the suffering of mankind, he decided to find the solution—the way out of this universal suffering. At the age of 29, soon after the birth of his only child, Rahula, he left his kingdom and became an ascetic in search of this solution.

For six years the ascetic Gotama wandered about the valley of the Ganges River, meeting famous religious teachers, studying and following their systems and methods, and submitting himself to rigorous ascetic practices. They did not satisfy him. So he abandoned all traditional religions and their methods and went his own way. At the age of 35, Gotama attained Enlightenment, after which he was known as the Buddha, "The Enlightened One".

For 45 years he taught all classes of men and women, without making distinctions between them. He recognized no difference of caste or social groupings.

At the age of 80 the Buddha passed away.

Today Buddhism is one of the major philosophies (it is not called a religion) in the world and is found in Ceylon,

Burma, Thailand, Cambodia, Laos, Vietnam, Tibet, China, Japan, Mongolia, Korea, Formosa, in some parts of India, Pakistan, Nepal, some parts of the former Soviet Union, and other locations of the world. The Buddhist population of the world is over 500 million.

The ethical and moral objectives expressed by the Buddha and those expressed by Jesus Christ are very parallel. Buddha advocated peace, tranquility of mind, development of one's mind to a higher plane, love of one another, unification in society, aid to those in need, action in goodness originated by the individual, actions of kindness, goodness, compassion, fairness, consideration, love, overcoming of jealousy, ill-will, and greed, and life in peace, harmony and contentment, direction toward the highest and noblest aim—the realization of the Ultimate Truth—Nirvana.

The Buddha lived in the 6th century BC, well before the time of Jesus Christ. Were the concepts of Buddha somehow transferred, or were at least common with those of Jesus Christ, as perhaps the religious concepts of Egyptians, and of other prior foreign cultures were possibly adopted to religious doctrines in early Christianity?

The teachings of Buddha are that there is no such thing as soul (on earth), I, or self. In arriving at that conclusion, Buddhism advances a complex linear expression that starts from ignorance, through actions, consciousness, mental and physical phenomena, application of the five senses of the body plus the mind, sensation, desire, clinging, becoming, birth, and death. It holds that there is no free will, that everything is relative. His philosophy connected ideas of God, soul, justice, reward, and punishment. This is the Buddhist doctrine of Anatta, no-soul, a no-self. Some followers of Buddhism deny this denial of soul, self, or I, even though Buddha professed this nonexistence 2,500 years ago.

Buddha maintained that the theory of soul brings grief, lamentation, suffering, distress, and tribulation, that any soul theory is false and imaginary, creating all kinds of problems. Buddha professed that "I" shall be in the universe after death, permanent, abiding, everlasting, unchanging, and "I" shall exist as such for eternity, that soul or self is nowhere to be found in reality, that one is one's own refuge and you have to rely on yourself and not on others. It is better for a man to take his physical body as self rather than mind, thought, or consciousness, because the body is more solid than the mind, which changes constantly day or night. A body should strive to become what Buddha calls in Sanskrit, an Arahant, free from all impurities.

Buddhism seems to focus more on the interrelationship of body and mind rather than recognizing that the two, body and mind, are separate, although common to each individual. Source: *What The Buddha Taught* (Revised Edition), by Walpola Rahula, published by Grove Press. New York, New York, 1959, second and enlarged edition copyright in 1974.

It can be seen that, although Buddha did not advocate the existence of soul on earth, he did advocate the development

Do We Live In Two Worlds?
PART IV - The Soul

Buddhism

of one's inner mind and the existence of the senses of the body. He taught that Nirvana (complete bliss without suffering or pain) is achieved from development of the mind and body senses, with actions and outlook on life.

He taught the existence of reincarnation, and in this it is difficult to reconcile his denial of the existence of soul and yet advocate a being that transcends lifetimes.

Could it be that Buddha, in teaching his philosophy, stopped only a minuscule away from recognizing, and could well have recognized the existence of soul on earth and a religion encompassing recognition of God? It can be observed that the teachings of Buddha were at least tangential to a religion that accepts the existence of God and an afterlife with souls.

"A rose, by any other name, would smell the same."

Could it be that one mission of the soul of Jesus on earth was an attempt to bridge this gap between the teaching of the Eastern religions with that of monotheism in God?

The verbatim and orally transmitted saying of Buddha correlate well with the teachings of Jesus and of Judaism. Buddha's discourse on Universal Love has many parallels with Jesus's Sermon on the Mount. The discourse on Blessings has many parallels with the recorded Ten Commandments. In many other discourses of Buddha he presents a clear and prolific expression of his concept of goodness and desired behavior, perhaps more clear and verbose than any of the reporting of the Old Testament, or of the reported sayings of Jesus, or of the teaching of Paul after Jesus.

In the Last Words of the Buddha, an individual, Channa, was denounced as in opposition to his teaching. This could be symbolized as akin to a devil. (The source, again, is from *What The Buddha Taught,* Ibid)

Hinduism, although many ways parallel in thought to Buddhism, incorporates a belief in reincarnation and worship of several gods.

The prevailing religion in northern India at the time of the Buddha's birth was Hindi. Hinduism dates from 1500 to 1200 BC, when Aryan (Indo-Iranian) tribes invaded India and settled in Punjab. These early inhabitants composed hymns (1,028, mostly to the Vedic deities) which make up the "Rig Veda", a document which is the oldest work of literature in an Indo-European language, and is the oldest living religious literature of the world.

The oldest cosmogonical myth in the Veda is the Indo-European one of the union of the Sky Father with the Earth Mother to produce the divas, or deities. This Brahmanism was the forerunner of later Country Hinduism, Jainism, and Buddhism.

Before the Aryan invasion, the Indus Valley civilization of 2300 to 1800 BC was the most widely dispersed urban civilization the world had yet known.

This is the religious atmosphere with which Buddha took exception, and set out to define a new philosophy.

I had dinner with friends one evening. The conversation got around to the spiritual life and mystical events such as Ouije boards, levitation, and tables rising to defy gravity.

I am frankly skeptical about such physical manifestations, but I can visualize how physical and mystical events involving matter can be reconciled with the world of spiritualism. The key word is energy, or more precisely, the POWER of energy.

I believe that God and souls are concentrations of energy and intelligence, to a degree that we in mortal life cannot, or possibly with great difficulty, imagine. We can at least theorize how mind over matter might be manifested.

If humans can demonstrate a power to communicate with a soul, not necessarily in a religious sense, but in a functional, real, and spiritual communication, the thought process of man could "team-up" with the energy available in a soul to accomplish the act of levitation and mysterious movement of matter.

My friend, who happens to be Latino and a devout Catholic, stated that she and others, in a family setting, jointly experienced an event of a table rising from the floor through no visible means. This person was speaking in all sincerity and I don't doubt that the event did in fact actually happen, and was not merely a dream, mass hypnotism, or figment of their imaginations.

A communication was apparently established that allowed merging of human mind and spiritual energy. If we can appreciate this relationship, we can more readily accept and understand what we commonly call miracles, but which I prefer to recognize as a merging of science and theology.

We are all familiar with the three dimensions that we see in everyday life. We see things as dimensions of height, width, and depth.

It is my belief that souls exist in another universe, perhaps in a 4th dimension of time, a 5th, or even a different dimension.

A 5th dimension is one with an existence whereby sometimes you see it and sometimes you don't, and may later not be aware of its existence at all. We can get an idea of this when we sometimes look at a star in the sky. We sometimes see it clearly, and later it seems to disappear. There are physical reasons for this "disappearance", but you can get the idea and perceive how things sometimes disappear and reappear.

In fact, an emerging theory in science is that there are no less than 11 universes, each with various dimensions, including in addition to the 4 dimensions mentioned, dimensions of curved, circular, twisted, and more.

To illustrate multiple dimensions, imagine a sheet, like cloth or paper, having two dimensions of height and width (there is a 3rd dimension of thickness, but relatively so small that it is insignificant). Now imagine the sheet, instead of being flat, is now lifted, which gives another, say, a 5th dimension.

(The 4th dimension, of time, was experienced during the interval that it took to, say, manipulate the sheet.)

Now imagine the sheet forms a continuous curve that meets itself. Let's call that a 6th dimension. The configuration would look like a tube. Now, what if our sheet is long enough that it not only joins itself to make a tube, but that it encircles itself, perhaps once, twice, or even more times. Let's call that a 7th dimension.

Now let's twist this tube (like common illustrations of a double helix), and we could call that an 8th dimension.

If the diameter of our "sheet-tube" is made so small, it essentially has no perceivable depth, but many parallel "walls", and can again be viewed as flat, like our original sheet, and may look like a pencil line drawn on a sheet of paper, or even like a dot, or the period at the end of this sentence. Let's call that a 9th dimension.

We could visualize manipulating our sheet into other configurations for even more dimensions. Our minute-size tube also would look like a hollow string as it would lie on a table, and in essence this is what science has called "string theory". This "string" could be sliced crosswise, much like pepperoni is sliced, into innumerable membranes of space and time, which is referred to by scientists as "space-time dimension", with each "slice" being a different event of history, future, and location.

This is an oversimplified illustration of a very complicated theory now emerging in the field of quantum science. Future developments by scientists, philosophers, and I think theologists, will be astounding.

Multiple dimensions, as illustrated here, are possible. I propose that the usually invisible soul is operating in a dimension different than the four dimensions we know of height, width, depth, and time.

The same can be said for God, that He operates in a dimension, and a universe, that is different than the three or four dimensions that we are familiar with. God and souls exist, but in another universe that overlaps our own known universe.

Science is just now, as we enter the 21st Century, beginning to "crack open the door" of quantum physics that may give insight to, and possibly reveal the world of God, souls, and who knows what else.

The Biblical expression, *"In my Father's house there are many mansions"* may have a significant and different meaning in the context presented here than that proposed in religious dogma over the past 2,000 years. NOTE: Further reading on this subject may be found in <u>Scientific American</u> magazine, February, 1998, pages 64-69, in the article, *The Theory Formerly Known As Strings*.

What does a soul in Heaven look like? What does God look like? What does Jesus look like? What do the souls of our deceased parents in Heaven look like? What will we look like in the spiritual world after our death? It goes without saying that I do not know. Nor does anyone now living know. I present here a concept based on reason and logic, reinforced by reports in the Old Testament.

The Book of Genesis, if it can be taken literally, states that Man was created in God's own image. To determine what the soul of Man looks like would therefore determine what God looks like.

Elsewhere in this essay the author proposes that God is an energy, an intelligence and a consciousness. It is proposed that God is not a worldly existence, does not have a body, legs, feet, hands, and face. It is proposed that God and soul exist in another universe, or frame of reference, completely different from the physical universe that we all know consisting of matter and material things.

The universe of God and souls, the author proposes, is in the universe of antimatter, which scientists are discovering, now in the 21st century, as consisting of qualities that science has recognized in our universe of matter, but strangely having qualities of just the opposite of matter.

The 19th century saw the rise and finally, the general acceptance of the atomic theory of matter, according to which there are unique and distinguishable atoms in each of the chemical elements. The combination of these atoms in various ways was understood to produce all of the

Do We Live In Two Worlds?

various chemical reactions and the vast variety of kinds of matter.

The 20th century, on the other hand, saw the decomposition of each of these chemical atoms into constituent parts. One constituent common to all atoms is the negative electron or, briefly the electron. Historically this was the first subatomic constituent to be identified.

Science recognizes electrons, and now in studies first formulated in the 1920s, also finds antielectrons. In 1932, C. D. Anderson announced the observation of positively charged particles with the same ratio of charge to mass as the negative electrons.

These soon came to be known as positive electrons, or positrons. The positrons can be produced in the free state only by rather violent processes such as occur in cosmic ray phenomena.

We find protons in atoms that make up our world, plants, animals, stars, and universe and now have found antiprotons. We know of quarks that are elements of electrons and have discovered and somewhat defined antiquarks.

Science has discovered and defined in particle physics the existence of:

baryons—*a class of elementary particles, including the neutron and the proton, which take part in strong interactions,*

bosons—*a class of elementary particles that include photon, X, W, and Z bosons,*

fermion—*a class of elementary particles that include electrons, protons and neutrinos,*

Do We Live In Two Worlds?

gluon—*an elementary particle of zero mass that binds quarks together,*

hadron—*any particle that participates in strong interactions,*

leptons—*particles that do not participate in strong interactions, that include the electron, muon and tauon (elementary particles with negative electric charge), and the neutrinos (electrically neutral particles having weak and gravitational interactions only).*

mesons—*strongly interacting particles that include pions and kaons, which are hadrons,*

neutrino—*element of cosmic energy that has no mass and can pass through the entire diameter of the earth without loss. The fact that this happens is evidence of the extreme strangeness of high energy particles that originate in outer space,*

neutron—*an elementary particle with zero electric charge, and heavier than the electron,*

photon—*an elementary particle associated with light,*

quark—*fundamental particles which are the components of electrons,*

rishon—*hypothetical internal constituents of quarks,*

W boson—*recently discovered electrically charged elementary particle predicted to unify the weak and electromagnetic forces,*

X boson—*a very heavy photon predicted to mediate transmutations between quarks and electrons,*

Z boson—*electrically neutral companions of the X boson predicted to exist in theories of the weak and, electromagnetic forces.*

zino—*on the cutting edge of particle physics research as hypothetical super symmetric partner to the Z boson, a fermion.*

———————————

Like the positron is an opposite, positively charged electron, each of the above elementary particles have their opposites such as antineutron, anti-photon, antiquark, etc. These antiparticles possess the qualities exactly opposite to those counterparts existing in matter.

This is assurance, as science progresses in its search for truth, that an existence is "real" and that parallels, although being "opposite to", are commonly recognized existences in matter.

The universe of antimatter has qualities in its existence which are far different than those qualities of matter, yet strangely are the mirror of those qualities of matter.

The story by Lewis Carroll, a published mathematician and son of a minister, written in England in 1865, of *Alice's Adventures in Wonderland* and later, *Through The Looking Glass* (1872), comes to mind. These books, originally written for adults, have become children's classics largely because their concepts are so unreal that, seemingly, only the not regulated and unrestricted mind of a young child can visualize and add realism to its concepts.

What is the image of a soul or of God? We are in the image of God. Look at your car, say, or some other object that is a physical entity. Now close your eyes and visualize that object. What your mind envisions is the image, without the physical presence. This is a demonstration of how an image persists without the physical matter and how a spirit can have an image, after death, without the physical presence of body.

God and souls might exist as like a wisp of smoke, with no embodiment as we presently visualize persons on earth.

God and souls may be as ethereal as a thought, existing in another universe. They may have the power to appear in this universe in some inanimate form, or to merge with an earth embodiment (person in body), thus again being the body of man and mind of soul.

This would include the power of transfiguration, or ability to transmigrate from one physical body to another, temporarily replacing, or joining, the existing soul of that body.

God could exist as Father, Son, or Holy Ghost. In soul, He could be any of these entities at any one time, or manifest in multiple existences at the same time. Souls or angels could perform the same as God's representatives.

So, to answer our lead question, we still do not know what God and soul look like, but perhaps we have gained a feel of His existence and that of souls.

As God and souls (including angels) in the spiritualistic world I visualize then:

- a wisp of smoke (Biblical)?
- a specter?
- an aura giving a sense of presence?
- an entity having ability to manifest into other physical objects, animals, and men?
- or some other presence?

We can each be assured that the last travel of each of us, upon our soul exiting this world, or even this universe we have come to know, will be one that we will never forget for an "eternity"!

The theory of the Big Bang is widely accepted by today's physicist as a probable way that the universe was created. The author personally feels that this also is a mechanism on how a theological universe of souls was created. *In synergy it turns out, science and theology do merge to support one another.*

Big Bang theory holds that before the moment of "ignition", of the Grand Unification Theory, of singularity, and of Annihilation, and later expansion, all particles presently comprising the universe were together in a singularity, inseparable in one extremely compact entity of inestimable mass.

There would have been absolutely zero space between the elementary particles found in quantum physics. There were no separate atoms (these would be formed later). There were no individual electrons, protons, neutrons, quarks, leptons, or other particles that are today found in the makeup of elements in atomic theory and elementary particle physics. All things except space and distance were incorporated in an undivided mass.

Initially this would exist at zero temperature (Celsius scale), because the temperature requires, by definition, existence of zero movement of particles. With zero space between, there would be no movement of particles within the singularity mass.

The mass existed before time began, or time counting started. Time is relative to space, and again, zero space existed within this mass. As expansion occurred, vectors of mass increased, with resulting increases in temperature and time to tremendous, inconceivable numbers. The rumble and vibration in illustration would resemble a volcano prior to eruption.

When the mass was caused to start an expansion, and during the subsequent expansion, certain particles manifested their qualities. Quarks are elements of electrons, and leptons are sub-elements of quarks, and Z particles, and photons are subunit qualities of quarks.

Further subdivisions will likely be found as efforts in scientific basic research continues. Science is still in search of the smallest particle in the generations of atomic structure. These too would be elementary particles of the singularity mass. (Approaching year 2013 scientist are investigating the existence of even smaller and even more more elemental components of quarks and leptons.)

For every positive quality in elementary particles, there is a negative quality, to give generally, a net neutral value of zero. Therefore, for each lepton, there exists an anti-lepton, for each quark, there exists an antiquark, and for each electron, there exists an antielectron (positron). Likewise for W particles, Z particles, photons, and other elementary particles.

These negative or electron-based elementary particles manifest into matter which makes up the physical features of our universe. In contrast, the "anti" qualities manifest into antimatter, that is, without physical and tangible qualities in their existence.

Positive and negative forces were continually attempting to come together into one existence, but the very coming together of opposites resulted in annihilation, or the destruction of one or the other, positive or negative, forces.

Invariably the negative force continued existence and the positive force was annihilated, with a very small proportion of positive elements, called protons remaining in the negative, electron-based world of matter. The imbalance was not perfect, and a small imbalance resulted in some positive forces existing in matter (those protons that exist within the nucleus of atoms). The annihilated positive forces became antimatter.

The remaining positive forces (qualities of antimatter) conceivably could form a sort of "base camp" within the world of matter. This would provide what little observation of antimatter activity we occasionally see or hear of from responsible persons, and which have reportedly been experienced in ghostly images, foretelling, thought projection and soul-to-soul thought communication between our worldly and additional dimensions, and other insight into another dimension of space and time.

It is reasonable, then, that the world of antimatter, even a universe of antimatter, does exist. The existence of antimatter would appear to be nonexistent because for centuries man observed matter, as what the eye and senses perceive, as the only form of existence. But antimatter does exist as surely as matter exists.

It is reasonable that the world, or universe, of antimatter contains a whole new existence that is not today commonly understood. In parallel with the world of matter, the world of antimatter is "peopled" by intangible souls. The master of the world and universe, of both matter and antimatter, is God.

The following is theory with various suppositions presented:

- *God is not theological in our normal concept of a religiously-oriented being, but is the Master of a world of antimatter, and might best be described as an energy of intelligence and consciousness.*

- *God existed from the start, before any of the thousands of various religions commenced.*

- *Souls exist (as antimatter) and are paired with physical human beings (matter), and perhaps, other nonhuman life forms.*

- *Souls are in the image of God. Contrary to Biblical dogma, God has no physical body. The physical body of man is not "in God's image", the soul and mind of man is in God's image.*

- *The physical body, as it exists today, is the result of an evolutionary development directed by God and carried out by the acts of souls and angels. This is done through manipulation of DNA and RNA within living objects by affecting the enzymes that in turn determine* the proteins comprising DNA that thereby control the various mutations. Evolutionary manipulation through directed mutations continue to exist today.

- *Souls have the ability to transmigrate from "the life hereafter" to a secular life on earth, and from one body to another. Perhaps from one of these existences, to existence in a nonhuman form, and at different times. They continue to exist and may manifest themselves even in the absence of a physical body. (This theory of animalism that supplements the theory that souls are unique to human beings is borrowed from Native American Indian, Hindu and other religions.)*

- *Souls are perpetual. They continue their existence even beyond the physical death of their inhabited matter (i.e., the body). There is no physical being to "die" in the case of a soul.*

- *Souls have a purpose in their existence, and that is to prove their worth and qualifications to eventually exist as an undivided portion of Godliness, which is an existence of energy, intelligence, and consciousness.*

- *The existence of souls is common to the various religions. The existence of souls is manifested in nearly all religions and humanity, whether it be Judeo-Christian, Indo-European, Buddhist, Native American, Voo Doo, "Black African" or other.*

- *The nomenclature, rituals, and dogma of the various faiths differ, but the essence of existence beyond death is the same in nearly all religions.*

- *There is no existence of time in the world of antimatter. Time difference is dependent upon physical distance within matter. In the world of antimatter, it is proposed, there is no distance, and therefore no time-point variation.*

- *God (energy, intelligence and consciousness) may have existed prior to the Big Bang, and God would have been the master of some preexistence before this event, which would have climaxed by the expansion and gravitational workings of a prior Black Hole.*

- *The Big Bang is the "funnel end" result of the accumulation act presented by the horizon (area of force for gravitational attraction) of a Black Hole. God, not having physical existence, would transcend the working of matter reduction in any Black Hole.*

- *Numerous "Big Bangs" might have occurred, resulting from the accumulation action of various Black Holes, with each "bang" resulting in a separate galaxy. Each galaxy therefore is independent of one another and spatially unrelated. Future Big Bangs somewhere in the cosmos, may occur in the future.*

- *It could be questioned and argued by reasonable men that it would be absurd to reason that God would manipulate the biological inheritance system (the genome) in a manner that would have negative effects on mankind.*

Mutations account for medical diseases such as disorders of the nervous system, mistakes in fetal development, schizophrenia, several cancers, and many other infirmities of the body that are attributed to gene disorders, i.e., attributed to faults in DNA elements of genes.

In turn, the author responds that DNA genes are adjusted to effect a good and a purposeful direction in development of a living organism. It is unfortunate that side effects of the gene manipulation have negative consequences. The changes (mutations) were made with good intent and no malice desired for any body.

Any later negative changes would be the result of extraneous influences not existent at the time of the mutation.

Each year, details of automotive design and manufacturing techniques are modified to produce a better automobile, one that is safer in design and construction, perhaps to have a faster speed potential, to ride easier, or to have a more functional appearance, to attain improved mileage per gallon of fuel consumed, to allow longer useful life of the automobile, and to have other improvements over the previously existing model.

Can the designers, engineers, and technicians be properly blamed or held accountable when a user of that automobile has an accident, caused by environmental conditions, perhaps from driving at a speed which the driver is unaccustomed to, or too fast for conditions of the road?

Can a manufacturer, the creator, be held accountable because, with the improvement, a fail-safe prevention system was not simultaneously developed, that perhaps the outside of the automobile be built as solid and heavy as an army tank, and that the inside be fully padded to prevent injury in event of accident, or that windows in the automobile be eliminated because those are a common source of injury at the time of the accident?

Perhaps, in our comparison, environmental and extraneous factors were main contributors in the unfortunate events following the manufacturer's creation. In parallel, perhaps conditions of living in modern day environment, with excesses in certain chemicals in the atmosphere, of foods, stress, living habits and the like, unforeseen at time of creation, are factors as partial cause for biological infirmities, diseases, and these would be amplified over generations in parents having an inherited weakness in prevention of these traits.

Condemning such total and concurrent "improvements" in nature would be just as absurd as accusing the designers and those who implement in industry, of error in offering a "design change" that is good, but results in unfortunate negative effects.

Mutations continue even today to effect change in biological, botanical, and microbic life on earth. Changes are dictated by the need to avoid threats to their existence or to allow a more efficient existence. Side effects may result, some of which are undesirable. Mutations may be derived to correct previous mutations. These mutations all occur in a grand, orderly, and programmed scheme to improve the existing well-being. Intelligent life could not have occurred by accident, or without an intelligent, guided program.

Successful cloning of mammals was accomplished in February, 1997 when Dolly, a sheep, was born. The pregnant mother's early embryonic egg cell was manipulated to remove the nucleus of a fertilized egg, which was replaced with the nucleus of another sheep with its own precise assortment of genes. The egg was implanted and allowed to develop in the womb of the mother sheep.

This procedure has been said to possibly allow cloning of humans in a like procedure. The ethics of cloning one human being to be an exact reproduction of another is highly controversial as "not being God's way". Humans are said to be playing God.

Contrary to that popular thought, it would be impossible to produce an exact duplicate of another human being. In the concept that human beings consist of two elements— the animal or mammal body, which could be cloned, and the soul or spirit which is individual to each person and would not be duplicated.

Psychologists have researched for years the question of nature versus nurture. Are two identical twins, raised in different environments during their maturing years, going to be identical in their thoughts and actions as well as in appearance? Many times they are. Although raised in different environments and cultures, they still retain certain similarities such as basic personality traits, preference for certain colors, numerical and art form aptitudes, creativity, and other intangible traits.

I recently talked with a mother of twin boys. They both had experienced having three successive sets of teeth, both had an inherited illness, and at the same time experienced other uncanny similarities in their childhood development.

Other twins who have lived their lives apart because of childhood separation, independently have unexplained preferences in color, hold their coffee cups in an identical manner, and in one case even chose for a spouse a person having the same first name as the other's spouse.

It is like not only inherited physical traits are determined by genes, but that life events too are guided by some entity during lifetime.

Conditions that are learned, such as culture, habits, discrimination, information, and the like will be unique to the environment.

Cloning brings in a third variable to join nature and nurture as determinant of a person's attributes. Even if nature and nurture prove to be identical, a newly cloned human would have a distinctive soul and spirit.

Supposedly identical cloned twins will not prove to be identical when intangible qualities of the soul are considered. The new human would vary from its brother or sister to some degree in the qualities of the soul listed elsewhere in this book. (See *Qualities Of The Soul* in Part IV.)

The "twin" would evidence different spiritual values, different facilities for love and affection, different values for aesthetics of art forms, and other similar intangibles.

Communication, mind to mind, such as thought transference, and ability to visualize or imagine, creativity, grace, compassion, poise, awareness, intuition, free will, morality, ethics, emotion, judgment, and humility, will vary from individual to individual.

A clone, derived from the brain of Albert Einstein, say, will not produce an individual that is the exact image and personality of Albert Einstein. The cloned individual could be a genius, as Einstein was, but, say, bent on mass destruction of civilization, or some such vector in his life goals.

He might not attain the academic accomplishments of Einstein, but instead be an extremely bright person in some operational job in industry or some other vocation.

He might be concerned with applying his original thoughts, and analysis to philosophical and spiritual concerns.

At any rate, it is highly improbable that he would end up his career with the same "resume" as had Albert Einstein, because his soul, spirit, and values would differ, regardless of any identicalness in physical traits.

He might rebel at society's attempts to direct him into a life plan paralleling that of Albeit Einstein, when that is not his own chosen course of living.

In the history of our civilization, the prince, to be later king, is invariably different from his father-king in many respects, even though sired from his father, tutored in his future responsibilities as king, and reared in a closed culture of the palace, castle, and the King's court. The newly crowned king cannot be a duplicate of his father because of the different composition of his soul and spirit, even though physically and culturally he might be nearly identical to his father.

We can reproduce the components of an object, just as manufacturers mass produce components of automobiles, but even in this commodity, surely not having a soul, it is extremely difficult to find two complete automobiles exactly alike in all respects.

The completeness of the soul in humans will make the difference.

Let us assume that the reporting in the Bible is basically, even though perhaps symbolic, correct. It can be argued that man was, or was not, created biologically from the soil of the earth, and that woman was, or was not, created from the rib of man.

It might be more logical, and perhaps more factual, that man as Homo sapiens which derived from primates, existed prior to Adam and Eve, and as this book contends, Modern Man (or Cro Magnon man) came into existence when soul was biologically merged with the existing Homo sapiens.

I

The Bible reports that man was created in God's image. The folklore of other cultures also hold that their peoples's creation arose from some precise moment and event.

It is the contention in this book that God, souls, and angels exist, not as human beings or in human form, but as a consciousness, intelligence, and an energy. This existence is perhaps in a universe strangely different from the universe that we each know and live in.

The existence of God, then, is in the same universe as the existence of souls and angels. The creation of man, as Adam and Eve, is symbolic to the mystical joining of soul to the biological man-form of Homo sapiens.

This theory holds that in other cultures as well, soul was joined by God with existing Homo sapiens. Man developed within races of Caucasian, Native American Indian, Asiatic, African, Indo-European, and perhaps other sub-races of the world.

Do We Live In Two Worlds?
PART IV - The Soul

Conceptual Relationship Of Soul And Man

Prior to this moment of creation when eternal souls were miraculously united with biological Homo sapiens, there was no such thing as death of a soul. Souls could exist in the universe of God forever (with some poor souls relegated to the kingdom of Satan).

Souls and angels had existed for eons prior to Adam and Eve in a world of God. Angels had been instrumental since perhaps the Big Bang as messengers from God to manipulate the gene structure of all forms of life in virus, bacteria, plant, insect, fish, and animal worlds. In this sense God did create life on earth. Adam and Eve were the first forming of combined body and soul recognized in the Christian-Judeo culture.

With the soul existing forever, physical death was known only as a "wearing out" of one or more biologic components of the animal body, or through some damage to the body such as when Cain murdered Abel as the Bible relates.

II

It is possible that reporting the existence of various historic personalities of Adam, Eve, Cain, Abel, Noah, Seth, Abraham, and others in the early historic Biblical period (cited in Genesis) are not biologic lifetimes of individuals, but instead periods of existence of series of personalities, perhaps all exhibiting a single soul or family of souls that continue on within several bodies over a period of years.

In a parallel illustration within the ancient Egyptian culture, comparable eras were known as dynasties, which were series of kings, princes, princesses, and court members who together formed a continuing body of government, policy, culture, and god worship. Each dynasty was identifiable in these regards.

This theory could account for the reported lengthy earth life of the early Biblical personalities, e.g., Adam was not just one body-person, but was actually a series of body-persons, perhaps with a continuation of soul. Other Biblical personalities were also embodiments of several, or a series of persons who, taken together, personify the character described.

Lifetimes, as described in the Bible, for Adam, Noah and Methuselah approached 1,000 years for each. Lifetimes later in the time of Jacob and Moses were more in line with lifetimes of 70 to 90 years for those who were given long life. (Probably an average life expectancy for the general population at this time being 40 to 50 years.)

This theory further holds that each race existing prior to Cro-Magnon, or Modern Man, was a localized form of Homo sapiens, mutated over eons to possess certain characteristics advantageous for best survival techniques in their respective environments. We can likewise detect even today the racial characteristics such as skin coloration, height, skeletal ruggedness, facial features, anatomy differences, and the like.

Racial features are different between races, but content of soul is universal.

III

Let us assume that in the universe of God there is some form of organization and communication that will affect action. Without this, in our worldly orientation at least, it would be improbable that intent and plan would be implemented.

We have learned that past philosophers in religion have somehow identified various levels of angels. In the Jewish literature, the Book of Enoch cites the names of 150 angels, with names of three angels revealed as Gabriel, Michael, and Raphael.

Theologians teach that the angels were elevated to a supernatural state and that they had to pass through a period of probation before being admitted to the beatific vision of God. Reverend Billy Graham, Jean Dixon, and other modern-era people, many Biblical personalities, and various church personalities have vouched for the existence of angels. As reported earlier, Thomas Aquinas, in the 13th century, stated that there were seven levels of angels. Theologians commonly divide the angels into nine orders differing in rank. They are Seraphim, Cherubim, Thrones, Dominations, Virtues, Powers, Principalities, Archangels, and Angels.

The angels, a hierarchical level of souls, are the implemental entities that carry out the plans and desires of God.

IV

The angels implement actions and changes in the development of species on earth, and in specific actions within individuals. Short-term plans are put into action by manipulation of biological components within individuals that will cause certain functional changes in anatomical or mental components of humans. (This is the functional cause of what are commonly recognized as miracles.)

Longer term plans are affected by changes in genes of an individual, and through planned mutations that cause activities or inactions of individual genes that control the various aspects of anatomy.

Angels then are the messengers of God and function to carry out the will of God.

The soul and the intellect work together like the hand fills a glove. The soul has evolved over the ages, much as does the human body evolve, to combine with the mind in an evolutionary progression. The intellect within the human body has undergone the various phases of evolution, dating from the very start of life on earth. As man was once a primate, the soul was once a purposeless, nondescript, unprincipled existence of undirected intellect.

The souls, during their early creation, would have been as unpurified and devoid of admirable qualities as were the sordid individual humans living in the Biblical cities of Sodom and Gomorrah. Only through purposeful and directed development did souls progress in a vector that would be headed for spiritual perfection.

Soul was incarnated into the human body and mind (some persons of animist cultures maintain that souls exist in various forms of living animals as well as in other objects, both material and ethereal) for the purpose of development and "proofing" towards a God-perfect entity, worthy of ultimately becoming a portion of the God substance, or at least to be accepted into His loyal domain.

Evolution of souls comes slowly, through incarnation and reincarnation, with many human bodies through many generations. The goal of soul evolution is perfection into the likeness of God.

As the soul directs, the intellect, brain and body react. Where inspiration for perhaps some irrational uplifting deed occurs, the "goodness" is manifested into the brain and the act is a choice the individual makes that is willingly performed by the body.

When an inspiration of reverence and understanding for one's Creator is intended for example, an actual mental or neuro electrical thought is generated in the brain, often times followed by some physical act, that demonstrates that reverence and understanding.

By the act or non-act choice of the human body, the soul becomes further spiritually refined in either a positive or negative direction. Examples of goals for soul development are detailed elsewhere in this book at *"Qualities Of The Soul"*. (PART IV).

"Good" inspiration by the soul results in "good" acts of the body, and "good" acts of the body promotes evolution of the soul in a positive way.

With the number of generations and incarnations occurring since soul and man were first joined, it would seem that all inspiration for negative thoughts and acts would have by now been dismissed, to the extent that the soul would have achieved perfection.

However, it is obvious that actions of human behavior, by at least many of the world's population, is demonstrably far from having reached a state of perfection. The twist of human frailty afflicts us all.

Many religions refer to this negative action of the body and mind as either sins of commission or sins of omission—performance of the negative act or the nonperformance when the act should have been performed. The positive acts flowing from inspiration are acts of salvation.

We must conclude that there is constant "tug-of-war" between those inspirations to perform good, and those inspirations to perform evil. In Biblical analogy, it is an example of the constant battle between God and Satan for control of the individual souls.

* * *

Gary Zukov, in his book, "The Seat Of The Soul", describes the 5-sensory man (possessing only hearing, sight, smell, taste, and touch), and the multisensory man who has all the emotions and appreciativeness that are otherwise experienced by man. The balance of the sensations in the multisensory man are properties of the soul. (Please see *Qualities Of The Soul).* His presentation goes far in explaining the relationship of soul and human beings.

Karma is the cause and effect of the immortal souls intentions that are reflected in the actions of the human body and of the mind, which in turn affects both ourselves and others. A person is said to have good karma or bad karma, depending on whether his intentions of the soul are reflected in body and mind actions in a positive or negative sense.

All thoughts are motivated by intentions of the soul, with intentions producing effect. A dynamic of karma is that for every action there is an opposite and equal reaction. The Golden Rule is based on the karma rule that we receive in proportion, and of a kind, to what we give. Our total actions create our karma, either positively or negatively.

Our balance of soul energy is not achieved within a single lifetime but is cumulative over several lifetimes.

Reverence is appreciation of that contact by the human mind with the essence of the soul energy and its power. Reverence is a perception of the soul.

In practical terms we cannot judge what we see. We know only that the road to our soul is through heartfelt actions. Zukov states that the time has come for a higher order of logic and understanding, and this comes from the feelings of the heart. Both Mahatma Gandhi and Jesus Christ, for example, with their inner calm did not judge but applied a nonjudgmental justice. Ethics were described and each individual was left to adhere, or not, depending upon his or her own choice.

The soul and the body complement each other, with the intention of the soul reflected in actions of the body and mind, and the result of the body and mind actions affecting development of the soul, either positively or negatively.

The soul, living in conjunction with the body, has many opportunities to express good karma or negative karma. The soul incorporates all previous souls of incarnation and reincarnation, which reflects past and present accomplishments.

The workings of the soul in conjunction with the body (described as dualism), or incarnation or reincarnation, is another kind of spiritual power that he calls "authentic power". From the perception of the 5-sensory human there is a universe that is only physical. But from the perception of the multi-sensory human the universe is alive, intelligent, and compassionate.

Soul adapts to functions within the physical world. Personality is a reflection of karma energy of the soul.

An evil personality is reflection of a mind that is unable to fully relate to its soul. As such, the personality of the evil person cannot fully differentiate in, and adhere to, the difference between the mind and the soul.

Does nonphysical reality really exist? Our cycles of life have been in existence for millions of years. We are evolving into a whole, decision-making being. Zukov states that we have to expand our consciousness to a level of further understanding and the quality of our consciousness. Our emotions are currents of energy, with different frequencies. Emotions are instantaneous. Thoughts are energy shaped by consciousness. We need to appreciate the thoughts of others.

Attitude comes to reflect our decisions. We cannot have a splintered personality but must be total in our intentions, thoughts, and actions. We have to create reality with our decisions. Physical reality is a reflection of the actual systems of life (the way it is).

The phases and effects of spiritual reality grow, like the cells of our body, moving outward in scope from ourselves, to others, to our society, our country, and to the world, continuously expanding towards the spiritual end goal.

We must make people see their inner worth and the worth of others, and convince them to share their goodness with one another.

From the start of time, at the moment of the Big Bang (or at Smaller Bangs as the author has earlier suggested) the evolution of the soul parallels evolution of life on earth. For probably 7 to 8 billion years souls developed from the original particle science creation which came out of singularity and the subsequent annihilation of positive-charged particles.

The author maintains that, before life on earth, souls existed in a universe of antimatter. The existence of soul would have been parallel, but opposite in its basic nature, to the created negative-charged particles of matter in our experienced universe.

Soul would have evolved over some 7 or 8 billion years or more, from its original creation out of the singularity existing prior to a Big Bang and the resulting subsequent annihilation of positive-charged particles.

The positive-charged particles were parallel, but opposite in its basic nature, to the created negative-charged particles of matter in our experienced universe. Soul existed in a created universe of antimatter.

Scientists today have assigned terminology to positive-charged particles as "positrons". Terminology further refers to anti-particles, with antiquarks, and "anti" for all of its component qualities that parallel those of matter.

Souls, from a universe of antimatter, were functional beings when original life forms of amoeba first appeared on earth. They were able, under direction of their Supreme Power, and in a mystical world of antimatter, to manipulate

Do We Live In Two Worlds?
PART IV - The Soul

Evolution Of The Soul

the elements that first combined to form basic life in the primordial seas some four to five billion years ago.

Souls, in antimatter, exist without physical form. They would each have ability to manipulate DNA within cells of this world of matter.

Such action was perhaps not unlike a concert musician (a soul) who manipulates his instrument (Protein and DNA) to form musical notes (genes) and plays musically in a unified system (intelligent evolution) that produces a planned, organized concerto (life development), all in unification with other musicians (other souls) also acting in concert, all under direction of the concert master (God).

At somewhere between 4 and 5 billion years ago first life appeared in the form of algae and amoeba. With this there came a greater needed function of soul. Life on earth needed intelligent evolution; evolution without direction would result in complete chaos in structure, function, and appearance of various, widely divergent and grotesque life forms. Each life-form would have adapted to its own particular environment but would have little uniformity in general anatomy within its biologic family. The family of animals, for example, would likely not have had the classic anatomical form of head (with mouth, eyes, ears, and brain), body, four appendages of arms and legs, lungs, and other features, say, that differentiate man and animals from insects, fish, deep sea marine creatures, germs, bacteria, and the like.

Three-dimensional algae was intelligently folded and molded into five-dimensional tubes. As tubes, intake mechanism for nutrients was formed, digestive systems evolved, and waste disposal was affected. With this, first worms existed, not by accident, but by intelligent manipulation and evolution of existing botanical/biological structures.

Soon, from basic "flow-through" worms, an elementary heart and circulatory system developed, self-powered to provide a blood circulation and pumping system that would distribute energy throughout the animal, and a nerve and brain system to sense changes in environment. A renal system converted nutrition to energy, with parallel development in evolution of plants from first algae to first vascular plants.

Again, this evolution was "engineered" intelligently and with a direction. Even at this, many grotesque organisms populated the ancient sea and beds of the Eozoic era, the likes of which can be seen by researchers today upon exploring in the dark depths of our oceans, and through microscopes to the world of germs and bacteria.

With each need for change in our universe of matter the evolution of soul became more and more complex. First RNA, and then DNA, developed in the nucleus of the ever increasing number of cells that comprised the increasing complexity of basic life, and with the diverse physical variations of life-forms itself.

In evolution, soul, in a parallel universe of antimatter, affected development of life on earth by manipulating the early, and then relatively simple compared with today's genetic code, DNA within each cell of each organism. Soul was able to affect change in the DNA composition that would, in turn, affect botanical and biological

Do We Live In Two Worlds?
PART IV - The Soul

Evolution Of The Soul

changes in the living organism. *Manipulation of DNA was accomplished by; (1) adjusting the genome, (2) that affected enzymes, (3) that control the proteins comprising the biologic organs and portion of the body and brain.*

From this basic cause (gene manipulation) and effect (botanical and biological change) the evolution of life became incredibly complex. DNA composition became a record of genome history. Souls had evolved to have a purpose in their existence. Souls operated as servants under the intelligent planning of a supreme power.

A diverse program of botanical and biological change lie ahead for souls to accomplish over the next 3 1/2 billion years, dating through the Archeozoic, the Proterozoic, the Paleozoic, the Mezoic, and Cenozoic Eras, to today. Each change in life and life form was result of gene manipulation by soul. Without change (mutation) each generation would be an exact physical clone of its parent (as in yeast or bacteria).

By continued refinement, souls had become "trained" through inherit traits to affect certain botanical/biological changes of a "routine" nature that was in a predictable and rational direction. DNA in a parent resulted in the same DNA in its offspring. Detailed instruction by the Supreme Power was no longer necessary, except in devising a "total system" concept. In terms of modern-day organization management, operation by the soul had become decentralized, with centralized oversight.

To guide biologic development of the fetus, let us assume soul becomes present from the first moments of conception and directs the development of cell growth, culminating in a human being at the moment of birth. Development of the unborn fetus is a product of the mystic action of soul.

This revelation and analysis may clarify thinking of persons in questions regarding abortion and Right-to-Life controversies.

In abortion, the body (fetus) dies, but the soul does not. The soul is "returned" to the parallel world of antimatter from which it came.

Each animal progressed into a more complex variety and different specie than was its predecessor, as grasses developed through complex evolution to form bushes and trees. With the advent of sex, offspring adopted a combination of features from both the male and female parent.

Many aspects of botanical and biological evolution progressed in a "need-and-change" manner, portrayed in the studies and reporting of Charles Darwin. Shape and composition of the bills of birds, for example, changed to meet local environmental needs of nut eaters versus insect eaters. Other rational changes occurred in all aspect of living organisms, including later evolution from primates, through early upright-walking pre-man, to Homo sapiens and Modern Man of today.

Soul today, in a parallel universe of antimatter, has a major function of facilitating change in biological and botanical beings of our world. The vehicle for change, as it has been since the Eozoic Era, 3 1/2 billion years or more ago, is mystical manipulation of genes in the genome

Do We Live In Two Worlds?
PART IV - The Soul

Evolution Of The Soul

system, which is unique to each living organism that has ever lived, is living now, or shall live in the future.

Surely a revelation in our secular existence in science and theosophy will eventually be forthcoming to provide knowledge, first of the fact, and then of how souls manipulate genes to affect physical change in the biology of humans and the botany of plants.

A CONTINUUM OF HISTORIC THOUGHT
IN DEVELOPING DUALISM

Presented here is a summary, or compacting of 12,000 or more years of development in philosophical thought as applied to religions. It is a history of philosophy in religions. The thesis of this book parallels those developments, and goes further in associating the acts of soul, with the relatively new science, since 1951, in the further study of the genome and DNA, and the even newer exotic studies of parallel universes and particle physics.

The story of *Do We Live In Two Worlds?* is merely a step forward in light of the state of knowledge regarding genetics, biology, and physics applied to the existence and purpose of soul to human development. It is a step forward in the path trod by recognized revolutionaries in development of philosophical thought. Only through this progression of revolutionary thought has humanity progressed to today's state of understanding in our relationship of man and God. The idea of dualism is not new.

Much of the summarized history of philosophy can be found in *The Last Two Million Years,* The Reader's Digest Association. New York, London, Montreal, Sydney, and Cape Town; first edition in 1973 and first revision in 1974, pages 284-293, and in the many other books detailing the histories and philosophies of the principles.

Through religion and philosophy, man has sought to determine the ultimate meaning of his existence. Religion has been one of the great shaping forces of human history, transforming the way of life of entire peoples. Religion, and its predecessor philosophy, have helped man to attain his highest ideals of justice and morality, and inspired many of his most noble achievements in the realms of thought, art, architecture, music, and literature.

Man's religious urge through the ages has found expression in a bewildering variety of beliefs, ideas, and practices. But one factor seems permanent and universal in religious experience: the sense of a supernatural other-world which, though invisible, is believed to have power over men's lives. Even in the few religions that do not recognize a God, or are indifferent to the idea of one, such as early Buddhism, this supernatural world is assumed to exist. Even prehistoric man seems to have shared in this most powerful of all religions ideas; the belief that in some way a person, in soul, lives on after the death of his body. The evidence of ceremonial burials, and the provision of food, utensils and weapons for the use of the dead on their journey into the next life, goes back to the Neanderthal men who lived in Europe more than 50,000 years ago.

With the rise of civilization in the lands of the Mediterranean and the Middle East—in Egypt, Mesopotamia, Greece and Rome—"the other world" came to be filled with innumerable gods and goddesses, most of them depicted in recognizable human or animal shape. Each culture had its own cluster of divinities, usually ruled by a supreme god. This multiplicity of gods, called polytheism, is typical of religious ideas in the ancient world.

In Egypt such growth was the pantheon of gods which emerged as a result of union, about 3200 BC, of the kingdoms of Lower Egypt and Upper Egypt. The story of Osiris, a major god of the Nile and ruler of the land of the dead, and his brother who killed him, was probably a mythical version of the conflict between Upper Egypt,

Do We Live In Two Worlds?
PART IV - The Soul

Beginnings Of Religion

where Osiris was worshipped, and the Nile Delta, where the religion was one of worshipping the sky and the sun. A similar growth underlies Greek mythology starting about 2000 BC, with their supreme god, Zeus.

The idea of one god was carried out in Egypt 1,400 years before the birth of Christ when the pharaoh Aknenaton turned his back on the traditional gods, the greatest of whom was Amun, and established the worship of one god, the sun god Aton.

It is possible that this monotheism influenced Moses, who set out to convince the Hebrews that the god Jahweh (really God) had chosen them and it as their duty to live by his Ten Commandments. This uncompromising set of rules was originally framed for an obscure tribe when it was wandering in the desert. It has become one of the most potent and enduring moral codes of all time.

Hebrew prophets, from about the 8th century BC, such as Amos and Hosea, tried to make sense of the apparent injustice in human life. In the 4th century BC the Book of Job provided the lesson that a man should worship God because He is God, not because He dispenses favors.

From the 6th century onwards, there was a stir of questioning in the Greek world about the nature of reality, led by the Athenian philosophers, Socrates, Plato and Aristotle. Socrates was sentenced to death because, by his relentless concern to establish the meaning of concepts such as truth, beauty and justice, he was corrupting the youth of Athens. Plato, his pupil, held that there are two worlds, the world of appearance, evidenced by the five senses of man; and the world of reality. The real world is one of eternal, changeless ideas which can be known only by the intellect. Aristotle believed there must exist a perfect, non-material and changeless being from which all ideas ultimately derive, and this being is God.

The Stoics, one of the numerous philosophical sects that flourished at that time in Greece, tried to rise above both pleasure and pain. Other appeals, such as Mithraism in Persia, carried the promise of fertility and power.

Christ ministered to the sick and preached "the Kingdom of God" is at hand. Some Jews saw Him as the expected Messiah who would lead them to prosperity. Christ held out the promise of eternal life. But to most Jews this idea was blasphemous, and resulted in His Crucifixion. St. Paul taught that Christ's death was represented as an act of sacrifice, undertaken to redeem man.

Emperor Constantine, in 313 AD, granted freedom of worship to all religions, and Christianity later became the state religion. He wanted to unite all religions under one church, but instead the church later split into the Roman Catholic Church, under the Pope in Rome, and the Eastern Orthodox Church, under the Patriarch of Constantinople as their leader.

The Byzantine emperors maintained a large empire covering much of Asia and North Africa. From this branch grew the faith of Islam, that drew on the austere strength of the Old Testament, honoring the Jewish patriarchs such as Abraham. Mohammed, founder of the faith of Islam, was held to be the greatest of the prophets, and the Koran was a book recording God's revelations to him. The Crusades

Do We Live In Two Worlds?
PART IV - The Soul

Beginnings Of Religion

marked a series of wars between faiths of Christianity and Islam.

The Muslim empire of the Mughals successfully invaded and conquered India, but powerful as that empire became, it never swamped the great civilization of India, with its ancient deeply conservative religion of Hinduism. About 2000 BC fair skinned invaders had entered India from the northwest. They were Aryans, related in language and culture to the ancestors of the Greeks, Romans, and to the earliest Germanic tribes. Their religion was similar to that of Homeric Greece, with gods who in character were like the human heroes of the Greek epics.

Hinduism, the world's oldest living faith, has many different sects and schools of thought. Underlying all its forms is the caste system, acceptable to Hindus by the idea that they are placed in their social positions by their Creator, and are graded according to their good or bad behavior in a previous life existence. No power on earth can change this, and so they must be content. This is the law of "karma". For those Hindus who are placed in the lower levels of society, the hope of advancement lies not in this life, but in the next.

Jainism, an offshoot of Hinduism, arose about the 6th century BC. Unlike Buddhism, a much greater development out of Hinduism, it has mainly remained in India. Jains carry the Hindu principle of respect for life to its extreme. Since man is only a part of the whole scheme of living things, he has no right to exploit even the lowliest form of life. In any case, he himself may have to endure, in some of his incarnations, the life of an animal or an insect.

Jainism might have been taken up into Hinduism, had not its adherents rejected caste.

Buddhism, which arose in India at about the same time as Jainism, also abandoned entirely the concept of caste. But, again, like Janism, it kept Hinduism's belief in reincarnation of souls. Its main teaching was that all life is suffering, and suffering is due to unsatisfied desires, so the only solution is to eliminate desire.

Mahayana Buddhism is so different from the mental and moral self-discipline of Gautama, Buddhism's founder, as to be virtually a new religion. Mahayana Buddhists encourage prayer and devotion to Gautama as a means of attaining salvation for oneself and others. Instead of facing an interminable series of rebirths, all worshipers might now hope that, by faith, they would be welcomed after death into a wonderful existence called the "Western Paradise" or "Pure Land".

Another form of Buddhism is Hinayana which has stayed nearer to the teaching of Gautama, with its pessimism and stress on individual effort.

In China, Confucianism and Taoism, originated in the teachings of two philosophers, Confucius and Laotse, in the 6th century BC. Confucius was concerned to help man to live in society, and since he took an optimistic view of human nature he hoped that by education men could be improved.

Taoism believed that there should be no deliberate attempt to lead a virtuous life, still less to save men from the consequence of sin and evil. A follower of Taoism does

Do We Live In Two Worlds?
PART IV - The Soul

Beginnings Of Religion

not want to change the world, but to find his proper place in it.

The "two-worlds" theory greatly influenced early Christian thinkers, notably St. Augustine (354-430). St. Francis of Assisi (1182-1226) performed missionary work by Christians in preaching for better contact with the followers of Islam. One of the declared motives of Christopher Columbus was the conversion of peoples (Chinese) he might discover when he sailed westwards in 1492.

The Inquisition was set up by Pope Innocent III in the 13th century to investigate and punish heresy, wherever it might be found.

MEDIEVAL PHILOSOPHY

Within the limits of faith, the leading intellects in the Church were often given the widest freedom to speculate on fundamental questions, such as the nature of God and the immortality of the soul. During the Middle Ages, the time of the Church's greatest power and confidence in the West, there was a remarkable flowering of religious philosophy. St. Thomas Aquinas, in the 13th century, was deeply influenced by the ideas of the ancient Greek philosopher Aristotle. He sought to close the gap between reason and faith, holding that reason can prove the existence of God, and that nothing in Christian teaching is contrary to reason. His ideas were intensely debated by other contemporary thinkers, and vehemently opposed by some; but in time his last system of thought came to be accepted as the official philosophy of the Catholic Church.

The most momentous and far-reaching conflict of ideas within the Church occurred with the Reformation, which began in Germany in the 16th century. Martin Luther challenged the authority of the Pope and replaced it by the authority of the Bible. Soon reformers in other countries, notably John Calvin and Ullrich Zwingli in Switzerland and John Knox in Scotland, took up the challenge against the Church. The Thirty Years War (1618-1648) was a war of religious ideals, terminated by the Peace of Westphalia in 1648. As result of the war, many men had permanently broken away from the Catholic Church. An era of religious toleration followed, with the emergence of numerous new Protestant sects and the establishment of national Churches.

THE SEARCH FOR NEW CERTAINTY

The spirit of humanism, born in Italy towards the end of the 15th century, placed a new emphasis on man. The Reformation of the 16th century shattered the unity of Christiandom, and the Church could no longer convince all men that it was the sole transmitter and guardian of universal truth. The powerful challenge of science, too, made by such men as the astronomers Copernicus and Galileo, further weakened the Church's intellectual authority.

The French philosopher, Rene Descartes (1596-1650), advanced a systematic new rationalist philosophy. He believed that a man should try to doubt everything until he arrived at first principles which could not be doubted. By the act of thinking he was an individual *("I think, therefore I am."),* he saw the material world as being a "machine", wholly separated from the mind. This approach is known as

Dualism. Only by God's intervention, Descartes believed, were the material and mental worlds connected.

Descartes's teaching influenced two later 17th century philosophers, the Dutchman, Benedict Spinoza (1632-77), and the German, Gottfried Leibniz (1646-1716). All three of these philosophers are known as Rationalists, for they based much of their thinking on the new science of mathematics, and had an unbounded faith in the power of reason to deduce, from self-evident principles, the whole nature of reality.

A new philosophy opposing that of the Rationalist became established in Britain, called Empiricism. The founder of the Empirical school of philosophy was John Locke (1632-1704) who set out to show the origin, nature and limits of human knowledge.

Influenced by the work of Isaac Newton, Locke held that some sensations accurately reflect the external (material) world whereas others (color, smell, and taste) do not, and derive from reflection on the act of thinking.

Bishop Berkley (1685-1753) took Locke's view further by pointing out that, if all our knowledge is of sensations, we have no way of knowing whether any of them truly exists, that all ideas are always in the mind of God, so the world still exists even when we are not perceiving it.

The Scottish philosopher, David Hume, (1711-75) took Empiricism further, holding that there is nothing permanent in this world, just sequences of sensations, and even the individual person is nothing but one such sequence.

The German philosopher Immanuel Kant (1724-1804) set out to mediate between the two schools, Rationalists versus Empiricists, by showing that reason can give true knowledge of reality, but only of things experienced by the senses. His view was that space and time do not exist independently, but are imposed by the mind on the world. For Kant, the mind largely creates what it knows.

George Hagel (1770-1831) developed a view known as "Absolute Idealism". On this view, matter is only an appearance or illusion; the only reality is "Absolute Spirit", which expresses its nature in an historical process of struggle and conflict. Out of this process emerges the true expression of Spirit—a perfect society where all conflicts are resolved in a higher synthesis.

Hegel's idea of a clash of opposites was taken over by Karl Marx (1818-83), but Marx turned Hegel's ideas upside down by making matter the basis of his system instead of "Absolute Spirit". Marx held that a series of class struggles will produce the lasting synthesis of Communism.

Numerous other church leaders and philosophers have added variations to existing dogma, providing an extensive choice from which seekers may select.

MODERN PHILOSOPHY

Today, philosophers are divided into two main schools, both of which have reacted against German philosophy. In Europe, the Frenchman, Jean-Paul Sartre, born in 1905, developed the philosophy of Existentialism, originated by the Dane, Soren Kierkegaard (1813-55). This starts from concrete individual experience, instead of abstract theories. It analyzes such features of experiences as anxiety and death, and stresses man's freedom to determine his own future.

In contrast, philosophy in the English speaking world has seen its main role as helping to analyze and clarify the nature of language and its relation to the world. It has tended to draw back from making pronouncements about the meaning of human existence. The works of the Austrian-born Ludwig Wittgenstein (1889-1951) are dominant in this branch of 20th century philosophy. Wittgenstein started his career under Bertrand Russell at Cambridge and his colleague, A. N. Whitehead.

RELIGION TODAY

The strongest challenge to organized religion comes from communism—an openly atheistic ideology which nonetheless has much of the appeal of a religion. The spread of materialistic values in many parts of the world, and the accompanying decline in religious beliefs are further challenges.

Yet religion holds powerful sway over the minds of millions. The major religions claim more than 2 billion adherents. Religion still appeals to a deep-felt need in man, and in church, mosque, synagogue, and temple the quest for spiritual truth continues.

Much of the above is from *The Last Two Million Years; The Quest For Truth,* pgs. 284-293. The Reader's Digest Association. London, 1973,1974.

A STEP FORWARD

Hopefully, this book will add *yet another step to the advancement of knowledge in the understanding of a*

Supreme Power that most religions call God. With this addition of the interlocking of quantum physics, genome, DNA, soul and parallel universes will provide a new philosophy involving the interwork of God in His universe, and man on Earth.

Plato, Aristotle, Constantine, St. Augustine, St. Thomas Aquinas, with many other philosophic and religious leaders, appearing in many different cultures and times, each believed and advocated dualism—that there ARE two worlds—the physical existence of matter, and a spiritual existence that continues on after earthly death.

The thesis of exploration in this book is not only that souls exist, but souls have a purpose in serving a supreme being. One of those purposes is to develop and cause the intelligent evolution of all living organisms. The soul activates this evolution by a mystical manipulation of genes, in a process not yet even basically understood, but whose connecting solution will be found in the new science/physics disciplines of quantum mechanics and parallel universes. By such intelligent manipulation, the physical qualities of the living organism are changed.

Because of, and until, needed work in the field of science and mechanics of this manipulation, the intricacies in the process of gene manipulation by souls must, of necessity, remain in the realm of faith.

Soul also is evidenced by the intangible and aesthetic functioning of the mind, more than merely providing the basic biologic and anatomy functioning necessary for continuance of animal life. Such allowed the evolution of Modern Man in what makes us human.

Do We Live In Two Worlds?
PART IV - The Soul

Beginnings Of Religion

This book may be a first exploration, given that souls exist and can be described in the unity within man, and in afterlife, into the purpose and nature of souls. Such revelation could be as remarkable as Plato's announcement of duality—2,400 years ago.

Qualities of the soul are described here with function and purpose detailed in a realistic, observable portrayal involving animal and man's past and continuing evolution. Attention is directed especially to the chapters: *Creation, Out Of Creation Came Souls, Qualities Of The Soul, Functions In Life—Basic Functions of The Body And Brain,* and *Functions In Life—Qualities Purely Of The Mind.*

The evidence is here. Irrefutable evidence is presented in this book that something, that we call soul, exists in the mind of man that is beyond the elementary brain functioning of the dumb animals.

There is high probability, based on reason, logic, and experiences of humans, that not only incarnation occurred in the anthropologic past to create Modern Man, but also that reincarnation occurs in present day life. There are testimonials by responsible persons, and further indications of continuing reincarnation.

Mystical acts of soul occur and are evidenced by numerous documented experiences in medical and religious history that are beyond the limits of medical knowledge or abilities in the known functioning of the brain, and theology of our worldly development.

It is evident that *"We Live In Two Worlds".*

PART V
TO THE FUTURE

- The Scheme Of History Is Already Written
- Near Death And After Death Experiences
- Time Comes In Little Glass Boxes
- Hyper Speed Is Possible
- Is There Anything To This Astrology Thing?
- A Challenge To Fundamentalists
- A Research Project In Fiction
- In Summary
- Update
- Gene Manipulation And Life Science Institute
- Woman And Man Were Separate Species

The scheme of Earth's history is already written. The events of the future are already scheduled in the scheme of the future.

Observing life in overview, is like seeing a three-act play, viewing the events of the first act, yet knowing that there is still other events to come, including the last. The script is written and will be acted out in accordance with the overall plan.

Such schemes allow the foretelling by seers such as Biblical prophets, Nostradamus, and by modern prophets, such as Jeane Dixon and Edgar Cayce. These individuals possessed the ability to "look ahead" in the book of history, into the future.

Nostradamus predicted in the 16th Century that *"the end of the world would be at year 3,797, but then the course of time runs much further"*. (Source: *Nostradamus,* Page 92.)

The present form of man as Cro-Magnon is merely a phase in the many forms of life that has existed in the past, and will logically continue to develop in the future. Life forms have existed as amoeba and algae, as worms and sea plant, as fish, reptiles, dinosaurs, ancient and modern birds, small and large mammals, various forms of primates, and anthropological man including Australopithecus, Robustus, Erectus, Neanderthal, Homo sapiens, and

Cro-Magnon. Why do we think that our present form of existence is the ultimate and the end of evolution?

What new types of evolution might be next? I propose the change will be not in the physical body, but in the mind and consciousness of life form. An evolutionary phase may thus develop where the intangible mind is supreme, and the existence of any form of body is superfluous.

The mind and consciousness in its extended form will be godly. It will be an extension of God and be in the form of souls, ethereal and invisible, but existent. There will be communication between souls and God, with Heaven being an empire on earth, to continue either forever, or possibly that empire too would evolve into some other phase of existence.

The souls developed will be considered, not in a religious sense, but in a spiritual existence, with variations between good and evil, slovenly and precise, immature and parental, and in other qualities outside of physical existence.

It is conceivable that our future may reveal that Satan will turn out to still be a servant of God, as Biblical History holds that he once was. Souls assigned to the kingdom of Satan may be only a "holding area" until that soul is reincarnated to a human body for another "try" at salvation, with subsequent joining of that soul with God in Heaven.

There have been at least five mass extinctions of life in the history of earth, and several more catastrophes that resulted in at least partial extinction of one form or another in plant, animal, fish, insect, bacteria life or Homo life on earth.

Listed here are some events that have, or could have, further results in mass extinction on earth. Some events may be global, whereas others may be localized to certain areas of earth.

With each extinction, like the Phoenix bird, earth has come back with a new creation, or as it were, re-creation.

Catastrophes can be caused by:

Celestial collision, drought, floods, warming, heat, cold, extremely high concentrations of oxygen, extremely low concentrations of oxygen, high carbon dioxide proportions (that suffocates animal life), low carbon dioxide proportions (results from lack of plant output), earth orbital fluctuations, earth flip in polar orientation (geologic evidence shows that this has happened before), change in magnetic poles, polar wandering or earth wobble, volcanic action, earth interior changes, man error (bombs, geophysical drilling, nuclear accidents, space accident, or miscalculations), huge gas clouds from magnetic forces or cataclysmic solar winds in space colliding with earth, attraction and disruption from a near-miss of earth by cosmic objects or forces (e.g., Pluto and Jupiter were not of our original Solar System), drop in ocean levels, rise in ocean levels, continental drift of movement that creates opening to seas or creating mountains by collision, anthropological change in anatomy or biology of man, victory of other forms of life over man (e.g., bacteria), starvation, bloating, bodily imperfections caused by radiation, cancer, etc., blizzards, storms of wind, water or snow, or any of many other events.

Any one of the possibilities could lead to either mass extinction or partial extinction of plant, animal, or mankind on earth. See Appendix: *Some Sources Of Cosmic Or Earth Catastrophes.*

I have never had a near death experience, summarily called NDE. I only can reflect on those reports heard and read about, reported by those persons who have experienced being clinically dead, but then for some reason, regained body functions of heart pumping and brain electrowave functioning.

Many of these persons report at least one of three scenarios: A common experience reported is one of traveling at amazing speed through a tunnel, and viewing an intensely bright light at the far end. (The bright light and passage through a tunnel are perhaps the transition in progress from our earthly world of matter to a parallel universe of antimatter.) Persons report a sensual calmness, and some have reported hearing beautiful music. We seldom hear of arrival at the end of this tunnel.

Another scenario reports an essence of the reporter himself, perhaps his soul, leaving his physical body, and his viewing of his own physical body, wracked in injury, or whatever would threaten his secular life. Those reporting such a scenario relate that their ghostly essence later rejoined their apparent lifeless body, and recovered to tell the experience.

A third scenario has been told by a person who had led a life of evil and met his death in a traumatic way. This person reports that after he had been shot he found himself on the shore of a sea, but that sea was a body of fire for as far as he could observe. He reports that he recognized certain persons that he had known who were now deceased, and some even that this evil person had himself killed during his lifetime. He reports that no communication took place during this scenario. He also reported seeing a senior-appearing figure that seemed to have a judgmental power to accept or reject the person into that scenario. That entity finally approved the reporter's reentry back into life.

There have been reports of some persons, in the moments before clinical death, whereby the dying person appears to recognize some person and has waved, as if in greeting, to that entity, an action of my own widowed mother.

There have been enough reports, and of a serious enough note, to convince at least this author that this experience may be a path that one follows upon death.

I think of the time I entered the U.S. Army Air Corps during World War II, and wonder if that experience parallels the experience of entering and existing in the hereafter.

I had never experienced anything like this routine before and perhaps there is a procedural analogy to the sequence of transition from civilian to soldier that compares to the death experience.

In my military experience, I was transported by train from my home to an army recruit receiving center. I happened to travel alone, but there could well have been others also traveling, even from my own local area to the receiving center. The closer I came to that location, the more I knew that others whom I met and joined were also destined for the same place. There was no doubt that all of the new people, save the service people who were stationed there for the processing work, were there for the same reason.

We stripped ourselves of the civilian clothes we wore in traveling to the center. We were judged and sized for military uniforms, underclothing and shoes. We were issued a number, and we stenciled that number on all of our "government issue" clothing, including our duffel bag that would contain all of our issue then and in the future. We had completed our transition from civilian-looking to military-appearing persons.

We were placed in groups, based mostly on our time of arrival at the reception center. We were shown to our quarters, which would be our military home, at least for the first night. We were told where and when we would eat next and other routines.

We happened to arrive at a period that the facility was crowded, causing insufficient barracks space (we were told this was because service veterans were being discharged and were being processed through this same center). Consequently, we were provided an overnight pass away from the receiving center.

What we did with the available time was our own choice. We could telephone home, or even visit there as long as we returned to the reception center by the next morning. *(Perhaps in my analogy, a deceased person might choose to return in spirit soon after death to comfort the family or a loved one agonizing over his death.)*

Upon return to the receiving center, we were placed on a train that traveled to a basic training camp. In my case the receiving center was near Chicago and the basic training camp was located in the state of Mississippi. The two day travel seemed to be enjoyable, we recruits now all being common in having the same induction experience.

Upon arrival at basic training camp, we were instructed on the routine that we would experience while we were there. We were assigned a drill sergeant (an angel in my analogy? My drill sergeant would have been amused by that comparison!)

After a passage of time (six weeks in basic training), we received more instructions in military protocol, expected actions on our part in our new capacity, skill training, and were tested to determine how we might best serve in our new status.

From that introductory experience, we would go on, individually, to whatever seemed to be the best program, considering our individual abilities and the needs of the organization.

The day came (eighteen months later in my case) when events were such that I was reinstated to my former status as a civilian. If circumstances required, I would again be required to experience this same scenario.

At any rate, I felt that I had improved myself, I had gained a new experience in traveling through this different scenario, and I believe that I became a more complete person by the induction and after-induction experience, and my later reentry to civilian life.

Perhaps the qualities of a soul might also be refined by the experience of secular life and the following experience in afterlife for subsequent reentry to some worldly existence.

It is easy to see the analogy of this military experience with a proposed "procedure" taking place after death: A deceased person "travels" to a certain location, often having enjoyable sensations, is joined by others in a comparable death situation, assigned a leader or sponsor (angel) during an indoctrination period, evaluated to determine future assignment, providing service to the organization, and later experiencing reentry to the former secular life.

Could this be the "life" in the afterlife that all "recruits" or deceased persons will experience upon death and reincarnation?

We think of time progressing from moment to moment, each moment being like an automobile traveling along a roadway or over a bridge. As a rider in the car, we look aside, out the window, and view whatever there is to see at that moment. Each moment provides a different scene. It is like time progressing with each moment being different than the experience of a moment before and the moment after.

In a sense, time comes in little glass boxes, with each content of that moment neatly boxed, adjacent to and viewed or "remembered" through the adjacent "glass boxes". This series of "adjacent glass boxes" can be likened to the history of the life that each of us experience, remembering the past or anticipating the future, as we would view through adjacent glass boxes in our passage through life.

We view existence in each "glass box", seeing into and through adjacent "glass boxes" that represent the past and, viewing through, memory of the past. To a limited extent we can also "see" by anticipation into and through the "glass boxes" of the future.

A variation of this travel horizontally along a roadway or over a bridge, say, is to conversely think of traveling vertically up a limitlessly high skyscraper building, with the view at each "floor" (or moment) different from the "floor" previously passed, and different from the next "floor".

What I am trying to state is that: perhaps there is no such thing as "time". All things or experiences occur at the same cosmic moment, a flash in the cosmos that incorporates all of history, and we merely experience different scenarios at a different moment, or in a parallel universe. There are multiple, parallel universes for each of us to experience, each occurring at the same cosmic moment. Each moment we travel in our own multiple universe.

With this concept, it would be conceivable that we could return to a former universe, or advance to a future universe, at our discretion, much like we can control the destination of an elevator in a building by depressing a particular button indicating the floor desired. In this way, we could experience directed time travel, once we have "found a way to make the elevator go up or down".

Perhaps some exotic civilization or being has done exactly that of controlling travel to parallel universes. The moment of existence of some civilization, culture, human type, or soul world of, say, 10,000 years ago, would be reachable from our present existence. Likewise, some future existence could be traversed to and from our present: existence, all with ability to return to our original base universe. All events of what we call history would occur and exist at the same cosmic moment. A new philosophical theory is now on the horizon. Such experiences are available in a theoretical system of parallel universes. Parallel universes exist because each moment presents at least two choices, with each choice creating a different scenario, and therefore a different universe. (Source: *Parallel Universes, The Search for Other Worlds,* by Fred Alan Wolf, 1988, Simon & Schuster, NY, NY)

For example, with parallel universes, at the moment of my own birth, or at some later moment, I personally might have continued to live, or I might have died. I may have married my present spouse, or I may have married someone else, never having met my present spouse. Of course, the entire future will vary depending upon the universe that developed from the outcome of some particular moment.

Each subsequent universe and moment also creates additional parallel universes, and so on, so that an infinite number of universes come into existence for each of us. We could theoretically travel up various paths, as in a maze, and experience any number of possibilities in human existence.

With this concept, it could truly be said that, with the number of moments existing since the start of "time", and the consequent number of parallel universes, there is truly "nothing new under the sun" and all things are possible.

Perhaps advocates of multiple or parallel universe theories may someday refine and resolve their concepts to provide an "intra-time" travel. Perhaps the reality exists today.

In his last major work, *Four Quartets,* T. S. Eliot speculated on whether the "arrow of time"—its apparent movement from past to future—was illusory. The poem, an exploration of the possibility of life outside of time, echoes Hindu and Buddhist philosophy:

Time present and time past
Are both perhaps present in time future,
And time future contained in time past . . .
If all time is eternally present All time is unredeemable.

Albert Einstein, amazingly enough, made the same assertion in explaining relativity. *"The distinction between past, present and future?* the great physicist argued, *"is only an illusion, even if a stubborn one."* (About Time, Wall Street Journal. January 1, 2000) *(Please see Appendix, "Time May Be Illusory".)*

Hyper speed, with velocities greater than the speed of light, presently exists. Upon death, the soul is projected into a phase that incorporates a new dimension, different than the four dimensions of height, width, depth, and time.

In this new, say fifth dimension, the soul is transported with zero restrictions of time. Almost instantaneously the soul finds itself in a new universe. We call this new universe "Heaven".

In this universe of Heaven, it would seem that time does not exist. All events of history supposedly are happening at the same instant, separated only by strata identified as moments similar to today, tomorrow, yesterday, the day before yesterday, etc.

In terms of our own, our commonly recognized universe, hyper speed theoretically allows transport to points that are light years away, at nearly zero time lapse.

In actuality, within a fifth dimension, space transport (relocation from point A to point B in outer space) may be nonexistent. We conceivably would remain still upon the surface of earth, but merely in a new dimension.

An indication of this concept of hyper speed and fifth dimension is provided in testimonials of persons who have experienced near death experience (NDE). Commonly, testimony from persons who have experienced NDE report the sensation of rapid transport through a form of tube or path towards an intense light.

Those individuals who return to life on this earth never report arriving at the observed light. Supposedly those who do arrive have entered "Heaven".

Hyper speed then is possible, once we have learned to control and travel, by the technique of "jumping" to another universe.

Note of interest:

Mathematician/philosopher Kurt Godel (1906-1978) demonstrated that universes in which time travels into the past is possible and compatible with Albeit Einstein's equations.

In science, theoretical physicists are conceiving the existence of "worm-holes" through space, that would allow travel through "folds of time", at experiences of several times the speed of light.

Here is a theory that will exasperate some readers, although it may make sense to those who either tolerate or are firm believers in astrology, some theologians, and persons interested in the eschatology, or phase changes, of souls in their continuing existence.

Astrology has stood the test of time, even grown in popularity over the centuries, and its analysis and predictions have proven so uncannily accurate that it has often quelled the skepticism of the most ardent disbelievers.

Study of Astrology and prognostications attributed to astrology have been recorded for at least 4,000 years, dating back to time of planning and construction of the great pyramids, and possibly before. When ancient Egyptians studied the stars and planets, they understood that there was more to be learned from them than just the cold data of astronomy. They perceived that as celestial bodies move in the skies, those celestial bodies have a profound effect on events occurring on earth.

Astrology holds that persons born at certain times of a year, on certain days, and even at certain times of the day, and in proximity to other astrological signs have certain personality, biological, and propensities in their actions.

There seems to be just enough "coincidence" to support those defining astrology to warrant some credence for their belief in the principles of the art. The science-minded or rational person will tend to dismiss the philosophy of astrology as not possessing any reason or verifiable basis that will support what they believe are unsubstantiated mystical beliefs.

Earth orbits the Sun, tracing a complete parabola approximately every 365 days. Let us liken this orbit to the track or path of a train, bus, or subway system having 365 different stops or stations, which are located in 12 different regions on its closed path.

Of course, the 365 stations are analogous to each day of a year, and the 12 different regions relate to the 12 astrological houses in astrology. A person born on the cusp, or at a time near that of the adjacent house, will have traits that merge with those strong traits or "centered characteristics" of their own astrological house.

Let us further imagine that when a person dies his or her soul is deposited at one of the 365 stations. (There seems to be no system, or little correlation in date of death with date of birth, as to which station or house to which the soul is left.) That station will be populated with other souls each of which possess similar personality or biological traits; certain traits are common to all souls existing at that particular station. A "newly arriving" soul will acquire those common traits, if not already possessed.

In the obverse, when a person is born, on a certain day, that person will acquire a soul from that station corresponding to his or her birth date. The soul "boards the vehicle", so to speak, through incarnation, and travels his or her lifetime with that defined particular set of traits. At death, the soul again is deposited at some "station" in space and at some point in time on the orbit of earth.

Therefore, the person, through his or her soul, will possess the traits common to those other persons on earth (also with souls) who have been, are, or will be born on that particular date, and in that particular point in time. (Please see *Qualities Of The Soul* for listed characteristics.)

This supports the theory of astrology that people born on a certain date of a year all possess generally the same traits in their personality, desires, and preferences. Persons born on a cusp of their astrological house will acquire some traits common to traits of an adjacent astrological house.

This theory would provide rationale of how certain souls, that are matched up at birth with certain physical bodies (incarnated), possess and demonstrate personalities, circumstances, and fortunes that relate to their particular time of birth.

Relationships relating to position of the stars relative to space location of earth is not the cause of events, but is merely a way of describing the relative space position or place in earth orbit at a particular time. When stars appear to be in a certain position, earth is at a determined position on its orbit of the sun.

Like a navigator traveling over an ocean, the relative location of stars in the sky to the earth do not dictate aspects of weather, temperature, calmness or fierceness of seas, and the like. The relative position of stars merely indicate the individual's position on earth, and it is that position on earth that determines the qualities that a person experiences.

Certain events are likely to happen to particular individuals, because of their relative position on earth. Rough seas or calm seas, or mild or cool temperatures, or other physical factors may be instrumental in promoting certain events. Likewise, periods of good fortune, or conversely negative acts, may be common to certain points in one's secular life.

The appearance of star patterns defines a point in time, for that individual, on a defined life progression. That point in time is causal to certain events happening to that individual. The Titanic ocean liner would not have collided with that particular iceberg, ceasing the lives of hundreds of people at one time, if the ship had been at a different place or at a different time. Likewise, an individual progressing through life would not experience certain events, with certain results, if he or she was not at that particular point in time and at that particular place.

There is a degree of fatalism here in that the fortunes of each individual is preordained, and therefore the future foretold.

The existence of soul and the moment of conjunction with the human body (incarnation) could affect the events concerning that body during its lifetime.

Key to this proposed theory is the belief in the existence of soul (which every Christian, Jew, Mormon, Hindu, followers of Confucius and Buddha, and nearly all other religions should observe), plus the concept that anything in God's realm is possible (and supported by new finds in particle science almost daily). With existence of soul, both in secular life and in transition during the Hereafter, the events portrayed here are entirely possible. Whether they are probable shall remain with the judgment of the reader.

Fundamentalists are Believers who generally hold whatever the Bible states as sacrosanct, the divine word of God, given through chosen men to report.

A third Testament could well be written to span the time from the period ending at the New Testament to the present time. Let us call this a "Modern Testament".

In a Modern Testament it could be reported that historical events have taken place in the past 2,000 years, in much the same manner as told in the Old and New Testaments. The ordeals of early Christians, the attainment of Christianity over pagan religions, the assemblage of church dogma from the many edicts of various church men, the wars of the Crusades, the church philosophy of the Dark and Middle Ages, the accomplishments in theology, philosophy, and science of the periods of the Renaissance, the "discovery" and populating of a New World, the advancements and shortcomings of a growing society, the great wars of the new world especially following the Renaissance, advancements in engineering, physical science, social science, and philosophical thought. A Modern Testament would tell of astronauts and space endeavors, computers, the genome study and other new revelations resulting from findings and advancements in knowledge and reason.

Reporting of these events in books is real and written. They merely have not been placed within black-covered bindings and labeled "Modern Testament". They have been recorded in books of history, and are perhaps more accurate.

Let us say that this multitudinous array of books were formally labeled "Modern Testament", or Holy Bible; and held in esteem equal to the Old Testament and the New Testament. These Testaments would then join and make up our Holy Bible.

With our Bible then covering all of time from biblical Creation to today, Fundamentalists could then, in all religious conscience, accept the history events of the past 2,000 years as God-conceived and Holy in reporting. It would be written evidence of God-ordained events. Fundamentalists could accept events of history reported in a Modern Testament as Biblical and Holy.

Upon this acceptance, Fundamentalists would be provided a new dimension to their views. They could accept and understand historic events of the past 2000 years, and view these events much as the present books of Kings, Isaiah, Paul, and Revelations are cherished. Fundamentalists could be converted to Realists in their beliefs of church doctrine. With such conversion, present barriers between Fundamentalists and Realists could vanish in a unified doctrine of reporting Holy events.

It is true that reporting of history may vary with the viewpoint of the author. Telling of history will be slanted in accordance with the author, varying with his or her viewpoint, cite telling the history of wars from viewpoint of the victor or the vanquished, or of political viewpoints depending upon the source as a Republican or Democrat.

This hypothetical story is presented here to portray how a research investigation and travel of soul from the matter universe of Earth to the soul existence of a parallel universe, and return, might be experienced.

It was our last day out at sea in the research project. Our hypothesis and goal was to establish that humans could soul-travel from the world on earth to Hereafter, and return. Everyone had been working incessantly in an attempt to devise an experiment that would prove that directed "round trip" soul-travel was possible—a link between the world on earth and the Hereafter.

Each person on the project had worked continual shifts, relieving others in their duties when they could no longer continue logical thought and needed a rest, but only for a short time. If a person could freely cause his soul to travel from the world on earth to hereafter, our goal would be met.

It would be a matter of projection. Many persons had been able for years to separate their soul from their body. It had started when persons had experienced out-of-body experiences, perhaps an actual viewing of their mangled body in a hospital emergency room while surgeons worked feverishly to restore life to their body.

Separation, the first step, had occurred. Instantaneous travel to Hereafter was now needed. Most of us on the project felt this was a matter of willingness and desire.

And once hereafter had been experienced, travel back by soul to the world on earth, and return to the body, must be accomplished.

Chuck, our project leader, had been successful many times in placing himself into a directed trance, separating soul from body. But each time he had lost motivation in his trance to continue on. It would be an instantaneous travel we were sure. We felt that in the hereafter there is no such thing as time.

Directed consciousness would need to be developed and maintained throughout a trance, with return instantaneous to the world on earth, but in a time compression in Hereafter. Time compression is merely a descriptive term—actually hereafter is a complete void of time span.

My first encounter with Separatism was when Chuck told me he had experienced viewing his sleeping body from a location that seemed to him to be from an upper corner of his bedroom, high in that apex where the three dimension planes of the ceiling and two walls met. He had returned, of course, to the world on earth where his soul had rejoined his body. Aside from the weirdness of this experience, he apparently had suffered no ill effects.

Others have reported Separation in more dire circumstances, watching their traumatized body in a hospital emergency room following an accident while surgeons worked to prevent death.

Still others claimed experience of travel during critical surgery. They had traveled through a seemingly endless tunnel, at an incredible speed, towards a bright light, but

Do We Live In Two Worlds?

returned, in body recovery, to the world on earth to tell their mystic tale.

In each, their had been absence of consciousness and motivation to pursue directed travel. They had traveled as if some force was controlling their destiny. Each had been subject to some predestination that directed his travel.

Chuck had developed his states of trance, by numerous encounters, to now be able to enter a state of Separation, and return, at will. He stated that he felt each time a progress in directing his state onwards into Hereafter, but had never been able to complete the travel back to the Earth and secular being.

It was following that accident when Chuck had been washed overboard during heavy seas, and only by the heroic act by Henry, after a long visual search, diving into the sea in rescue, that the seemingly lifeless body of Chuck was given artificial respiration, bringing him back to a coughing reality.

Chuck had told of separation and that he had progressed in travel, willingly, to Hereafter.

His soul, was conscious, and traveled at some extreme speed through some kind of tube. He traveled towards, and arrived at the source of light.

He said he found himself in a very odd situation. He described a kind of empty room, except there were no containing walls. Yet he felt the presence of a multitude of others in the same mode as himself.

He knew that he had, himself, directed his soul to Hereafter. He also had retained control of directed travel, and had desire to return to the world on earth.

Chuck told of his conscious decision to return to the world on earth and reverse his travel back down that time tube and away from the light he had experienced.

The next conscious event of Chuck's tale was lying on the deck of the ship, with the ship surgeon pumping on his chest to expel water from his lungs.

Chuck had experienced not only Separation, but also a Directed Travel to Hereafter, and a conscious decision to return to earth, followed by Directed Travel back.

Chuck felt that our project goal had been met. Conscious and directed travel to, and return from, Hereafter had been made.

Apparently, when Chuck was washed overboard and floundered in the sea water, he had given up hope of being saved. Separation of soul had occurred quite easily. He had motivation to continue in Directed Travel towards Hereafter, and had arrived there. He experienced Unity of his self and some greater power and, at the same moment, with all souls who had ever existed. He had traversed from the universe on earth to a parallel universe. Motivation was weak to return, but he had desire, prompted perhaps by his research mentality, to return to the world on earth.

Success!

I don't know positively whether the premises outlined in this book are actually existent. I have tried to relate a possible and comprehensive account, based on knowledge current in the years leading to the 21st Century, of how such events could have taken place. I believe the "pieces" fit together quite well.

The existence of "Big Bang" is widely accepted today by the scientific world. The process of General Unified Theory (GUT) is also widely accepted. The dynamics of original cosmic evolution following "ignition" at the Big Bang is theorized with reasonable credibility by respected particle physicists.

The explorer satellite, COBE, has identified cosmic radiation existing in space, a remnant of the Big Bang. An unexplained existence of Dark Matter is theorized to explain the partial void of matter calculated as created at the Big Bang event.

The process of annihilation of positive and negatively charged elementary particles after singularity at time of the Big Bang is also credibly theorized. The destinations (purpose) of positrons, positively charged electrons, has not yet been determined by science. The existence and world of such positive-charge elementary particles is a basic tenet of this book.

The first portion of cosmos existence following the Big Bang, that period of gaseous existence with later gravitational effects to later form gaseous and localized stars (planets, asteriods, etc.) and the period of debris accumulation of other space substances followed by chemical changes resulting in molecular formation of the various elements which are now identified in the chemist's Periodic Table.

However, at the estimated age of two-thirds to four-fifths of the way back into earth's history, geologic evidence has been found of the oldest rock formations. The "book" of geologic history can be seen and read today in such places as the walls of the mile deep Grand Canyon. Here, layers of historic existence are laid out as evidence, several hundreds of millions of years old, in parallel rock formations exposed above the current level of the Colorado River. Even older artifacts of Archeozoic rocks, scientifically dated to at least four billion years, have been located in Australia and Iceland.

By approximately four billion years ago the table had been set for life to exist on earth. Biologists have assembled a history of how first cells originated, how multi-celled creatures would have come into existence, how cells adopted specialized tasks in plant and animal organ formation, and with specialized organs and systems that facilitated sex and reproduction for continuation of their species.

As of this writing earliest Prokaryotic (one celled) life has been discovered at 3.85 billion years ago, shortly after storms of meteors, matter, and "space junk" had bombarded the planet. Archeologists have discovered rock formations fossils as evidence of life forms on earth during various time periods, allowing a comprehensive reporting of biologic and botanical evolution leading to the state of evidence observable today. History of primate evolution, starting perhaps with Lemurs in Madagascar, with Tarsiers, or with Shoshones found in the state of Wyoming, has been developed. This history exhibits successive life forms, lacking only a mind (as segregated from the brain) to differentiate them from life forms having a human existence.

Religion has been a part in humanoid civilization for at least 100,000 years of Homo sapiens existence, with archeological findings and analysis showing an apparent purpose in the burial of their deceased. Philosophers in ancient China, Mesopotamia, Egypt, and elsewhere in the world, evidenced, in their art, a life beyond their secular existence on earth and the existence of gods or supreme beings. Philosophers of these cultures elaborated on the purpose in life as they opined at the time.

The Old Testament records the thoughts and actions of people in the Mideast regarding religious matters. Comparable thought must have also taken place in parallel civilizations elsewhere in the world, where fossil evidence has proved their existence.

Unfortunately, oral and written records have generally not survived to document those histories outside Mesopotamia and Egypt. In these, we have only archeological finds and presumptions on which to base a continuum of their life and history.

The New Testament records the existence and life of Jesus Christ and the philosophies advocated by Him, as reflected by others at His approximate lifetime. The Christian world has based dogma of religion upon words and interpretions . . . the Bible, as agreed upon by conventions of various interests for 2,000 years without substantial change. Other religions have based their cultural philosophies on similar revered recordings.

This book has attempted to pull together many aspects of history in many specialties of knowledge and study, into a comprehensive, continuous, possible, and believable story of mankinds development, although cursory in the depth of any one field.

The author has attempted to show the universe of God as being in some ways comparable to the workings of our own secular life, although the "mechanics" of operation are far different than those of modern industry and organizations. Even at that, comparison can be made of the imagined world and administration of God's realm with the administration by a President or Chairman of a country, or the court of a powerful king. (See *God's Empire* chapter.)

To facilitate accomplishment, organization must exist and tasks must be performed by various components of the organization, working with the tools that are available, and having a purpose for its existence.

This is observed, not just in today's corporate life, but also in the evolution of nature's plants and animals since the start of time, with each change in appendage or organ having a purpose.

Perhaps the purpose on earth of Homo sapiens, Modern Man, and Thinking Man, is to think. In this, I believe, this civilization has responded well. Early man evolved a set of morals and ethics to focus his behavior and standards. Early Assyrians and Greeks produced unique thoughts and philosophies regarding the meaning of life. Pythagoras contributed in mathematics, Copernicus for our position in the cosmos, Galileo for solar system discoveries and introspection, Newton and St. Thomas Aquinss for bridging religion and science, Einstein for relating energy, space and time to a unification, Hawking, and other physicists of this century, developing advancements in a Grand Unification Theory and particle science. Others have made like contributions in the arts, government, philosophy, and collateral fields of study.

This has lead the common man of Earth to seek a deeper meaning to life. We wish to determine where our own position in the scheme of life exists. We wish to determine, or have assurance, that we are on the correct road to the greatest peace.

The HAL computer of the movie *2001, A Space Odyssey* (HAL = Heuristically Programmed Algorithmic computer; Heuristic meaning to allow or assist in discovery, or proceed to a solution by trial and error), has not arrived quite yet, and when it does, it is highly unlikely that it will possess the ethereal qualities of the human mind.

We, as Cro-Magnon man, may be only a transitional phase on earth, as Homo sapiens, and Neanderthal before us were, in a total plan whereby, at some future eon, physical life forms may have become extinct, and only souls will inherit the earth and cosmic systems, leaving the world of matter to bacteria, virus, and the insects, as near the start of life.

There have been several recognized mass extinctions of particular forms of life in Paleo history. Four mass extinctions took place during the Neoproterozoic era from 800 million to 543 million years ago. Other mass extinctions took place at 438 million, 367 million, 248 million (the well documented K-T Explosion between the Cretaceous and Tertiary periods), and 206 million years ago. The well known dinosaur extinction occurred about 65 million years ago, possibly caused by some form of cosmic collision with Earth. Other extinctions have since taken place for one reason or another since then, accounting for the absence of evidence that would prove previously existent life, identified by formerly living fossils discovered in earth, swamp and rock. (Source: *Death By Seltzer,* Discover Magazine. January, 1997).

We are in continual jeopardy of another event, similar or novel, occurring again, either by slow, ecological change in the earth's systems, or by instantaneous elimination of life by cosmic collision or other happenings. The next mass extinction might coincide with some celestial, ecological, or geophysical event.

These thoughts are not new. Probably every thought and idea expressed in this book has been previously thought of, discussed, and presented by someone during the course of civilization, including:

Prehistory man and their shamans
Ancient Egyptians
Socrates

Plato
Aristotle
Old Testament writings
New Testament testimonials
Councils of Nicaea, Constantinople, Ephesus, and
Chalcedon
Constantine
Any of several Popes and church men
Thomas Aquinas
Isaac Newton
Albert Einstein
Pioneers in natural science
Pioneers in atomic science
Pioneers in social science, psychology, and
parapsychology
Pioneers in particle science
Pioneers in computational and computer science

Here I have merely reflected thoughts of these great men and their minds. I have attempted to merge certain concepts into one possible summary scenario of what our culture and religious thought might be.

If this has been accomplished, I believe substantial numbers of "on-the-fence" believers in God will exercise a new look upon this faith, seeing now that the eventualities are logical, rational, possible, and probable, whereas they previously looked upon many aspects of Christianity, as illogical and improbable.

My intention upon nearing publication of this book was to assume a pen name for fear that acquaintances might think me somewhere between a heretic and mentally unbalanced. However, I now, realizing the honorable company with whom my thoughts reflect, will be proud to lend identification to these writings.

I have drawn upon many fields of interests to develop these thoughts. Ideas and concepts have been borrowed from theology of prehistory, the Old and New Testaments, and current day church denominations; from cosmology and astronomy; from anthropology and archaeology of archaic, the ancients, the regional civilizations, American Indians, and of Middle East excavations and writings; from biology, botany, anatomy and psychiatry; from geology, history, and culture of American, English, Middle East, Asian and world focus; from evolution and nature; and from physical, medical, social science, psychology, and other schools of the sciences and the arts.

To fully comprehend this writing, one would do well to have a cursory appreciation of at least some of these disciplines.

I believe my contribution is primarily to place various concepts of theology in perspective, with a relation to each other in a logical, reasonable, and understandable way, and as one layman communicates an idea to another layman.

In appreciation of advancements in knowledge occurring during the past 2,000 years, I have tried to not be constrained by dogma set down by writings of 20 centuries ago, and to recognize how these testimonials might have been written earlier if the writers had the benefit of today's state of knowledge in science and the arts.

Do We Live In Two Worlds?

PART V - To The Future

If this sounds a little weird, you are not alone. You may have a response that you "don't believe it!" But it does, very nicely, explain many events. This exploration explains:

- Evolution—Charles Darwin explained the existence; this exploration suggests how and why evolution transpired
- Mutation and its purpose. The opposite of mutation is perfect cloning, such as in insects—millions of insects within a species are absolutely identical
- Culture variations
- Race differences
- Man vs. animals—the differences
- Differences in men
- Differences in women
- Differences between men and women
- Sex—why mutations, limitations, clones
- Emotion, rational and irrational acts
- Different findings in anthropology
- DNA—What it is, what are the determinants, relationship of DNA and cell composition, genome "engineering", and results of DNA changes
- RNA—the instructional program and the system program for DNA
- A purpose in life
- Souls—their creation
- Souls and their purpose
- God—Tangible evidence of His existence; an understandable system in His universe

- Understanding biological and neurological changes in one's body and mind following heartfelt prayer, and causation that effects change
- Differences and compatibility of earth's nature and the mystics of life
- Relating our solar system and cosmos to mystical life
- Catastrophe, and return of life after
- Specie creation and refinements to meet new environments
- Specie extinction
- The seeds of forming civilization—benefits of many vs. one acting in a society
- Development and progress of civilization
- Theological theory and dogma—probable errors and possible corrections
- The difference and relationship of brain and mind
- *"In God's own image"*—a true meaning and rational possibility

I believe I have, in writing this book, taken a step to having figured out the Hereafter, the mind and soul, creation, the genome and evolution, while reconciling these with theology and science. I hope the reader believes the outcome is magnificent.

"At midyear in the year 2,000 researchers will announce that they have successfully mapped the human genome, the famous DNA strand of more than 3 billion chemical "letters" that spell out instructions for how to "build" a human being.

"Yet, despite the grand aura of the double helix, knowing its code is really only a means to a greater end. To learn what makes the human body thrive or falter, scientists will now brave an endeavor that dwarfs the genome project. Welcome to the age of "proteomics", jargon for the study of proteins, the most complex of all known molecules.

"Proteins are, in essence, everything that a DNA blueprint calls for: workers that build the body and keep it in good repair, and warriors that battle invaders. By watching what goes right or wrong, as proteins attempt to carry out genetic instructions, scientists hope to finally attain a Holy Grail of medicine, such as the prevention of breast cancer and the cure for heart disease." (Source: U.S. News and World Report. July 3, 2000, Pg. 47.)

Today, entering the 21st Century, several leading universities in advanced learning are probing into the untapped academic areas of life sciences. The Life Science Initiative will investigate all factors that affect the existence of life in an interdisciplinary cooperation among different academic disciplines.

The institutes will tap the knowledge and resources of all disciplines of knowledge in search for better understanding of those factors concerning life. Studies will encompass medical science, physics, anatomy, chemistry, biology, theology, anthropology, genetics, microbiology, computer science, and whatever other studies that might affect life commencement, existence, and continuation.

This is a relatively new concept in science, one that is hoped to flourish under the Life Science Initiative, a campus-wide effort to expand research in genetics and related field.

One Institute that seeks to take a leading position in this regard is the newly formed *Life Sciences Institute at the University Of Michigan* in Ann Arbor, Michigan. Construction is now underway to house the Institute and to develop its esoteric program.

It is the author's vision that the essence of this book, the manipulation of genes by souls operating in a parallel universe of a different dimension, one associated with the new field of particle physics and antimatter, will be included in the study program.

Boys are different from girls. We learned this early in childhood, even before starting elementary school. Once in school we noticed further differences. Girls seemed to be quicker in coming up with answers to the teacher's questions. We later learned that girls mature quicker than young boys, and also that the gestation period, on average, for girl babies is somewhat shorter than for boys, and that women often have a longer life than men.

As we progressed in school and into our preteen years, boys noticed other intangible sensations about girls—that they provide some aspect of emotional or erotic appeal to boys (and boys to girls) that makes them attractive to each other. The differences often excited the developing male sexual qualities and organs. At puberty the girlish voice quality of the boy drops in pitch as the boy approaches age 12 to 14 or so. The girl has already started to notice change in her physical being, with enlarging breasts and perhaps menstruation.

At high school ages we learned, either formally through books and academic instruction or by discussion with others, of the biological differences between male and female. The female can become pregnant through union with the male, the female person developing a fetus within her body in a strict system of biology unique to being a women.

We notice that the posterior muscles of some females traverse a greater horizontal span when walking than does that of most males. In comparative study of anatomy we observe that the pivot point of the female femur bone is often more forward on the pelvic bone, the better to support the additional weight during pregnancy, thus prompting a "wiggle" in the anatomy of some females.

The psyche of women differs from man. She is frequently more responsive to artistic and sensual events. Men often are attracted to operational and mechanical happenings—not always, but many times. We learned that women possess a layer of fatty material beneath the epidermis of the skin, insulation that retains their body heat, a trait useful for protecting the growing human embryo within her body. They develop breasts for the purpose of nursing their young, different from that of man.

It seems strange that women are like men in many ways, yet so different in others. Analytically we wonder if we are really from the same origin. The Bible summarily professes that woman was created from the rib of man, and that man was formed from clay. This is myth formulated by a mentality of people living 2,500 years ago, before the subsequent advance of knowledge occurring since that time.

Indeed, if some anthropologist discovered the skeletons of today at some future time, he could make a good case that the male and female remains were from two different species. He would consider the cranium, teeth, pelvis, hands, feet, general anatomy, skeletal structure, bone features, size, and even evidence of cultural differences, perhaps reflective of differences between Neanderthal and Homo sapiens, or at least between the first Homo sapiens and Cro-Magnon or Modern man.

A book was popular during the 1990s *"Men Are From Mars; Women Are From Venus"* by John Gray, Harper Collins, published in 1992. The book makes a wonderful presentation of various differences, primarily in psyche between women and men. The book describes differences in expectations and in methodology between male and female of how to accomplish those goals.

The author advances here a theory that originally male and female descended from different species of life. Taxonomy is the methodology of making a systematic description of life in botany and zoology, and sets up a system for the arrangement of species in plants and animals in the form of hierarchies of superior and subordinate groups. In animals, the like study is referred to as Phylogeny.

Sex plays an important role in the development of society. In the protozoa sex itself may have originated as the result of selection based on the mutual stimulation to more rapid division. The story begins with the flagellate protozoa, that is claimed by botanists to be feature of the algae. The variety of sexual changeability occurs in several invertebrate animals, including some Echinoderms, several Molluscs, some Annelid Worms, and certain Crustaceans.

In at least one order of the annelid (segmented) worms, laboratory research shows they function in early maturity for a while as males, and then switch over and become females. The female phase may continue until the individual dies or the male phase may be resumed. In addition, many adverse conditions, including starvation, cause females to revert to maleness in some annelid worms and in boat-shell snails.

In some other varieties of worms, the large female harbors small parasitic males within her uterus, that either directly or indirectly fertilize the female. In other varieties of worms the female alone carries the specie for many generations.

In certain aphids, outbreaks of sexuality occur, usually at a sustaining pond that becomes dry, or as autumn sets in.

Crowding female worms of a population into limited space can effect inducing bisexuality. This production of either male or female, when needed, frees all members of the race to be egg-producing members of the community when environmental conditions favor rapid expansion of the specie population.

In protozoa, individuals belonging to the same sex do not conjugate with each other; they do conjugate readily with a member of the other sex of their own variety. Sometimes, but not often, they will conjugate with a sex type of a different variety (specie).

Social facilitation refers to increase in frequency, intensity, or complexity in the behavior of an individual resulting from the presence of another in mutual interaction. Asexual divisions occur at a faster rate when working together, compared with the result if each works alone.

Increased social facilitation in behavior is noted in several varieties of animals when the participants are active in a group rather than as individuals. Under some conditions competition is a factor of social facilitation. Likewise, there is greater cooperative behavior when varieties such as male and female work together than when each work separately.

In studying behavior of numerous animals, birds, and fishes in groups, flocks, and schools, psychologists have reached the generalization that throughout the higher reaches of the animal kingdom, man included, males tend to be sufficiently aggressive so that they exert a disruptive social influence, in contrast to less aggressive females.

Plant life as a whole and land animal life as a whole are referred to as the plant and animal Kingdoms. The subordinate groups are successively the Phyla, Class, Order, Family, Genus, and Specie, each such category including one or more of the groups next subordinate to it. (Source: Encyclopaedia Britannica, Volume 1, Phylogeny of Animals, pgs. 970-989)

In summary, the author theorizes that feamales were created, or first existed, as a separate specie from male, quite early in the divisions described by taxonomy as a separate Class, Order, or Family. Female and male cooperated closely over the subsequent eons as a matter of synergy and of improved efficiency in evolution and natural events or social facilitation, through mutual interaction.

Male and female existed separate but closely parallel. The cooperation, through sex, allowed continuation, with frequent mutation to promote desirable physical or biological changes, often but not always, as improvements.

Prior to division of male and female sex, reproduction occurred from hermaphrodites, much as occurs today whereby yeast, virus, amoeba, and algae reproduce without sexual interaction, each generation being a clone of its parent.

Over the eons men and women have become as compatible as were Neanderthal and Homo sapiens in their heyday. Men and women existed, practically as one specie, for at least 4 1/2 million years. We previously existed on earth, as separate species, existing much the same as did the somewhat communal relationship of Neanderthal and Homo sapien species from about 100,000 to 25,000 BC.

The merging of two species, man and woman, are examples of reverse evolution where species combine, rather than divide. (Please see *"A Rosebud Theory Of Evolution"*). As stated elsewhere in this book, the operation of change, inter-species and intra-species, may have been accomplished by angelic manipulation of RNA and DNA in the living organism to effect biologic and physical change within the body. Once change is effected, laws of genetics pass that quality down to the offspring and to subsequent generations, subject again to mutation and intelligent evolution.

Will male or female become extinct in the future, as did Neanderthal man? Will there, at perhaps 50,000 years or so, like when Neanderthal man became extinct, exist a single sex in Homo sapiens, as sexless organisms existed at the beginning? Will there be biological need for two sexes, or will technology of that time allow birth of genetically engineered offspring from a single parent, as happens today in certain primal forms of life and in so-called test tube babies and clones?

In the earliest forms of life on earth, were all forms of life one sex within their specie? Was there no such thing as male and female, but that each specie was hermaphroditic, that is, was able to reproduce within itself, as even today happens in some forms of algae, fungus, yeast, amoeba, bacteria, and even lone plants, moss, some isolated bushes, and perhaps certain trees in the botanical family, and elementary animals in the biological branch of life.

Without dual sex there exists a drawback for evolution in that each specie and generation is sterile for development. There is no provision for universal developing variation, mutation, or crossbreeding. Each generation would be an exact clone of its prior generation. Life would reproduce, perhaps much like grass, moss, and strawberries grow and reproduce their own today without sexual mating.

With creation of male as a sub-species that would unite sexually with the existing female-like species reproducing organism, it would then be possible to "engineer" biological and botanical life that would provide a physically stronger and more aggressive sub-species, the male, and leave the former hermaphrodite as the female that would reproduce the species.

As biology matured, in that embryonic state of life on earth, with both female and male within the species, great strides would be made in reproducing and improving the next generation with combined strengths of both the female and male, and sex was here to stay in evolution.

PART VI

PERSPECTIVE AND LOOK-BACK

I realize that many of the thoughts advanced in this book are controversial. To some, including even myself before my attempts to realistically analyze the events were completed, the concepts might seem so impossible as to be categorized as ridiculous.

But in a time of advancing research and knowledge, by seeing constantly new findings in archaeology, anthropology, geology, and the Hubble Telescope, each month seems to bring a new research report that supports these conceptual proposals, adding verifiable substance to the somewhat nebulous explanation of reasoned interpretation in the events. The author was largely enlightened by articles in monthly issues of Scientific American and Discovery magazines, as well as numerous other readings.

By proposing revisions in our understanding of certain facts and interpretation of some of the Biblical lore, I certainly do not think less of Jesus Christ as an extension of God. By His soul and mind He was exceptional, to say the least. He had unique insight and communication with God, therefore capable of a performing and foretelling, that others could not do. The realism of having a human body, however, I believe, made Him biologically equal to other human beings.

The exploration in this book, on the other hand, has increased our understanding, appreciation, and conception of God. We now visualize a realistic entity, although ethereal, that exists in a way that we can better comprehend. We no longer are limited to thinking of God as some unimaginable function, existing largely because ancestors, associates, and cultural lore said it was so.

I think of God as an energy, an intelligence, and consciousness which is a controlling, driving force in the existence of the cosmos, earth, humanity, and our so called "Heaven".

We can see a system, organization, and a purpose in life. I have separated spiritualism from religion, not at all denying religion, but recognizing the various religions, and their various rituals, all as a means to celebrate their own spiritualism. We recognize that there are many forms of religion spiritualism, all parallel, to celebrate the existence and power of God, even though their supreme power may be recognized differently and called by different names in different cultures. It is hoped that others in reading this book might experience the same revelation that I have stated here.

A person often has a quandary in his mind over certain questions that seem to just gnaw at his mentality. Often he visualizes the pros and cons of a questioned situation, but is not firm in his mind which tack is correct for problem solution.

Often it is advisable to step back, so to speak, in order to look at the problem objectively. It is necessary to "distance" one's self in order to place the various components of the problem in perspective. I have found it helpful to reduce my thoughts to writing.

I have attempted to do this in studying the components of the quandaries approached in this book. For example, persons are raised since childhood with an understanding of "what is correct" in church dogma, without necessarily knowing the why or reason, if any, supporting the accepted approach. Questions of a natural science are often well defined and reproducible, even though not fully understood.

I have attempted, in writing this book, to perform this necessary "step back" and to approach suggested alternatives for interpretation of the facts presented here. I believe the interpretations are generally correct.

I believe much of the evil, as religion calls it, or crime as civil law refers, or immorality as society is damned, are caused by the basic frustration that certain individuals feel in not knowing, in a way that satisfies their own mind, that a God does in fact exist.

Not knowing, they are not resolute in controlling their own behavior, and therefore become a scorn against society, and even themselves. An understanding and a renewed belief in God or some superior power will go a long way in abolishing evil, crime, and immorality.

Often it is the lack of a code of ethics that is instrumental in the wandering of ethical and morality standards that guide persons.

A code of ethics and morality exists in many organizations. Formulating the Ten Commandments provided rules of conduct for Hebrews in the exodus from Egypt. Egyptian pharaohs were guided in their conduct by the rules promulgated in the *Book Of The Dead.* For 2,000 years and more the Bible has set forth standards, yea, demands, for conduct and belief to guide Christians as well as Jews and other followers. The Koran defines rules and examples for Muslim adherents.

The Magna Carta in the 13th Century reduced to writing certain agreements between King John and his nobles. The United States Constitution and the Bill of Rights reduced to writing certain agreed standards. A corporation has a mission statement with an image and policy supported by their procedures, rules, and practices. Civic and professional organizations often develop a code of ethics from which all members are guided.

I believe that even a lawless, street corner gang in the inner city has certain understood rules of conduct. If each of the street gangs were to formulate and reduce to writing their exact rules of conduct, ironically, they would actually have produced a respectable code of ethics, even though justified only in their own minds. All members, present and proposed, would know exactly what standards of performance exists for membership.

A code of ethics will have one prevailing theme: *Treat others as you would want to be treated yourself.* The Bible states this poetically at Matthew 7:12, *"So whatever you wish that men would do to you, do so to them, for this is the law and the prophets"*. These words state the concept that we should not rob the possessions of another, whether it be material, life, or affection.

The author believes that a person having a more close spiritual relationship with God will be a person of quality. By person of quality, this is not necessarily meant in a sense of social stature or economic wealth. Rather, person of quality is meant in the sense of a person displaying admirable attributes of soul, and acting in a responsible manner, as desired by his God.

A person of quality may be found in all religions and in all cultures, whether that culture is recognized and esteemed, or held privately by few. Each individual has the choice of strengthening his own personal desire as a person of quality.

Hopefully, the compilation of thoughts in this book allowed the reader to have a better understanding and love for God, a transition not unlike a son who, not knowing his father well in his adolescence, comes to better understand the same father once a close emotional understanding has been attained to bridge past chasms.

Finally, let me repeat, now with more truth than poetry in Afterlife, as in our modern-day vernacular colloquialism might voice in a parting, *"I'll see you later"*.

In reading thus far in this book one will sense that the author visualizes a practical and realistic realm of God. As an educated businessman, I think of "delegation of responsibility" and "span of control" in an organization. I view the empire of God as not necessarily "churchy" (i.e., heavenly music, prayer, sermon, ritual, even expressions of love and worship), but of souls definitely respectful, loving, and functional to accomplish those desires of God.

A business organization will have a mission statement. Likewise the precepts of this book could be reflected and expressed in a creed:

"Creation of soul dates to the creation of the cosmos itself. The soul has a dutiful junction in the intelligent evolution of all life forms. Soul was incarnated into the ancient animal form of man to become Modern Man, which we are today. Soul is evident in the qualities of man beyond the functions of merely sustaining a physical animal existence. Soul is the essence of God, Christ, prophets and man."

It seems that whenever a populace has a leader, certain responsibilities and procedures develop and become defined. This is noted whether the leadership is that of a flock of geese, or of a complex government. In a business or dictatorship those concepts of leadership that will exist are often determined at the very top of the organization.

I wish to compare the mystical realm of God with the realism found in that of a president of a country, or the reign of a powerful king. A president is chosen for his publicized slate of desires and objectives. A king, although not chosen by his subjects, also has certain goals or accomplishments that he wishes to attain.

To accomplish his program the president will, of necessity, have secretaries to head sub-functions within his administration.

There will exist a judiciary system and an executive system. An organization will be formed and exist to accomplish those functions that must be done.

Likewise, a king will form a court to assist him in his goals and responsibilities, and to provide the basic and necessary functions of his reign.

In parallel, the realm of God might be thought of as an administration or an empire. We recognize God as the supreme being. There are an unlimited number of souls that comprise the realm of God. This can be likened to the citizens of the president's country, or the subjects of the King's realm.

The "religion" practiced in God's realm parallels the philosophy, program, and ideals set forth by the president or king.

Hopefully the programs of the president or king is followed by the majority. In the Hereafter, opposition to those programs is headed by the devil, and supported by demons, his followers. In administration of a country this opposition is known as party politics or disagreement, and a king will have his detractors.

A penal system exists to confine persons of ill will and actions. In the empire of God this exists as assignment to "Hell" and withholding of the pleasures of "Heaven".

Likewise, a reward system exists for souls which have met the prescribed program of God. The reward is everlasting existence in the presence of God. Refinement of soul is accomplished by incarnation with living organisms (joining mystically with the human body, or with another entity as Animist followers believe), and in continual reincarnation until the soul is sufficiently purified and proven to enter and participate in the rewards of "Heaven", and oneness with God.

Subjects exist on earth to advocate and promote the perceived programs of God and acts necessary to be accepted into Heaven. This would be manifested in the clergy and "good" men and women on earth performing worthy acts.

A court system exists to determine outcome of questions, mainly that of assignment of souls from earth to either "Heaven" or "Hell". A processing system will exist to assign the more routine decisions, that will be numerous, with the Judiciary deciding more complex determinations. An administrative agency would exist, of necessity due to volume, for reception of souls from deceased persons from earth, and for assignment as later reincarnations.

An agency of "Environmental Control" would be necessary to audit the need for necessary changes in earthly DNA of humans, animals, plants, insects, bacteria, etc., and to affect those desired changes by corrective actions by souls.

A "Department of Guardian Angels" will give care and guidance on a daily basis to each of the earth's 4 to 6 billion population.

A function comparable to a "king's court" or "president's cabinet" will give executive implementation regarding day-to-day matters of concern within the realm of God and upon earth (and the rest of His realm if that is indeed the fact).

A "security force" is reluctantly recognized to protect the administration of the president or king. Whenever there are dissenters (the devil and his demons) there is need for opposition, and to protect the security of the realm.

Religion, that philosophy, dogma, and conducting the worship ritual, like the intangible program of a president or king, is only part of the total administration of the Supreme Being. Equal effort is necessary to affect accomplishment, or putting into practice those concepts that are to be the goals and will of God.

Exposure, or presence before the citizens or subjects, and promoting an understanding of the workings of God's program, and making known the mechanics of administration, is a worthy effort that builds support and love for the magnificence, with a sense of Summan Bonum (the recognition of a supreme being or highest good).

We pray to and respect God, but we realize that "behind the scenes in Heaven" there must be a sizable organization to accomplish the will of God in all respects. Angels are a substantial aid to God and are the "work force" in the Hereafter, a "Heaven" in a suggested parallel universe.

A multitude of assisting entities are mentioned in the Bible. Angels and saints are the "administrative staff" in Heaven. They are chosen representatives of God and exist to carry out the will of God. Angels are the messengers between Heaven and earthbound individuals.

Angels have been elevated to a supernatural state and had to pass through a period of probation before being admitted to the beatific vision of God. It is considered that every person on earth, even though he or she is not baptized, and may be a sinner or infidel, has his or her guardian angel.

Saints are designated, by various levels of sainthood, to "administrate" different functions, and each of different scope. In the Old Testament, angels are variously called "messengers", "sons of God", "spirits", "holy ones", "watchers", "host of the Lord", and "host of Heaven". Their functions are to praise God and to attend upon His throne, to execute His commands on earth, to protect the faithful, to punish the wicked, and to drive away evil spirits. They manifest themselves in assumed or apparent bodies in humans. (Source: Encyclopedia Britannica. 1959, Vol. I, *Angel,* with Bible citations.)

Saints are in modern history, and supposedly throughout church history, authenticated when canonized, an event performed mainly within the Catholic church, as having superhuman spiritual powers or have performed acts promoting on earth the conceived will of God. Saints and souls could be a link between the matter and antimatter worlds, and prompt "unworldly" acts in this secular life.

Three angels were revealed in the Old Testament: Gabriel, Michael, and Raphael, each of different rank. Many saints have also been designated by earthly religions, Saint Peter and Saint Paul being only two of a myriad of saints designated in a wide variety of churches. Saints Anthony, Augustine, Barnabas, Christopher, Gregory, Ignatus, Jerome, Olaf, and Zeno are only a few of well over 100 saints declared by various churches as possessing the qualities of sainthood.

Theologians have divided angels into nine orders, differing in rank. In the book of Isaiah, the attendants upon the divine throne are called Seraphim. Cherubim are said to be the guardians of paradise. In organization, functional officers in the earthly Vatican and the Swiss Guard come to mind here as having a parallel form of hierarchy as Seraphim and Cherubim in Heaven.

Other ranks of angels, in order, are Thrones, Dominations, Virtues, Powers, Principalities, Archangels, and Angels. The various officers of a church might parallel these ranks of angels, such as Cardinals, Bishops, Priests, Ministers, and Laymen.

Souls in Heaven will possess certain ethereal qualities that were once an integral part of their recognized human existence.

This is not considered a religious book, although God and religion are frequently cited. The author prefers to have you view it more as an exploration into particle physics, philosophy, anthropology, chemistry, biochemistry, geological, archeological evidence, and Biblical history, with overriding principles of logic and reason.

Laid out here is a rather comprehensive model for man's existence. This model spans all of time, and of events in this span that reflect evolution of earth, plant and animal life leading to man on earth, soul in man and in afterlife, God, and the possible demise of humankind.

Some of these concepts may seem strange. The author asks merely that you keep an open mind.

Singularity and Unity existed in a Black Hole, emanating from a previous cosmos.

  A. A previous physical cosmos of cosmos energy did exist, was compressed to its elementary particles in singularity, and was void of space.

  B. Unity is a consolidation of all basic qualities in elementary particle physics and "theosophy-physics".

  C. Unity of elementary particle combined with singularity, was the source of our Big Bang.

   1. One, or more, Big Bangs did exist in the cosmos.

PART VI - Perspective And Look-Back

Essence Of "We Live In Two Worlds"

Souls manipulated development of life on earth by mystical changing (mutating) of genes.

   A. Is this possible?

      1. A science principal—No change takes place without cause. Intelligent changes since cosmos creation have obviously taken place.

      2. This applies also to genome construction and development.

      3. Evidence exists that physical change in the body affects health and well-being.

         a. Exercise and medicine.

         b. Change in a gene (mutation) will effect physical change in the body.

         c. Death occurs upon ceasing of functioning of certain body organs.

      4. Faith

         a. Traditional view: God works in mysterious ways.

         b. Enlightened view: Intelligent changes have and will take place.When absolute knowledge is not available, we must rely upon faith for "miraculous events".

         c. Some day we may better understand the process.

   B. Various examples exist of return to life from a recognized state of death.

      1. Experience in today's hospitals.

      2. Lazarus (Biblical)

      3. Christ's resurrection

C. Various examples exist of physical healing (Shrine at Lourdes, France, Quebec, Canada, and others).

D. Need for change can result in mutation.

E. Answering of prayer is proffered evidence of a directed change in genes (by angels).

    1. Manipulation of genes will effect biological (body and brain)change.

    2. Manipulation of genes will allow change in mind functioning.

    3. Answered prayer is request, with the enabling act.

    What are the processes of accomplishment:

        a. Genome engineering.

        b. DNA is manipulated by changes that effect composition of DNA.

        c. Research still is needed in the state of miracles and faith.

    4. Physical change takes place in the body (via genes) to manifest (cause) certain miracles or change in body cell activity.

    5. Rule of inertia (from physics): Objects at rest tend to stay at rest and objects in motion tend to remain in motion.

        a. Genes will remain without change unless mutation occurs.

        b. Cancer is a runaway change (production) in body cells.

Souls (angels) manipulated development of life on earth by mystically changing (mutating) genes.

A. These changes were intelligently guided.

B. From these changes all life evolved:

    1. Algae, amoeba, bacteria, plants, worms, early sea life, fish, reptiles, mammals, primates, erect walking creatures, early man, and Modern Man.

    2. Animists believe that animals, plants, and some inanimate objects existences also have souls (e.g., Native American Indian, Hindu, African tribal, others).

Homo specie (Homo robustus, Homo ergaster, Homo sapiens) are the result of a joining (biologically) of robust creatures (such as primal ape and gorilla) from smaller, analytical, intelligent creatures such as lemur, monkey, chimpanzee, orangutan, and others leading to Homo species.

God incarnated (joined) soul into the existing primate.

A. Man and soul are each evolving in parallel.

    1. Man evolving in the universe that we experience.

    2. Soul evolving in a parallel universe.

B. Mutations are guided by and performed by angels. Angels (a selected group of souls) have the ability to mystically change genes.

C. Some physicians hold that their ability and medicines can go only so far in continuing life of a patient. The patient's recovery is often beyond medical understanding.

D. Man has spiritual beliefs that foster a sense of wellbeing.

Soul and animal body of man are different, joined, and separable.
- **A.** At death, soul leaves the animal body of man.
  - **1.** Physical bodies do not "rise" to Heaven.
  - **2.** Only the soul enters "Heaven".
- **B.** Souls enter humans at—
  - **1.** Birth (with reincarnation).
  - **2.** Rebirth (at reevaluation by existing persons of their soul).
- **C.** God and souls (including angels) are of the same essence.
- **D.** Supreme Being, that Judeo-Christians call God, is the same entity in all cultures and religions, varying only in name and dogma.
- **E.** Angels are souls in the direct service of God.
- **F.** Physical evolution is a product of geology and biology in science; soul evolution is a product of God. God-directed evolution lead to human body, human being, and Modern Man.
- **G.** A primary goal of soul is development, evaluation and validation of its worth and purity.

A purified soul will merge with God in eternity.
- **A.** Jesus was a purified soul.
- **B.** There are others—
  - **1.** Angels

2. Saints
3. Purified individuals.

C. An unpurified soul will be prohibited from After life and relegated to the existence of Hell.

Eventual elimination of the human race by catastrophe is suggested:

A. Souls will continue in a different, nonphysical, parallel universe.
B. Many causes of catastrophe are possible.

AS RADICAL AS IT MAY SEEM, THE MODEL DOES RECONCILE SEVERAL CONFLICTS AND PRECEPTS WITHIN THEOLOGY AND WITH SCIENCE:

A. Original creation of earth (An evolutionary, physical event, not by God).
B. Creation of man (Evolution directed by God, accomplished by angels in gene manipulation).
C. Continuance of God.
D. First souls (Created from Singularity and Annihilation)
E. Creation and existence of soul within man (Incarnation)
F. Evolution of man (Directed by God; performed by angels).
G. Adam and Eve, Garden of Eden (Symbolic).
H. Is Jesus God, Son of God, or Holy Spirit? (In this model He is all three!)

I. Miracles are facilitated by directed change in genes.

J. Virgin birth (may have been normal pregnancy with soul of God incarnated or may have been affected mystically by angel manipulation of genes) exampled even today in single-sex reproduction in bacteria, virus, yeast, others.

K. Return from the dead (Lazarus, Christ).

L. *"You must be born again"* (by either reincarnation, or reevaluation of relationship with one's soul).

M. Conflict of man with man (e.g. war, crime) is contrary to will of God.

N. Is the future ordained (predestined)?

O. New Books of the Bible could be written based on events since the time of the New Testament (new individuals, new events, new wisdom).

P. Genome determines personal traits.

Q. Genome code regulates individual body cells, proteins, and enzymes.

R. Genome code regulates brain functioning. Brain functioning effects mind, which interacts with the soul.

S. Mind functioning (personality, Id) is a function of the soul.

T. End purpose of the soul? (Perfection)

U. The "Second Coming"? (Muhammad?)

V. "Heaven"? (Afterlife)

W. "Miracles"? (Genome manipulation by soul)

X. Revelation (the things which shall be).

Y. Possible future of mankind and souls.

Z. Corrects some basic Biblical thought:
1. Dogma (interpretations by man)
2. Miracles (knowledge vs. faith)
3. Biology (present vs. biblical)
4. History (accuracy refined through research).

This model hopefully adds an understandable comprehension to our story of existence, considering the knowledge gained in over 2,000 years since bible books were written and assembled.

The author believes that the end goals that souls are instructed to strive for are accomplishments in:

A. Recognition—Of just what God (or Supreme Being) is.

B. Humanity—Love, tolerance, and to help one another.

C. Ethics—Treat others as you would be treated.

The Homo sapiens' body and mind are vehicles for souls to prove worthiness for afterlife. There is relationship between spiritual well-being of the mind and future of the soul in an afterlife. Secular wellness, in a total sense, including continuation of life, is related to the designated path of the soul.

PART VII
EPILOGUE

- Explaining *"Two Worlds*

I once had what I consider a near ideal opportunity to verbally explain my thoughts as expressed in this publication. In May of 1996 my wife and I vacationed for a few days at a location we have frequently enjoyed before.

Berea, Kentucky is the location of a small Christian college near the foothills of the Appalachian Mountains. It is close to the "Bible Belt" of the United States. My wife and I like to exercise by walking the athletic track of the college, as many local residents of the community also do. The track has a rubberized surface and is especially appealing to walk on.

On a Friday night we were walking this track and had made nodding acquaintance with two ladies walking who were local residents of the town. At a resting spot, we stopped to converse with these persons. My wife struck up conversation with one nice lady, who was a Sunday School teacher. I spoke with the other lady who started our conversation by asking if we knew the location of the Danforth Chapel on the campus, which luckily we did because we had attended a wedding there several years before. The lady said that her daughter had also been married there.

The lady went on to ask me what religion I was. I stammered a bit and said that, "I kind of had my own religion, but generally was a Protestant, although I respect all religions", I told her. The lady confirmed my guess that she was a Southern Baptist. She volunteered that her daughter was "educated", but that she (the mother) wasn't.

She stated that her daughter reads a lot. In talking with her I suspect that she respects education, that she probably had not completed high school herself, although her questions and thoughtfulness were probing.

She asked if I knew anything about the Catholic religion, because she "wasn't too knowing about it". I stated that I thought the main difference from Protestantism was that Catholics largely rely upon the priest to interpret the Bible to the congregation, whereas the Protestants believe in individual determination, and their own interpretation of the words in the Bible.

The lady volunteered that she had frequently asked "her daddy" where we came from, and when we arose from the dead, will life be just as it is here and now?

With this comment, I had to let down the "flood gates" of my thoughts on the subject, and I think we both found the next few minutes interesting, although I am sure that when we parted I hadn't convinced this lady any differently than her Southern Baptist, fundamentalist upbringing had engulfed her.

I stated that I don't believe 100 percent in what the Bible states. I stated that, "We can see evidence right here in the Kentucky hills of the geologic events that took place in the evolution of the earth, which conflicts with the creation idea expressed in the Bible."

I stated that much knowledge has been gained in the 2,000 years since the New Testament was written, and that many of the Books of the Bible were written 600 years and more before the time of Christ, and other books were finally reduced to writing only after several hundred years of oral history, with good intentions, but inaccuracies resulting in the repetitions.

I stated that faith is necessary only when there is inadequate knowledge to support the facts. I went on to state that much knowledge has been accumulated since the Books of the Bible were first written. Some acquired knowledge supports certain statements in the Bible, and some dispute certain events.

She stated that she had asked "her daddy" where God came from. I stated that I believe we all exist in two parts, an animal body, that will someday rot in our grave (why was I so blunt?) and a soul that will continue on. I told her that I believed in reincarnation, and that her soul today might well have existed in the body of another person, perhaps some 100 or 200 years ago, and that her soul might well exist in some person in the future. The soul is in a stage of striving to attain perfection for eventual joining with God.

I stated my theory that souls are a part of God, relating that souls break off from the God-substance, much like a drop of oil breaks away from a larger body of oil on the surface of water, and that upon human death, the soul is rejoined with the God-substance, much like the drop of oil rejoins the main body of oil, perhaps losing all its individuality.

I stated that regarding reincarnation, some religions believe in animalism. I mentioned Native American and Hindu religions which believe that after death, some souls may be reincarnated into lower forms of life, such as wild animals, or even inanimate objects. The lady added, "maybe snakes", to which I replied, "snakes". Later reincarnations would provide for elevation back to the status of human, and perhaps beyond.

Many people are convinced, I said, that certain animals, specifically their pet dog or cat, and certain other animals too, have souls, or have a communication and empathy with the owners or masters of the pet, or communicate with the wild animal. Hindus believe the Brahma cow is sacred and with soul. Many Native American Indians, and people of other cultures too, speak of the soul in wild animals, birds, and even inanimate objects such as stones and the Earth, as well as trees, the winds, the moon, and the sun.

I stated that Jesus Christ is one soul who has met the criteria of God for perfection. Their may be others, (I thought, but didn't say saints) and that others, perhaps each of us, can someday also meet perfection in our souls.

My new-found friend asked if I thought a person could ever get out of Hell. I stated that I hadn't thought too much about this, or whether there would be a "reevaluation". I did recall to her that Catholics talk about Purgatory, an existence of indecision, or holding period, after which determination is made, after consideration of the person's deeds while on Earth, of whether to advance on to Heaven or Hell.

I began to lose my credibility to this lady, I'm sure, when I related my thoughts of antimatter and the "Big Bang". I had to explain in elemental terms about Grand Unification and that annihilation would occur with creation of antimatter when matter was created. This left my uneducated, mountain-area-reared, Southern Baptist lady pretty befuddled I tried to explain the Grand Unification

Theory. I thought of making popcorn balls. I stated that if we wanted to make popcorn balls from a big volume of popcorn, we could mix it with syrup and compress it all down with our hands, as I put my hands together like I were to form small balls. I tried to relate how the solar system is composed of the sun and planets, and if this were all to be "squeezed" down to where all the space is gone, it would be like making those popcorn balls. She had only a "heard of conception of what the solar system was like.

I further explained how atoms are constructed, much like the solar system, with a nucleus, and electrons circling the nucleus, and often having several concentric belts of electrons. I stated that if this, too, were "squeezed" down to eliminate all space, there would be tremendous reduction in size.

I took a chance of further losing the conceptions of my lady friend by suggesting that even the electrons consist of smaller elements called quarks. I left the further explanation of this aspect in the field of particle physics, or quantum mechanics alone.

I then tried to explain the creation of antimatter by annihilation. These were terms she knew nothing about, as she stated. She had never heard of antimatter, and the concept of annihilation was completely out of her understanding.

I explained that matter was all of the things that we see and touch about us, such as the earth, the trees, I touched her sleeveless blouse, and her arm, illustrating our bodies. I stated that antimatter is an existence like matter, but just the opposite. I'm afraid I further lost her on this concept.

I went on to state that at the moment of the Big Bang (I didn't really argue or take the time to explain "Big Bang") that all matter was created, and that positrons (the basis of antimatter) were eliminated, or annihilated, except for a small portion, which is the world of antimatter, and my theory that this is the world of souls and God.

I gave brief mention that God might well have existed prior to the Big Bang, but that the Big Bang was the moment that souls could first come into existence in the image of God. The souls were incarnated into humanoid forms with the coming of Homo sapiens and Cro-Magnon man. Souls perhaps had a function on earth before the time of incarnation into man.

She stated that "her daddy" had made some mention that "all things are today". This opened the conversation to my discussion of time. I stated that we commonly think of time as going horizontally, like lengthwise over a bridge, with each movement likened to a change in time. But, I went on to say, we could also think of time as going up, like an elevator into a tremendously high skyscraper, with each floor of the building being a different time unit. With this vertical time concept, all things could be "today", as her father had suggested. My friend showed no reaction to this concept.

I stated that Heaven might exist right here on the surface of the earth, and not up in the sky, as people seem to commonly think.

I stated that in the future, perhaps after "Judgment Day", the Earth may be inhabited strictly by souls. I stated that in terms of anthropology, we are Homo sapiens, and before this, the world was populated by Neanderthal man, and before that by a succession backward in time of a variety of humanoid types, as fossil remains dating back millions of years were identified by the Leakey family studying in Africa, and by other anthropologists throughout the world.

It is possible, I stated, that, say, half a million years from now, Homo sapien man will be replaced by souls on this earth. I quoted a Biblical saying that the lady had heard before, but stated that she didn't know what was the meaning, that the *"The meek shall inherit the earth"*. I said that perhaps this explanation of souls would provide the meaning.

My friend then asked if I believed in Jesus Christ and I replied, "Definitely." I couldn't resist relating my thoughts about Christ, and I am afraid it broke up the conversation. I stated that Jesus Christ was a great teacher who instructed people of Earth on the ideals of God's world, and how to qualify for existence with God.

I went on to say that it is possible that Jesus Christ did not come to clinical death on the cross, but instead suffered medical shock from the crucifixion. I related that during crucifixion the organs of the body drop within the body, and the person actually dies from strangulation. I said this is a slow form of death and unlike a quick death that would occur if a person were, say, shot. She replied, "but there was the stone at the tomb." I replied that in the hours following being laid in the tomb Jesus could have recovered from the medical shock (and perhaps exited the tomb by Himself).

Do We Live In Two Worlds?

I said that it is improbable that the physical body of, say, a 150 pound man would physically rise up into the sky as described in the Ascension, although it is conceivable that the aura of His soul was seen, or visualized as leaving the body, as He later suffered secular death, and His soul departed from this world.

I would have liked to have continued our conversation at this point but it seemed to both of us as the time to break. I wish that I would have explained more clearly that I am indeed religious by my thoughts, perhaps more religious than most.

I suspect that my friend, and her friend, the Sunday School teacher, further discussed my views on religion, perhaps summarizing that I will surely be condemned to Hell.

PART VIII

EPILOGUE II

With surrogate mothers commonplace, can surrogate fathers be far behind? Two new studies in Nature and Nature Medicine bring that possibility to the fore. Researchers at the University of Pennsylvania School of Veterinary Medicine transplanted once-frozen tissue from the testes of one mouse into another's and found that the recipient produced the donor's sperm. The technique worked even when rats were the donors and mice the surrogates. The mice made rat embryos along with their own.

The new approach holds advantages over freezing sperm itself, says Ralph Brinster, the studies' coauthor. Sperm storage can be troublesome, but freezing testicular tissue seems to require no special handling. Also the genes of already-made sperm are fixed, while the sperm-generating testicular cells still hold all of the male's potential gene combinations.

The work could help preserve the genetic diversity of rare animal species, Brinster says, and treat male infertility. One day men who face chemotherapy, for example, could bank their own tissue for later re-transplantation or even use another individual—human or animal—as a host. That's one of many eye-popping scenarios that 21st Century ethicists will have to wrestle with.—(U.S. News And World Report. June 10, 1996).

(Comment: The author theorizes that in the billions of years since the creation and evolution of the earth, virtually all forms of life have existed. Satyrs, a combination of animal and human, are commonly believed to be myth.

Some philosophers have reasoned that all of time, from pre-time (Big Bang and before) to oblivion (in the future) all occur at the same moment. Some particle scientists have lent support to this theory, and that we live in multiple universes, all at the same moment.

They reason that time passage is merely within our own minds and is illusory. Thought is separating the many scenes, or states of the world, into an order, perhaps like the multiple frames on the film of a moving picture film for projection viewing of the different moments, projected in our minds to form a continuum of hours, years and eons.

It follows that a change in the ordering of various time separations would experience different time scenes. This can be partially experienced when we view a moving picture show filmed, say in 1930, we are viewing the experience of 1930 in that particular location. Of course, when the movie is over, we return our mentality to the present day.

One of the hottest themes in theoretical physics today is the theory that time itself is illusory. We are not accustomed to perceive events as proceeding in a cyclical, nonlinear sequence, in a world of multiple universes, that in which theoretical and particle physicists explore. Such concept of instantaneous time lapse might be conceivable and possible in this newly discovered universe of antimatter.

Time may be conceived as merely a series of images, all occurring at the same moment. All time is like a snap of the finger. Variation in illusion is like the different actions, namely 1) placing the fingers together, 2) rapid separation, and 3) listening to the sound vibration. Different events all happen instantaneously and at the "same moment" in time.

Likewise, all events of "history" happen at the same moment, differing only in our own perception of order, memory and recall (past), and vision (future).

Albert Einstein, in his holding regarding relativity, denies any absolute, universal significance to the present moment. Simultaneity is relative: Two events that occur at the same moment, if observed from one reference frame, may occur at different moments if viewed from another. For example, an observer standing on a train station views passengers moving by in a passing train, whereby an observer within a car of the passing train observes no movement of passengers. The reference point is relative to what the observer sees and reports.

Time does not flow. To the contrary, we as people, flow in our experiences within the "tube" of time. We are like electricity, that does not "flow" within a wire, but is merely the reaction from adjacent atoms or molecules agitating within the wire, that will evidence presence of electrical power.

Spontaneity of time can be illustrated by describing "time" on either a horizontal or vertical scale.

Time is a function of matter, or rather the distance between two points of matter. It is assumed that there is absence of time in the antimatter of Hereafter. With this thought of instantaneous time, time in this universe and time in the Hereafter would be the same, that is, zero time lapse in both.

Do We Live In Two Worlds?

PART VIII - Epilogue II

The evidence of age, such as maturing and seed production of plants, and the aging of matter such as deterioration, rot, calcification, decay of half-life radiation, geologic formations, rock structure, archaeological finds, etc. of chemical and physical existence, are real. But these can be portrayed as happening instantaneously, such as in viewing time lapse movies, or even still photographs, of certain aging processes. The time of viewing is now, but the illustration of aging is said to create in the mind an illusion of aging.

In defense of reality, a person appears older, and indeed feels older, as he or she advances further and further from his birth date. This is not an illusion. However, an observer citing pictures taken at two different times may observe an illusion of age.

It appears that the theory advanced by philosophers and psychologists is incomplete.

I am writing this analysis in the Spring of 1997, the time that 39 bodies were found dead, neatly dressed, for a self thought, purposeful, self-inflicted death, supposedly to be transported to the "next level" in existence. This group consisting of 21 women and 18 men. 21 of the victims were in their 40s, eight were in their 50s, four were in their 60s, and one was 72. Five were relatively young.

The backgrounds of each would indicate that they were rational and sincere individuals, who were driven by their own prevailing philosophy. One was a mother of six, and another was a grandmother. They believed the time had come for them to leave this earth, to be carried by an unidentified flying object (UFO), following in the visual path of, and heralded by, the Hale-Bopp Comet.

In one sense, we can understand and empathize with these people, but in another sense their extended philosophy appears to be irrational. This writing advocates that each of us has a soul as well as a body. When our secular life is over, our spiritual self leaves the body and proceeds into a world of Afterlife, to be reborn, reincarnated to another person or creature at some future time, existing meanwhile in a "world of souls"; a world of God.

The author does not advocate self-destruction or suicide. The Bible states that it is wrong to take one's own life. We also believe there is a time for everything—a time to be born and a time to die. Perhaps this is preordained and we as mortals should not interfere with this program.

The individual members of "Heaven's Gate" did commit suicide. I can understand such action, even though we may disagree with the act. By death, one's soul is released, to which members of Heaven's Gate termed, "the next level". The soul is not physical, but is ethereal and without material substance.

The method and philosophy of Heaven's Gate members was illogical and ill-conceived. They apparently saw a continuing physical world after death, with transportation via a UFO. They each dressed themselves well prior to death, with neat clothes, new shoes, and even a $5 bill and quarters in change in their pockets. They apparently had no thought of their soul or soul conversion. Perhaps this care for after death can be likened to ancient Egyptian pharaohs that were dressed in their finest clothes and were buried in their tombs with creature comforts that would be useful and designed to gain acceptance in the afterlife.

If a person is to die on this earth, he or she needs no physical accoutrements to accompany his travel of soul, and in fact, all physical things such as body, jewelry, clothing, and mementos will remain on earth in the tomb. Only the spirit, or soul, will exit to "Heaven", wherever that may be.

The author sees no rationale for the philosophy of the members of Heaven's Gate in their action of self-destruction, nor in other events of mass suicide carried out by various cults, supposedly of a spiritual nature, in various locales of our world.

My thoughts are much the same as those expressed about Heaven's Gate regarding the James Jones debacle in the South American country of Guiana in the early 1990s. It is believed by some that Reverend James Jones, although a sincere minister of his church early in his career, had later convinced himself, and those who believed in him, that he was God reincarnated.

In this instance Reverend James Jones had built a following of perhaps 300 persons and convinced them to flee to a religious "freedom" location in Guiana, South America where their beliefs could be practiced without governmental influence or chastisement which they had found in the Los Angeles, California area.

Later, fearing exposure, interference and control, Reverend Jones convinced all but a few to commit suicide by drinking a potion of cyanide mixed into *Kool Aid* drink.

This mind control and mass suicide is difficult to explain, irrational, and immoral in conventional rules of morality and ethics, and the taking of the life of another, by whatever means.

Do We Live In Two Worlds?
PART VIII - Epilogue II

Reincarnation

Reincarnation: In religion and philosophy, rebirth of the soul in one or more successive existences, which may be human, animal, or, in some instances, plant. While belief in reincarnation is most characteristic of Asian religions and philosophies, it also appears in the religions and philosophical thought of primitive religions, in some ancient Middle Eastern religions (e.g., the Greek Orphic mystery, or salvation, religion), Manichaeism, and Gnosticism, as well as in such modern religious movements as Theosophy.

Among the ancient Greeks, Orphism held that a preexistent soul survives bodily death and is later reincarnated in a human or other mammalian body, eventually receiving release from the cycle of birth and death and obtaining its pure state. Plato, in the 5th-4th century BC, believed in an immortal soul that participates in frequent reincarnations. (Source: Encyclopaedia Britannica, Vol. 15)

Metempsychosis: The theory of the transmigration of souls is usually associated with the ancient Egyptians, who are said to have practiced embalming. With the teaching of Pythagoras and the Buddha, this was also held by a sect of early Christian heretics. The idea, however, much older than any of these creeds, exists throughout the world. Where the passage of the soul, or the vital essence, into some particular form is associated with ideas of retribution for the sins or accidents of this life, the influence of Buddhism or Hinduism has probably been at work.

Attempts to find metempsychosis in early Jewish literature have met with little success, but there are traces of it in Philo and it is definitely adopted in the Kabbala. Within the Christian church it was held by isolated Gnostic sects during the first centuries, and by the Manichaeans in the 4th and 5th centuries, but was invariably repudiated by orthodox theologians. In the middle ages these traditions were continued by the numerous sects known collectively as Cathari. The doctrine is found at the Renaissance and in the Theosophists in the 17th century A.D. During the classical period of German literature metempsychosis attracted much attention. Modern Theosophy, drawing its inspiration from India, has taken metempsychosis as a cardinal tenet. (Source: Encyclopaedia Britannica. 1959, volume 15)

The existence of soul is, today, a basic tenet of most Christian churches. The realism of reincarnation, or metempsychosis, is also believed widely in Judeo-Christian and other cultures.

Are there families in the spirit world? Are there associations of family members that include not only blood relationships but also relationships by marriage? And how about just good friends and second or multiple marriage partners while the mortals were on earth?

In reincarnation, do spirits or souls, return to mortals on earth only that exist in the blood lines? And if so, why is there a biological and soul relationship of certain bodies and souls? Is a person who is moral and ethical to a high degree more advanced in development of soul than say a person who is not as advanced in morality and ethics?

What is the time interval between when the soul of a mortal enters Heaven after a worldly death and when the moment of reincarnation takes place? And at what moment does soul join the mortal being—at the moment of conception, time of birth, or some other time?

Do souls return to mortality in non-human forms as some animist religion/cultures hold, or do souls return in reincarnation only to humans? If souls return to earth for the purpose of refining their quality, is there some guiding quality in the ethical and moral thoughts of that human that are ties to past quality of soul?

These are only a few of the questions that arise concerning life on earth, souls in Heaven, and reincarnation.

Are you your own ancestor, reincarnated? You may have heard family stories about your great-grandfather, great-grandmother, grandparents, or others as to their personalities, accomplishments, motivation, drive, leadership, good or bad deeds, or the like expressed in that person's lifetime.

It may have occurred to you that you just happen to possess many or some of those personality traits yourself. Never mind the physical traits—these are a matter of biological inheritance. But the qualities of the mind (not the brain) may be within you as a matter of reincarnation.

We cannot remember from one life experience to our present one, but in reincarnation, there could be semblances of those intangible traits.

For example, was your great-grandfather, say, a pioneer who shed comforts of home to explore life's possibilities? Was he, or she, a "born or natural" explorer who seemed to live for the goal of experiencing the unknown of tomorrow, or of a new place? Do you also seem to possess this quality of pioneering? Do you explore roads and pathways "off the beaten paths", simply for the purpose of learning what lies down those paths? Was your great-grandmother a rather pious person, or perhaps a social renegade? Did one of your ancestors contribute significantly to the goodwill of mankind? Or was that person even an outlaw? Was he or she good as an administrator, as leader of men, or as a peace maker? Did that person seem to possess extrasensory powers beyond what normal persons had?

If you possess any of these traits that seem common to those of one of your ancestors, you might be exhibiting certain traits of reincarnation from a previous existence.

General George S. Patton (World War II) and movie actress Shirley McClane are two notable personalities that claim to have lived in a previous life.

SOME SOURCES OF COSMIC OR EARTH CATASTROPHE

- Emission of heat or solar wave from sun, incinerating everything on earth
- Collision of earth with some cosmic body
- Near collision with earth of some cosmic body that would pull atmosphere of earth away from our surface
- Ignition of the planet Jupiter, which has all elements of our sun in its composition
- Extreme atmospheric warming or cooling
- Collision of our galaxy with another cosmic force, such as dark matter, perhaps the essence of stars.
- Collision of galaxies—Forecasts exist that the Andromeda galaxy(our closest galaxy neighbor) and our own Milky Way galaxy will collide in 6 billion years
- Atomic or hydrogen bomb warfare
- Worldwide plague, illness, disease, climate, or geologic conditions
- Cosmic cloud and cosmic rays (actually forecasted to arrive at earth some 10,000 years from now) and radiation exposure
- The earth would enter the attraction area (horizon) of a Black Hole
- A "Brown Dwarf" (former stars that have burned out) entering the proximity of our Sun and solar system, with gravitational pull disrupting all mechanisms and orbits of planets in our solar system.

Source: The October, 2000 issue of <u>Discovery Magazine</u> lists *Twenty Ways The World Could End Suddenly:*

Note: Some of these events have already happened on earth or in the cosmos since its creation.

Further reading is available in the chapter "The Scheme of History Is Already Written".

NATURAL DISASTERS:
Asteroid Impact
Gamma Ray Burst
Rogue Black Holes
Giant Solar Flares
Reversal Of Earth's Magnetic Field
Basalt Volcanism
Global Epidemics

HUMAN TRIGGERED DISASTERS:
Global Warming, Ecosystem Collapse, Biotech Disaster, Particle Accelerator Mishap, Nanotechnology Disaster, Environmental Toxins, and more

WILLFUL SELF-DESTRUCTION:
Global War Robots Take Over, Mass Insanity

A GREATER FORCE IS DIRECTED AGAINST US:
Alien Invasion
Divine Intervention
Someone Wakes Up And Realizes It Was All A Dream

Time Span	Events Of The Period
Timeless	Prior to the Big Bang: A prior existence of collapsing neutron star, Black Hole, accretion, Grand Unification to Singularity. Like a cosmos-size vacuum cleaner, a Black Hole, created perhaps by a collapsing neutron star, would gain unimaginable gravitation within itself. Such gravitation would have continued feeding by attracting cosmic nearby matter, such as stars, planets, comets, space debris, and whatever matter and antimatter elements that might exist, into a substance of intense mass and temperature, terminating in a grand unification of all particles, forces, energy, and qualities.
	Such an object, increasingly diminutive in size while increasing greatly in mass, would have had a complete metamorphose of qualities in its particles, as space is completely removed from atoms, electrons, positrons, neutrons, quarks, and any other particle components. Time ceases to exist in the Grand Unification or Singularity, and in fact time would reverse in decrease of space. The Grand Unification awaits only the moment of ignition from its own internal temperature, mass, and qualities of its particles, to finally explode and expand, as would fuel in a diesel engine once its own critical points of mass, temperature, and changes in element qualities have been achieved.

Robert Greenough

Big Bang, from state of Grand Unification, estimated between 12 and 20 billion years ago.	Particles from the Grand Unification Theory (GUT) change their qualities during about the first three minutes after the initial moment of the Big Bang ignition. Time intervals expand from zero (no time) during GUT, to increasing units of time, as change in distance within atomic structuring takes place during moments of expansion.
Big Bang to 4.6 billion years ago	Gaseous clouds swirling to form gravitation, pulling gases inward, gases and space debris inward. Solid earth core of molten iron and crust, extreme volcanic action mixes crust of earth from depths of 20 to 40 miles up to the surface.
4.6 billion years ago	Recognized origin of earth; asteroids form.
4 billion years ago	Accretion of earth changed from comets and asteroids to dust and meteorites.
3.9 billion years ago	Oldest known sedimentary rocks (in Australia); micro fossils.
3.5 billion years ago	Start of ARCHEOZOIC ERA
	Archeozoic Era is earliest division of geologic history; time of larva life. No known fossils. Most physical records destroyed or covered over by up to 18 miles of earth surface, by erosion, or meta-morphism of physical or chemical change in composition.
3.5 to 3 billion years ago	Single land mass of Ur, which grew slowly. Volcanoes spewed magma; surface and crust of earth thickened and cooled; time of larval life, first deposits indicating life in elementary single plant cell (Prokaryote) organisms of moss, algae, yeast, amoeba.

Do We Live In Two Worlds?

PART VIII - Epilogue II

About 4 billion years ago	Moon created when a large outer space object collided with earth. Earth would then have been in a "viscous" state. Note: This is a questionable theory—nearly all planets have one or more moons of varying size. Frequency of all moons in space being created in this physical manner is beyond likelihood of creation only by chance collisions. (AUTHOR'S THEORY).
3 to 2.5 billion years	First additional land mass divisions of Arctica (later Canada and Siberia).
2.5 billion years ago	Start of PROTEROZOIC ERA
	Proterozoic Era is oldest form of life. Iron and copper deposits formed. Proterozoic rocks underlie much of the iron and copper country of Northern Michigan and Ontario. Alternating glacial and moderate climate. Great mountains uplifted. Primitive life, first multicell animals of tubes and worms, first heart, brain, nerve, circulatory, renal systems. Widespread glaciations.
1.9 billion years ago	Second and third land masses of Baltica (Baltic states) and Atlantica (east South America and west Africa), complex Prokaryote cells in algae and mosses (cells had nuclei, RNA, DNA, specialized and multi-functions).
1.5 billion years ago	Land mass of Nena formed by collision of Baltica and Atlantica.
1 billion years ago	All land masses of Ur, Atlantica, and Nena collide to form single land mass of Rodina.

700 million years	Rodina land mass separates again into Ur, Atlantica, and Nena of which all continue to expand.
580 to 490 mya	Paleozoic (marine and terrestrial plants and animals) Era, Cambrian Period (many forms of invertebrate life of Tribolites and Brachiopods): First well-preserved fossils of Tribolites, Brachiopods, and Gastropods are abundant. Climate cold, becoming warm.
490 to 430 mya	Paleozoic Era, Ordovician Period (First vertebrates and abundance of marine invertebrates: First corals, crinoids, starfish, bryoza, pelecypods, and fish-like animals. Graptolites and Tribolites abundant.
430 to 410 mya	Paleozoic Era, Silurian Period: Evidence of first fish and land plants, formation of mountains and new land areas. First scorpions and goniatites. Many coral reefs. Eurypterids abundant. Greatest development of nautaloids. First land plants. Climate warm, salt deserts.
410 to 355 mya	Paleozoic Era, Devonian Period: First amphibians and tree forest. Armored fish abundant. First lung-fish, ganoids, sharks, fresh water mollusks. Decline of tribolites and graptolites. Climate moderate, becoming warm. Volcanoes in Maine, Quebec, and Nova Scotia. Alpena and Rockport limestone quarries and Michigan oil are in rocks of Devonian age.

Do We Live In Two Worlds?

PART VIII - Epilogue II

355 to 27 mya	Paleozoic Era, Carboniferous (Mississippian and Pennsylvanian) Period: Coal formed in eastern North America and mountains in Europe. Solution of carboniferous rocks formed Mammoth Cave. First reptiles, insects and ceratites. sharks, lungfish, ganoids, brachiopods and blastoids abundant. Climax of crinoids. Coal forest flourish. Climate warm at first, becoming glacial.
275 to 220 mya	Paleozoic Era, Permian Period: Development of reptiles, amphibians and deposits of red sandstone. Original Appalachian Mountains raised. Widespread glaciation. Rock of Bridges National Monument is of Permian age. Climate warmer, deserts, glaciation in Southern Hemisphere. Last of most tribolites, blastoids, eurypterids, graptolites, and tetracorals. Spread of reptiles, amphibians and insects.
220 to 180 mya	Mezoic (middle) Era, Triassic (red sandstone rocks) Period: Trees of Petrified Forest of Arizona grew in Triassic time. First mammals, first dinosaurs, Plesiosaurus, Ichthyosaurs. True ammonites and modern corals. Plants represented by rushes, ferns, cycads, conifers. Climate warm and equable, deserts.
214 million mya	Great collision of earth and a space traveler. Origin of moon from area of present Pacific Ocean, Grotesque changes in DNA forming variety of dinosaurs.

180 to 135 mya	Mezoic Era, Jurassic Period: Many large dinosaurs, first birds, including Archadopteryx, and mammals. Mountains formed by upper movement from horizontal movement of continental plates. Predecessors of Coast Ranges and Sierra Nevadas begin growth. Rocks of Zion Canyon are of Jurassic age. First birds, large marine terrestrials and flying reptiles. Abundant ammonites and cycads. Climate warm and equable.
135 to 70 mya	Mezoic Era, Cretaceous Period: First flowering plants. Extensive deposits of chalk. Birth of American and Canadian Rockies and The Andes. Canyons of Mesa Verde are cut in rocks of Cretaceous age. First abundant plants with conspicuous modern type flowers and fruits. Climate moderate, becoming cool.
90 million mya	Madagascar, a former part of Gondwana, becomes an island.
70 to 15 mya	Cenozoic Era, Early Tertiary Period: Evolution and development of mammals, birds, flowers. Extinction of dinosaurs and ammonites. (Paleocene Epoch— development of mammals; Eocene Epoch—small horses, bats, amphibious whales; Oligocene Epoch—first primates). Rocks of Bryce Canyon of early Cenozoic age. Mammals become dominant. All major modern groups of species represented. Early mammals relatively small and not specialized. First primates. First grasses. Climate moderate, becoming warm.

Do We Live In Two Worlds?

PART VIII - Epilogue II

40,000 to 20,000 mya	Hawaiian Islands formed, in horizontal movements rising from volcanic action at sea floor 15 to 18,000 feet below present surface. Highest mountain is 13,784 feet altitude, with evidence of glacial action on north slope. Mauna Loa erupts on average of every 3 1/2 years. Prehistoric horse vanishes in America about 30,000 years ago.
15 to 1 mya	Cenozoic Era, Late Tertiary Period: Miocene Epoch (diversification of primates including early apes), and Pliocene Epoch (extinction of many mammals and development of hominids): Rocky Mountains, Alps, Himalayas uplifted. Yellowstone Canyon cut in rocks of Late Tertiary age. Extinction of Archaic mammals. Widespread appearance of modern families of mammals. Invertebrate life and plant life much like that of today. Climate warm, becoming cool.
1 mya to present	Cenozoic Era, Pleistocene Period: Marked by great fluctuations in temperature with glacial periods followed by earth warming and interglacial periods. Southern Michigan landscapes owe form to Pleistocene glaciation. Culmination of mammals with extinction of many groups. Advent of man. Climate glacial.
250,000 to 65,000 and present	Cenozoic Era, Pleistocene Period: Holocene Epoch—Quaternary time: Evidence of pre-human development and invertebrates. Extinction of large mammals.

TOPICAL INDEX

Topical Index

Topical Index

Topical Index

GLOSSARY

For: Do We Live In Two Worlds?
   Wonderful Worlds
   Afterlife

AFTERLIFE—Occurrence following secular death, comparable to Heaven. Souls will be judged and evaluated, with souls held satisfactory in meeting Heavenly guidelines of God. Souls held unsatisfactory will be withheld from entry and assigned to Hell. Heaven is one aspect of Afterlife.

ALGAE—Group of one-cell plants. Perhaps first plans on Earth.

ALGAE, GREEN—Non-flowering stem-less water plant, especially seaweed and phytoplankton.

ANGEL—A soul selected in Afterlife to serve the Kingdom of God in any various capacities. Certain angels may serve as Guardian Angel providing guidance to a secular human.

ATOM—Until discovery of quarks, were believed to be the smallest elements in existence.

ANDROMADA GALAXY—Closest galaxy to our Milky Way Galaxy.

AMERICAN INDIAN—Race of humans in America, originating from Siberia.

AMINO ACIDS—Building blocks of life on Earth.

AMOEBA—A first life animal of prokaryote cells.

ANGEL—A soul from Heaven.

ANNIHILATION—Cancellation during Big Bang event of positive charge elements by negative charge elements.

ANTIMATTER—Elementary particles having positive charge. All elements of antimatter are exact opposite of like particles in matter.

AQUINAS, SAINT THOMAS—Religious figure of the 13th Century. Promoted philosophy of dualism of soul in body.

ARISTOTLE—Philosopher and teacher from school of Socrates and Plato.

ASTRONOMICAL UNIT—Distance from Earth to Sun.

AUGUSTINE, SAINT—Struggle with temptation, yet love of God; dissolute youth, yet conversion to Christianity at age 32. Describes searching for truth beyond the material world, of struggle between good and evil.

AUSTRALOPITHICUS afarensis—Pre-human being living about 3 million years ago.

BASES, CHROMOSOME OR NUCLEOTIDE— Adenine, Thymine, Cytosine, Guanine.

BIG BANG—Documented theory for origin of the universe.

BLACK HOLE—Cosmic gravitation attracts space matter or cosmic energy, reducing to a singularity of elementary particles, followed by expansion into space, forming starts, new elementary particles, forces, electrons, protons (base of soul), and other qualities of the cosmos.

BONOBO—An intelligent member of the Monkey family.

BUDDHISM—Belief in a doctrine expressed by the Buddha, or "The Enlightened One".

CLONE—Exact reproduction of another body.

CONFUCIANISM—Belief primarily concerned to help man to live in society. By education men can be improved.

CONSTANTINE, SAINT—(272-337 A.D.) First Roman Emperor to convert to Christianity. Issued edict that proclaimed tolerance of all religions throughout the empire.

COPERNICUS—(1473-1S43 A.D.) Astronomer, Mathematician. Founder of modern astronomy and Copernican Theory that Earth is not center of the solar system, and was chastised by Catholic Church that theory is contrary to Holy Scripture.

COSMIC ENERGY—Non-matter element of energy found in the cosmos.

COSMIC MATTER—Matter material located in the cosmos of largely negative charge particles.

COSMOS—The universe as a well-ordered whole.

CREATION-BIBLICAL—Creating of the universe regarded as an Act of God. Bishop Berkley (1685-1753) calculated from Books of Bible that this was done at Year 4004 B.C.

CREATION-SCIENCE—Event held by science as originated at Big Bang, 13.7 billion years ago. Creation of Homo species (like humans) about 600,000 B.C.

CRO-MAGNON MAN—Tall, broad-faced, European race of our Late Paleolithic time.

DARK ENERGY—Undescribed energy appearing in the cosmos.

DARK MATTER—Undescribed matter appearing in the cosmos.

DESCARTES. RENE (lS96-1650)—Philosopher. Believed that a man should doubt everything until he arrives at first principles which could not be doubted.

DIMENSIONS (ADDITIONAL)—Concept of additional existence beyond known four dimensions of height, width, depth, and time.

EVOLUTION, DIVERGENT (An original concept of the author)—Various species of man are like a rose blossom, and each petal offering a separate mutation, the organism closes to bring all organisms together, with next generation including all mutations.

EVOLUTION, CONSOLIDATED—See Divergent Evolution.

DNA—Deoxyribonucleic acid that describes the genome of living objects including
all animals, humans, plants, and sea life.

EARLIEST LIFE FORMS—Lived about 500 million years ago in forms of amoeba, yeast, bacteria in prokaryote cells.

EUKARYOTE CELL—A cellular organism in which the genetic material is contained within a distinct nucleus. Form of cell having a cell wall.

EINSTEIN, ALBERT—(1849-1955) Considered a great scientist with exploration in molecular and cosmic science. Developed formula of E=Mc' and Theories of Relativity.

EGYPTIAN CULTURE—System of beliefs and culture developed and recorded by Egyptian royalty over about 8,000 years.

ELECTRONS—Negative charged atoms.

ELECTROMAGNETIC—Magnetic force actuated by electricity.

ENERGY—Force with power to cause movement.

ENTROPY—Change in qualities of two sources and will eventually blend together.

ENZYMES—Reactor from genome that creates change in body and brain organs
EUGENICS—The act of selective breeding.

EUKARYOTE CELLS—An organism in which the genetic material is contained within a distinct nucleus. Combination of several prokaryote cells. (Also see Prokaryote Cells).

EVOLUTION—Gradual development from simple to a more complex form. Process by which species develop from earlier forms.

FORCES—Four forces in cosmos of gravity, strong force, weak force, and electromagnetism.

GALILEO, GAlILEI (1564-1642)—Astronomer, developed telescope and close observations of Moon.

GENE MANIPULATION—See Genetic Engineering.

GENETIC ENGINEERING—Intelligent surgery of genome, designed to affect a desired outcome.

GENOME OPERATION—Chromosomes are arranged like rungs of a ladder, twisted, and of which there are hundreds of thousands, and in various combinations of the four base pairs. These genes define qualities of each specific cell of the body. Environment requires mutation change in specific chromosome base pairs. Message is energized from chromosomes to enzymes that cause action of protein at cells and cell groups on specific organs of the body.

GOD—The concept of an omnipotent intelligence, spirit, and soul having power to control all activity on Earth and in a Hereafter.

GORILLA—Member of the Great Ape Family.

GRAND UNIFICATION THEORY (GUT)—Process in Big Bang system of reduction of elementary particles, annihilation, and expansion of matter and energy into concise, but expanding cosmos.

GRAVITATION—Attraction of one body of matter to another.

HEBREW—Civilization of Jewish origin in Israel portion of Mideast, later believed emanating back from Egypt at undetermined time.

HEAVEN—Concept that events in afterlife exist in an unidentified locality (in an additional Dimension) in reward for acceptance of religious understanding.

HELL—A concept of existence contrary to that of Heaven. A recipient of rejected souls is not accepted into status of Heaven.

HINDU—Civilization in India believing in reincarnation and worship of several gods.

HOMINID—First creatures possessing basic traits of man.

HOMINOID—Family of quasi-man creatures resembling future humans.

HOMO ERECTUS—Species having basic physical, mental, and spiritual qualities of future human species. First existed on Earth about 800,000 to 600,000 years ago.

HOMO NEANDERTHAL—Species emanating from Homo erectus, and as predecessor of Homo sapiens.

HOMO SAPIENS—Species possessing qualities of Modern Man. Species either 1) evolved from Homo neanderthal, 2) evolved from Homo erectus, or 3) developed as a separate species.

INCARNATION—Original joining of soul to the body of man, estimated to be about 600,000 B.C. with species Homo erectus.

JAHWEH—Ancient Hebrew name for their God. Believed to be the same entity as present God.

LEMUR—An early-developed animal of Madagascar having small size, furry, and four legs.

LUTHER, MARTIN—(1483-1546) For 1500 years popular religions of the world were predominately Catholic until Martin Luther questioned acts of the central Catholic clergy. Orientation of Catholicism was for priest to interpret and present views of the Pope. This changed with Luther instituting a protestant view that each Christian may interpret the Bible as seen fit.

MIRACLE—An event that appears to have no worldly explanation.

MITOCHONDRIA—An organelle found in most eukaryote cells containing enzymes for respiration and energy production.

MONKEY—Primate of the Great Ape family.

MOSLEM—Group of religious followers of Muhammad. Controversy results from different philosophies of sects regarding successors following death of Muhammad.

MORMON RELIGION—Church of Jesus Christ of Latter Day Saints, founded in 1830 by Joseph Smith following his revelation experience and told in the Book of Mormon.

MORTALITY—The process of life and death.

MUTATION—Change in nucleotide pairs that reflect into future generations.

MYTH—Concept designed by man to describe origin and existence of an event; may be promulgated by folklore without evidence of fact.

NEUTRON—Neutral-charge component of cell.

NUCLEOTIDE PAIRS—Elements in genome that actuate enzymes, originating specific actions in physical body, organs, and brain.

NEAR DEATH EXPERIENCE (NOE)—Commonly a reported travel preceding death, to a light designating arrival at death. Some experience a return, and report their experience.

NEUTRINO—Are electrically neutral elementary particles of near-zero mass that are capable to pass clearly through the Earth. They shift qualities of three varieties and may then have counterpart properties of both matter and antimatter. Neutrinos and antineutrinos may be one and the same.

NEUTRON STAR—Star that has exploded due to extreme gravitation and heavy mass, but then return, attracted by gravitational energy. May be source of a future Black Hole.

OMNIPOTENT—Having great or absolute power and influence.

OUT-OF-THE-BOX Thinking—Expression of ideas that are not previously accepted, were held as truths, or are conservative in nature; new, radical, creative ideas or concepts.

PARALLEL (Generation of Physics and soul)—Maturing of both soul and body in parallel development.

PARTICLE—A minute substance possessing definite qualities.

PARTICLE PHYSICS—Science in study of elementary particles and their qualities.

PAUL OF TARSUS—An Apostle of Jesus; Was a Jew who had Roman citizenship and tried to stamp out Christianity, until he had a vision on the road to Damascus; One of most influential early Christian missionaries of the first generation of Christians.

PHOTON—A quantum of electromagnetic radiation energy, proportional to the frequency of radiation.

PLATO—Early philosopher in Greece. A follower in Socrates' teachings.

PROKARYOTE CELL—Original form of cellular organism in which the chromosomes are not separated by a membrane.

PROTEIN—Enzyme that affects growth in body muscles.

PROTON—Component of cell nucleus having positive charge.

QUALITIES (Of the body and brain)—a distinctive attribute or faculty; a characteristic trait.

QUANTUM MECHANICS—Study of ultra-small elementary particles and their actions.

RACE—Each of the main divisions of humankind having distinct physical characteristics; a tribe, nation, etc. regarded as a distinct ethnic stock.

RECOGNIZE (EXISTENCE OF SOUL)—Realization of soul in man is additional to the physical being.

REINCARNATION—Return of soul to join the body and to be an integral part of human existence.

RNA—Ribonucleic acid that outlines plan of operation for DNA.

SINGULARITY—All elementary particles attracted by gravitation into one extremely small and concise mass at Big Bang.

SOCRATES—Philosopher in Greece about 500 B.C. Was convicted and condemned to death for unpopular abusing minds of youths in Athens.

SOUL—A property of antimatter and higher dimensions of space/time, proposed to unite with the human body and brain in reincarnation, as a quality of mind, soul, and communication with God.

SPECTER—Gaseous image of a soul.

SPIRIT—An intangible quality of belief or essence.

SPIRITUALISM—Doctrine that the spirit and soul exist as distinct from matter. Concept is older than recognized religions and should be recognized as such.

STAR FORMATION—Cosmic energy from Big Bang entering low mass area of cosmos, developing spin, gravity, increasing heat and light, and chemically forming new elements and particles.

STRONG FORCE—One of four forces of cosmos: gravity, strong force, weak force, and electro magnetism.

TAOISM—Religion holding that there need be no deliberate attempt to lead a virtuous life in order to save from consequences of sin and evil. A follower of Taoism does not want to change the world but to find his proper place in it.

TIME—Change in moments required from change in space location. Time and space are proportional per Albert Einstein. No change in space (as prior to the Big Bang) is no change in time.

WEAK FORCE—One of four forces in cosmos: gravity, strong force, weak force, and electromagnetic force.

WORMS—Theorized first animal having entryway for energy food, alimentary canal, and method for discharge of waste.

YEAST—A first animal, having prokaryote cells. Variations of ancient yeast still exist and multiply today.

BIBLIOGRAPHY AND FURTHER READING

Alaska, Random House, NY, 1988

Anatomy of a Phenomenon, Ace Books, Inc., N.Y., 1965

An Introduction To The Philosophy Of Religion, Oxford University Press, 1982

Anthropology, Harcourt, Brace, Jovanovich, NY, 1948

As *Seeing The Invisible,* Harper & Bros., N.Y., 1961

Astronomy For Everybody, Garden City Publishing Co., 1902

The Ascent of Man, Little, Brown and Company, Boston, 1973

Astronomy Today, Random House, NY, 1986

The Atlas Of Early Man, St. Martins Press, NY, 1976

Atlas of Great Lakes Indian History, University of Oklahoma Press, Norman, OK, 1986

Bedrock Geology of Michigan, State of Michigan, Dept. of Natural Resources, Lansing, MI, 1987

The Bermuda Triangle, Doubleday & Company, Garden City, N.Y., 1974

The Bible As History, Werner Keller, William Morrow and Company, Inc., 1981

Bible Characters From The Old Testament and The New Testament

The Bible: Fact Or Fantasy, Lion Publishing Co., Oxford, England, 1989

Bible History For The Finnish Youth Of America, The Finnish Lutheran Book Concern, Hancock, MI, 1929

Biological Science, W W. Norton & Company, N.Y., 1972

Birds, Their Life, Their Ways, Their World, Reader's Digest, Pleasantville, N.Y., 1979

The Birth Of The Gods—origin Of Primitive Beliefs, University of Michigan Press, Ann Arbor, MI, 1974

The Book of Darwin, Washington Square Press, N.Y., 1982

Black Elk Speaks, University of Nebraska Press, Lincoln, 1979

Black Holes And Time Warps, W. W. Norton & Company, N.Y., 1994

The Celts, St. Martins Press, N.Y, 1975

Chemistry, Random House, N.Y., 1981

Civilization In The Western World, J.B. Lippincott Co., 1971

College Physics, Addison-Wesley Publishing Co., Reading, MA, 1982

Comets, Charles Scribner's Sons, N.Y, 1976

Coming Back: The Science of Reincarnation, The Bhaktivedanta Book Trust, Los Angeles, CA, 1984

The Confessions Of St. Augustine, Airmont Publishing Co., Clinton, MA, 1969

The Conscious Universe, Springer-Verlag, N.Y., 1990

Contemporary Physical Geography, Saunders College Publishing, N.Y., 1981

Cosmos, Earth, and Man, Yale University Press, New Haven, Conn., 1978

Crossing The Threshold Of Hope, Pope John Paul II, Alfred A. Knopf, Inc., N.Y., 1994

Discovery Magazine—Various articles

Doctrine And Deed, Thomas Y. Crowell & Co., N.Y., 1901

Earth In Upheaval, Doubleday & Company, Garden City, N.Y., 1965

Encyclopedia *Britatadca-"Angels",* Encyclopedia Britannica, Inc. 1950, Ibid, "Souls"

Encyclopedia of Pre-Historic Life, McGraw Hill Book Co, 1979

Essentials Of New Testament Study, Ronald Press, N.Y., 1958

Fantastic Voyage, Doubleday, N.Y., 1987

Five Stages Of Greek Religion, Doubleday & Company, Inc., Garden City, N.Y., 1955

From Physics To Metaphysics, Cambridge University Press, Cambridge, England, 1995

From Stone To Star, Harvard University Press, Cambridge, MA, 1992

From The Tigris To The Euphrates, The Dorsey Press, 1978

The Fur Traders And The Indians, University of Washington Press, Seattle, 1965

General Anthropology, D.C. Heath & Co. Boston, 1938

General Chemistry, John Wiley & Sons, N.Y., 1982

Getting Acquainted With The New Testament, Macmillan Co., N.Y., 1927

God Was In Christ, Charles Scribner's Sons, N.Y., 1948

Good Grief, Fortress Press, Philadelphia, PA, 1982

Good News Testament, American Bible Society, N.Y., 1977

The Greatest Book Ever Written, Pocket Books, N.Y., 1966

Harper Study Bible, Revised Standard Version, Zondervan Bible Publishers, Grand Rapids, MI, 1965

A Historical Approach To The New Testament, Harper & Bros., N.Y, 1960

The History Of Man, Charles Belser, Stuttgart, Germany, 1961

A History Of New Testament Times, Harper & Bros., N.Y., 1949

Holy Bible, Revised, Standard Version / *Claudius,* Harrison Smith & Robert Haas, 1934

The Idea Of Revelation In Recent Thought, Columbia University Press, N.Y., 1956

Indians Of The United States, Doubleday, N.Y. 1966

Indian Names In Michigan, University of Michigan Press, Ann Arbor, 1986

In His Steps, G. D. Putnam's Sons, N.Y, 1988

Interpreting The New Testament, Holt, Rinehart and Winston, N.Y, 1961

In The Age Of Mankind, The Smithsonian Institution, Washington, D.C., 1988

The Image of God, Oxford University Press, N.Y, 1965

Is There Life After Death?, Bantam Books, Inc., 1977

Jesus Of Nazareth, Harper & Bros., N.Y, 1956
Jesus The Man, Harlow Publishing Co., Oklahoma City, OK, 1924

The Journals Of Lewis And Clark, Houghton Mifflin Co. Boston, 1953

Knowledge Of The Higher Worlds And Its Attainment, Rudolph Steiner, The Anthroposophic Press, Spring Valley, N.Y., 1977

Kon-Tiki, Pocket Books, NY, 1968

The Land Of The Ojibwa, Minnesota Historical Society, St. Paul, MN, 1973

The Last Of The Incas, Dorsett Press, N.Y., 1963

The Left Hand Of Creation, William Heinemann, Ltd., London, Eng., 1983

Utters To The Air Force On UFO's, Dell Books, N.Y., 1967

Life After Death, Bantam Books, N.Y., 1977

Life After Death, McClelland & Stewart, Toronto, Can., 1991

Life Among The Apaches, Indian Head Books, N.Y., 1991

The Life And Times Of Muhammad, Stein and Day, N.Y., 1971

Life—How Did It Get Here?, Watchtower Bible & Tract Society of PA, 1985

The Life Of Greece, Simon and Shuster, NY, 1939

Life Science Library, Time-Life Books, N.Y., 1968

The Living Bible, A.J. Holman Company, Philadelphia, PA, 1973

Looking At Earth, Turner Publishing, Atlanta, Ga., 1993

Lost Horizon, Grosset & Dunlap, N.Y., 1936

The Making Of A Continent, Times Books, N.Y., 1983

The Man From Nazareth, Harper & Bros., N.Y., 1949

The Master: A Life Of Jesus, Victor Books, Wheaton, IL, 1979

The Maya And Their Neighbors, Dover Publications, N.Y., 1977

The Mind Of St. Paul, Harper & Bros., N.Y., 1958

More Than A Carpenter, Tyndale House Publishers, Inc., Wheaton, IL, 1989

My Answer, Billy Graham, Pocket Books, N.Y., 1967

Mysteries Of The Ancient Americas, The Reader's Digest Assn., Inc., Pleasantville, N.Y., 1986

National Geographic magazines, National Geographic Society, Washington, D.C., (Various articles)

A New Look At The Dinosaurs, Facts On File, Inc., N.Y., 1979

The Northwoods Reader, Avery Color Studios, Au Train, MI, 1991

The 1980s: Countdown To Armageddon, Westgate Press, Inc., King of Prussia, PA, 1980

Old Rome And New Italy, Harper & Brothers Publishers, 1873

Organic Chemistry, D.C. Heath & Company, Lexington, MA, 1984

Our Magnificent Wildlife, Reader's Digest Association, Pleasantville, N.Y., 1975

The Outline Of History, Garden City Books, Garden City, N.Y., 1956

An Outline of Occult Science, Rudolph Steiner, The Anthroposophic Press, Spring Valley, N.Y., 1979

Parallel Universes, Simon & Shuster, N.Y., 1990

The Particle Garden, Addison-Wesley Publishing Company, Reading, MA, 1995

Patterns Of Transcendence, Wadsworth Publishing Co., Belmont, CA, 1990

Peace With God, Billy Graham, Pocket Books, N.Y., 1974

Physical Geology, Prentice Hall, Englewood Cliffs, N.J., 1965

Physics, Worth Publishers, Inc., N.Y., 1976
The Power Of Positive Thinking, Dale Carnegie, Prentice Hall, Inc., 1953

Prairie Smoke, Minnesota Historical Society Press, St. Paul, 1987

Principles Of Cosmology, Princeton University Press, Princeton, N.J., 1993

Psychology And Life, Scott Foresman & Co., Chicago, IL, 1948

The Purpose Of The Temple, The Church of Jesus Christ of Latter Day Saints

Quantum Mechanics And Experience, Harvard University Press, Cambridge, MA, 1992

The Rape Of The Nile, Charles Scribner's Sons, NY, 1975

Readings In The History of Civilization, Michigan State College Press, East Lansing, MI, 1947

Recognizing Islam, Pantheon Books, N.Y., 1982 Scientific American magazine, (Various articles)

Six Chapters Of Canada's Pre-History, National Museum of Canada, Ottawa, Can., 1976

Steven Hawking's Universe, Avon Books, N.Y., 1985

Stones From The Stars, Prentice-Hall, Inc., 1980

The Story Of English, Elizabeth Sifton Books-Viking, N.Y., 1986

Story Of The Great American West, Reader's Digest Association, Pleasantville, N.Y., 1977

Tales Of The Frontier, University of Nebraska Press, Lincoln, NE, 1963

Television: The Learning Channel, Ancient Mysteries, National Geographic, various other science, cultural, history and documentary programs

Understanding The New Testament, Prentice-Hall, Englewood Cliffs, N.J., 1965

The Universe History Of Arts And Architecture-Early Medieval, Universe Books, N.Y., 1974

The Universe and Dr. Einstein, Lincoln Barnett, William Morrow & Co., 1949

UP Country, Hertland Press, Minocqua, WI, 1989

Virtual Reality, Simon & Shuster, N.Y., 1992

Vital Dust, Basic Books, N.Y., 1995

Volcano Watching, Hawaii Natural History Assn., 1980

The Wall Chart of World History, Dorsett Press, 1988

Western Civilizations, W. W. Norton & Company, N.Y., 1947

When We Were Colonies

Wonderful Life, W. W. Norton & Company, NY, 1989

Worlds Apart. Nature In Cities And Islands, Doubleday and Company, Inc., Garden City, N.Y., 1977

The World's Great Religions, Time Incorporated, N.Y., 1963

World Religions, Facts On File Publications, N.Y., 1971

Wrinkles In Time, William Morrow and Company, N.Y., 1993

THE AUTHOR

Robert Greenough was born into a very normal family life at the start of the second quarter of the 20th century. His young and growing years were characterized by curiosity into nearly all fields of interest.

In his mature years, he attempts to assimilate all fields to explain man, our purpose in life, and more importantly, the "mechanics" of how we were created, developed, matured, and differed as human from animal life.

Along the way of his energetic and inquiring life, he obtained two university degrees in business. He built upon his MBA by reading extensively in science, anthropology, cosmology, geology, psychology, anatomy, particle physics, the mind, logic, various religions, and into whatever his inquiring mind might lead him.

He never felt completely comfortable with some of the traditional concepts taught in his Christian upbringing and assembled a rational logic and history of man's creation and development in "two worlds" of rational existence and soul existence.

He lives with his wife of over 60 years, has raised four children, and has a wealth of grandchildren. Greenough has lived 50 years in Ann Arbor, among questioning minds, to intermesh, living literally "across the street", from the intellectual University of Michigan, where he earned a Master of Business Administration degree. To date, Greenough has written more than ten books and papers on a variety of subjects. About half are published, others developed mostly as an analytic tool for a better understanding of the subject at hand.

Now semiretired, he has assembled and integrated the products of his lifetime curiosity, his reading, and his God-given logical and analytic ability, into a compendium of thought, inquiring and responding to the question, "Do We Live In Two Worlds?"

The author in his study

Books And Articles By The Author

Flatlander in the North

Timelines of the Physical Earth and of Evolution

A Bit of Philosophy (Unpublished)

We Were the Youngest (Unpublished)

Thoughts (Unpublished)

Magnificent Change (Unpublished)

English Kings and Queens (Unpublished)

Indians in the Americas (Unpublished)

Indians, Old West and Civil War (Unpublished)

Timeline—The French Period in North America

When We Were Colonies (Unpublished)

Memories (Unpublished)

History of World Countries (Unpublished)

Notes Concerning the History of Thought Regarding the
Soul Within Man and the Spirit World (Unpublished)

Bible, Science and History (Unpublished)

The Dansville House

Do We Live in Two Worlds?